*f*

# The End of Gay
## *(and the death of heterosexuality)*

Bert Archer

*This book is dedicated to David Mazerolle, who'll never amount to anything.*
*And to David Gershater, who, just at the last moment, did.*

First published in Great Britain by Fusion Press, a division of Satin Publications Ltd.

Fusion Press
101 Southwark Street
London SE1 0JF, UK
e-mail: info@visionpaperbacks.co.uk
website: www.visionpaperbacks.co.uk

Originally published in Canada in 1999 by Doubleday Canada, a division of Random House of Canada Limited.

Publisher: Sheena Dewan
Typeset by FiSH Books, London WC1
Printed and bound in the UK by Biddles Ltd.
ISBN: 1-904132-07-3

# Contents

*Acknowledgements*                                             *ix*

Introduction                                                    1

Part One                                                        5
    The End of Gay                         22
    Sexual Identity                        24
    Identity Politics                      27
    Sex                                    36
    Gender                                 38
    Bisexuality                            51

Part Two                                                       61
    The End of the Beginning               77
    Meanwhile, Back in Germany…            81
    Harlem                                 85
    Nineteen-Thirty-Three                  87
    World War Two and the Great Decommissioning   96
    Start Spreading the News              106
    Science and Surveys and Sex           126
    The End                               145
    The Consumption of Gay Identity       146

Part Three                                        151
    One False Move                                153
    Porn                                          162
    Nineteen-Ninety-Four                          167
    The Word                                      176
    Ex-Gays                                       193
    Queerness                                     208
    Monkeys on Each Other's Backs                 214
    The Stories We Tell Ourselves                 217
    Categories                                    229

*Notes*                                           *235*
*Bibliography*                                    *249*
*Index*                                           *259*

Dykes On Bikes thrummed slowly down Market Street last Sunday past the curbside perch of a 6-year-old girl. The first grader, who recently learned to ride a bicycle without training wheels, was fascinated by the squadrons of Harleys and Hondas that launched San Francisco's 27th annual Lesbian, Gay, Bisexual, Transgender Pride Parade. Out-of-towners must have been amused, or scandalised, or both, at the costumery. Miles of leather. Two bridal gowns. One torso clothed in blue paint. Nighties. A tuxedo. Cowboy chaps. Creative tattoos. Bare breasts. Bare skulls. Bare buttocks. It wasn't Kansas. The little girl from San Francisco was staring. 'Mommy,' she said. 'They're not wearing helmets!'

— Editorial, *San Francisco Examiner*, July 6, 1997

We continue to confuse each other into more complicated, less easy, truer understandings.

— Christopher Bram, 'Slow Learners', 1997

Who is more contemptible than he who scorns knowledge of himself?

— John of Salisbury, 1159

Some people in the community talk as if there's no choice involved, I'm gay and that's it and I'm just being carried along in this great river of emotion and sexuality by no volition of my own. That's bullshit. That's complete bullshit.

— Patricia Nell Warren, *The Front Runner*, in an interview with the author

Some men see things as they are and say Why? I see things that never were and say Why Not?
— Robert Kennedy

# Acknowledgements

To Rachel Giese, Dan Smith, Eleanor Brown, John Kennedy, Genevieve Stuttaford, Jack Murnighan, and Susan G. Cole for letting me try some of this stuff out along the way, and giving me most of the books that have ended up in the bibliography;

To Sheena Dewan, for finding this book;

To Andrew Moore, for always being on the other end of the phone, and to Andrew Daly, too, for so much hospitality at that apartment on the Plateau;

To Laura Stewart, for the house and everything else;

To the Lentons, Sumina, John, Rachel and Eleanor, for the invitation and the extreme hospitality that let me see the big *Queer as Folk* billboard in Charing Cross Station; and to Todd Lynn, for that and more;

To Leslie Lucas, for the talk, Lofty and otherwise;

To Jay Blotcher, for the apartment and some great e-mail;

To Bruce Benderson, for the apartment, great e-mail and a fine, fine book;

To my editor, Maya Mavjee, who came very close in the final days to living up to her namesake, the heavenly architect;

To Bruce Westwood, for turning a conversation into a book;

To Martha Kanya-Forstner, encouragingly and enthusiastically there when needed;

To Keir Douglas Wilmut, my first reader;

To Carsey Yee, who read the section on China and suggested it didn't really need to be there;

To Mark Kingwell, for early conversation, encouragement, and inspiration;

To Hamish MacDonald – most of these ideas sifted through him;

To Rick Bébout, for remembering;

To Ted Mumford, for that first job;

To Christian Bailey, for being a good friend on a cool summer patio over a half dozen tequila and sevens;

To the University of St Michael's College for being the freakish petri dish that threw so much of this stuff into such high relief;

To Grenfel Featherstone, who laughed at my shoes and told me I shouldn't write;

To Wil Bowman, for that kiss on the forehead;

To Frank Groves Ferris, for that trick with the wrist he taught me to do;

And to Solange, Ashley and Alison, to Mark Osbaldeston and now to Jason Gilbert;

– thanks so much.

# Introduction

SEX, SEXUALITY, SEXUAL IDENTITY. All very big and very different issues. And whether they've become trite before their time through too much too cursory discussion, or are still only tiptoed around for whatever reasons our still anti-sexual societies tiptoe around such things, there have been a pile of books and magazine articles and talk shows and television documentaries about them all.

And so, as I stumble into the same muddy territory, I've chosen to overlook those bits of it I figure we've all seen enough (or too much) of. I'm not going to talk too much about AIDS here, for example, or about the generations that still seem to figure they invented sex in the sixties and seventies. I am going to look at history, but gloss over Greece and Rome in favour of, say, Renaissance England or the eighteenth century in Holland or – and this came as a surprise to me as I was reading through everything I read through – World War Two. (I'd always thought the First World War had been the big one, the war to begin all sexual identity wars.)

Something else I didn't do was poll. Though I frequently find myself convinced by arguments when I have numbers pushed under my nose – 82 percent of people like their mothers more than their fathers, 14 percent vote strategically rather than directly – I think it's becoming increasingly obvious that such numbers serve whatever

1

purpose they're put to. And so, though I toyed with the idea of talking to 500 people thirty and under to be able to provide numbers to back up the central questions in this book, I figured it would be fudging, even if it was more convincing. Human behaviour, especially sexual behaviour, doesn't take well to quantification. So there'll be none of that.[1]

*The End of Gay (and the death of heterosexuality)* is also not a self-help book; it will not tell you what to do or how to act. It is, in fact, the opposite of a self-help book. *The End of Gay (and the death of heterosexuality)* is a tool to be used to redefine the role sex plays in our lives and in our sense of ourselves. Though we generally may be said to progress as a society in our understandings of ourselves, our place in the world, and the various workings of that world, in matters of sex and sexuality, for a whole host of reasons, but mostly because of religion, we have not. In sexual matters, we have taken paths with dead ends, doubled back, gone long distances in good directions only to run into roadblocks, and in general it may not be said of any society in any time that it has been sexually liberated. Though there have been opportunities from time to time: England immediately before Cromwell, for example; or Canada and the States from, say, 1967 to 1972 or so; and if John Lennon had talked about his little thing with Brian Epstein at the time, who knows what could have happened in Britain. This book suggests that we are now in the middle of another such opportunity.

*The End of Gay (and the death of heterosexuality)* provides no conclusive evidence to breed absolute assurance. It demands introspection rather than providing definitive exposition. And it asks you to accept sex as one of the parts of life, along with love, leisure time, family and friendship that, if indulged expansively and intensively without boundaries set by anyone other than yourself, lead most directly to life's ultimate end, which is happiness.

An essay appeared in the October 14, 2001 issue of the *New York Times Magazine* called 'Polymorphous Normal'. 'Has sexual identity,' its author, Stacey D'Erasmo asked, 'outlived its usefulness?'

'It seems that something different is emerging on the street these days, a new music coming out of the cultural radio. It is composed of, heard by, ordinary women and men of all varieties who sleep with, fall in love with, live with and break up with both women and men over the course of their lives, the current of desire flowing easily over the gender divide and leading them where it may. At the moment, these people tend to be artists, students and other cultural explorers,' the essay continued, 'but they probably won't be lonely for long.'

That ain't the half of it.

# Part One

G AY ENDED FOR ME on a late afternoon in March of 1991 in a
men's residence in a small Catholic college in Toronto. It was
an inauspicious ending to something that had begun so nobly
the century before, that had earned its stripes so bravely on that June
New York night in 1969 in front of a little tavern on Christopher Street
called Stonewall, and not only survived but flourished through a
decade of a plague that any reasonable Bible-literalist could only
assume was heaven-sent. Who would have guessed it could be snuffed
so easily by some big Italian guy named Vince.

The common room was populated on that day, as it usually was,
almost entirely by suburban men in their first and second
undergraduate years, sitting around in front of the television flipping
through the channels and newspapers, casually meandering in and
out of conversations, like the one that was going on around one of
the tables about Madonna's 'Justify My Love' video, which was
getting a lot of play on talk shows and in the news. MTV had
refused to run it, and *Entertainment Tonight*, *Saturday Night Live*,
CNN's *Showbiz Today*, *The Howard Stern Show* and *Nightline* all
decided to air it and discuss it and make sure everyone was talking
about it.[2] The video was filled with gender-blending images of men
kissing women kissing women humping men licking other men,
against the backdrop of some breathily erotic throb-pop music.

'The video transcends its function as a marketing tool,' *Time*
magazine said in an article about Madonna the week the video hit,
'and becomes something closer to a statement... The common
coolness of each role she plays keeps everything at a safe
distance... In that way she can be provocative and protective at the
same time.' A couple of months earlier, Luc Santé in *The New
Republic* direly observed of Madonna that 'her face and body and the
attributes of her legend appeared on and in every general-interest
magazine and newspaper and magazine-format television program,
her name was heard as a reference and a figure of speech in the
routines of comedians, the banter of TV news co-anchors, the
fulminations of media moralists, in bar-talk and gym-talk and water-
cooler-talk and supermarket-line-talk. In the night sky of the
American imagination, Madonna looms.'

Madonna was at the height of her celebrity and she had chosen to make a big fat same-sex statement. I remember thinking it was all sorta sexy, the attention and mostly tacit approbation a sign, for sure, of the gaying of the Western Madonna-loving world. I even continued thinking that for a little while after Vince, a first-generation Calabrese-Canadian friend of mine, said, 'Y'know, I could see myself doin' a guy. I mean, I'm not a fag or nuthin', but y'know, if I was totally horned up, sure.' There were general nods and murmurs from two others (also Italo-Canadesi) around the table, and shocked and guarded silence from the fourth. When I realised it wasn't some sort of entrapment ploy to flush me out (a constant concern of mine at the time), my first thought was, 'Whoa, Vince is like this total closet case. Cool.'

At the time a real garrison mentality was being cultivated on our part of the campus as a result of the intense political correctness of most of the other colleges on the University of Toronto campus. St. Michael's College, at least in its residences, had become in the late eighties and early nineties fiercely proud of its Catholic conservatism. Misogyny was often worn on the sleeve in the face of widespread No Means No campaigns and sexual harassment sensitivity training courses. It was also a place of playful racism and quick and fierce homophobia, reactionary and brutal. 'Just line 'em up and shoot 'em, man' was the sort of line I heard more than once from an otherwise friendly face across a plate of pork chops. 'Fags're fuckin' gross.'

I was a bit of an outsider in a lot of those common room and dining hall discussions. By this time I'd been sexually and more or less romantically involved with a guy in residence, Mark, for about four years. We'd met in first year, had separate rooms on the same floor of the same residence, and we'd known each other about six months by the time we took a long walk, I think drunken, late one night and he told me that he might not be entirely heterosexual, and wondered about me.

I'd wondered about me too. For the few years leading up to college, and the first months in it, I'd been pretty excited about the whole boy thing. And like many others, I hadn't ever bothered to think of myself as gay because of it. Less, I think, out of any internal homophobia than out of a sense that gays were essentially girls in boys' clothing, readily identifiable creatures that I didn't feel my own fascination with Jon Griffin's chest in grade eight or Bill Dawson's stomach in grade eleven had much at all to do with. Round about age twelve or thirteen, I started figuring girls' tits were pretty cool, and I had the good fortune to have access to a couple of nice ones, belonging to a sixteen-year-old named Shelley. A couple of years later, in grade eleven and twelve, I had a girlfriend. Pretty in a luscious sort of way, but frustratingly intransigent on the whole sex thing. A familiar story – she was about a year younger, liked the idea of being coyly sexual, but wasn't sure about actually having sex. Not as sure as I was, anyway. Front seats, back seats, ocean-front piers and waterbeds all resulted in bits of exposed flesh, a finger here, a tongue there, tussle, try, tickle, poke, pout, give up, go home.

It was only later, once I'd started something up with Mark, that I looked back and figured that they were anything other than your standard, frustrating, exciting, confusing teenage relationships.

When I got to college, I met a couple of women during orientation that I became friends with and was thinking might eventually become girlfriends, but the way the college was structured, women and men were kept quite separate, and since I wasn't a big drinker and didn't much like the pub nights the college held every Friday, I never really mixed with women. Nor did a lot of other guys in res. I did become closer and closer to the guys I lived with, eventually focusing on a core of three, Kevin, Dino, and Mark. I was probably closest to Kevin, and when Mark, his roommate, first asked me if I was entirely heterosexual, and then, when I said probably, um, maybe bi or something, he asked me out, it came as a total surprise. I liked him but had never thought of going out with him, or with any boy. There was a floor of my residence house made up of athletes and phys-ed majors that had me kind of entranced. I remember getting drunk with some guy with abs like I'd never seen (not even Bill's had been this impressive), going back to his room in a state of only semi-consciousness, him taking his shirt off, lying down on the bed, and, maybe having seen me looking at his glorious tummy, asking me to put my head on his stomach. Which I did, and we both fell almost instantly asleep. I liked the closeness, and his stomach was a wonder. Sounds odd now ten years later, but despite this kind of thing, I had no concept of boys being boyfriends.

Then I got a new lens to look at the world through when, about two days after I'd told Mark no, thank you, I sat on the edge of his bed as I often did and talked to him and Kevin as they were going to sleep, and put my hand slowly and discreetly under Mark's covers and took his hand. He was nineteen and I was seventeen.

I think we probably had sex the next day. I don't remember much about this losing of my boy-boy virginity except that it was in his room, on his bed, and I tried to make it look like I knew what I was doing, though the only experience I had was a guy who lived with us in grade seven prodding me while he thought I was asleep, and once seeing an almost microscopic picture of two guys doing something not entirely distinguishable and maybe a little awkward at the back of a *Hustler*. Turned out okay, though. And we got better at it before long. And after about a year, I was in love with him.

We kept it secret, each of us telling just one friend, variously figuring our careers, whatever sort we finally decided on, would be over before they began if we let anyone know. And we also weren't frankly sure if we wanted to be seen, or to see ourselves, as the sorts of fags who hung out at Mykonos, the all-night Greek restaurant underneath the liveliest of the half dozen gay bars within five blocks of the campus. A little too fey, I think we thought. We didn't want to be reduced to that.

By the time of the Vince Incident – four years on – I was nonetheless convinced I was gay, though maybe not a fag: I had a boyfriend whom I found sexually interesting and with whom I was thoroughly in love, and had pretty much eliminated women from both my social scene and my sexual prospects. The process had been slow, and since Mark and I had the courage to go to a gay bar precisely once, it had all been pretty petri dish, too.

So I hadn't reached the Doc Martens and slogan T-shirt stage yet (that'd come later), and I did, when I cared to think back, remember more early crushes on girls. But as time went on, I was more and more sure they had been sisterly sorts of things, social attractions to something safe and away from what must have been my more disturbing feelings for boys. Things seemed, in my twenty-second year, pretty much settled, my impression being that girls who had sex with girls and guys who had sex with guys were gay. The ones who did and didn't think they were, were closet cases. Simple. Satisfying.

Then what was up with Vince? I'd never encountered this sort of thing before, never had any of that adolescent sex with otherwise straight boys that might have immunised me against the shock of what Vince said. Sure, I'd heard all about the pubescent sex-play that went on, but I'd obviously been in the wrong scout troop. And I guess I always figured that all the participants, whatever their public identification, were really gay. But as I thought more about it in the days and weeks after the Vince Incident, it became clear that he, for one, wasn't gay. At least not by my working definition. He'd clearly rather have sex with women. But he seemed to have a notion of a sort of interzone I couldn't quite get my head around. It bothered me.

I've since found lots of similar anecdotes, like the stories Stan Persky tells about his days in the US navy during the fifties in his memoir, *Autobiography of a Tattoo*, and then there were all those randy sailors Quentin Crisp ran across on the dark streets of blackout London during the Second World War. Of course, the cultural contexts of Persky and Crisp's experiences were nothing like the context in which I'd listened to Vince. Several decades of rapid and fundamental change in the thinking about and assimilation of sexual habits – from the pill to the decline of Christianity – made the shift that Persky experienced when he heard guys talking about blowing each other against planes on the airfield at night of little practical or long-term value. He learned, as countless other early- to mid-century gay boys did, that if you catch a straight boy on the right evening, anything's possible. This is not what I ultimately got from Vince.

Crisp, in that way of his, didn't bother to take much away from his wartime loving than a slight disappointment at the outbreak of peace. But Persky, being a philosophy teacher, did think a little more about it, as I did about Vince, and our respective experiences, neither of us having encountered this sort of sexual attitude before, did shift things for us. This shift was on the most immediate level a personal one, the result of Persky and me spending overwrought hours thinking about sex and sexuality, figuring we were quite different, perhaps even unique, running up against a vastly different, apparently generalised, and far less complicated way of looking at what could very possibly be the exact same thing. At first blush the effect can be very much like having thwacked your way through weeks of underbrush to get to the top of a mountain, only to find a Starbucks at the peak and a fifteen-minute tramway built up the other side.

My first reaction, to assume that Vince was gay, was a result of my belief in the binary nature of sexuality. Though there had been times when bisexuality was considered a viable third option, too many of those who ended up gay had gone through a self-professed bisexual period as a way of easing themselves into gay for that to be taken too seriously. But when I realised that whatever sexual possibilities Vince entertained, he was simply not gay, his statement did more for me than imply that straight boys could waver. It eventually resulted in the ungaying of me.

Vince's wasn't a new way of thinking. It was in fact a very old way of thinking, a way of thinking that hadn't been too affected by all the sexual progress made in the name of gay in the almost two decades since my housemates had been born. It was a way of thinking that was once again becoming workable in a North American and Western European context. Madonna had done an end-run around gay, lifted up her dress and flashed everybody in a characteristically rowdy version of what the ancient Greeks called *anasyrma*. And so, though it was odd to encounter these attitudes in a young North American like Vince, it was precisely that (and similar notions and feelings that remained dormant in others of the same generation), when mixed with a sexual culture steeped in fifties bohemianism, soaked in sixties softening, dripping with seventies glam and abandon, and shot through with cold eighties realism culminating in a nineties present represented by Madonna – and Prince and Morrissey and Rufus Wainwright and Sandra Bernhard and Michael Stipe – that allowed for the beginning of the end of gay and the death of heterosexuality. A process of cultural benediction had begun, and desires, tendencies, ideas that had lain dormant at least since the seventies and eighties were beginning to poke their heads up and find they weren't being instantly lopped off.

I received an alumni newsletter a couple of years ago with a little note in their happy-news column about Vince's marriage. I never had any notion that he'd go off after that table talk and start boffing girls and boys left and right. I even doubted, as I began thinking about him and thinking about using his offhand observation for this book, that he'd remember the afternoon in question, or even recognise his comments in the context I've put them in here. That talk around the table in that upper room was more signifier than signified. It's what alerted me to what was going on, both around me and within me.

It gave me the first hint as to what to think about and what to look for. And as I said, I continued to think about gay and straight and sexual identity in much the same ways that I had for some time, but something had shifted. I realised that Vince and I were on different paths, though they were paths I came to figure would ultimately converge.

About a year later, by which time I was studying in Dublin and Mark was in law school back home, Mark decided distance was not in fact all that strong a force for fonder hearts and called it off. I was crushed and hermetically single for about a year, during which time I began to realise how tough it was to be gay without a boyfriend. You have to make a real effort to alert people to your hidden identity if there's no one around to kiss or hold hands with or even refer to ('oh, my *boyfriend* really likes Blossom Dearie, too'). There's an old Creole proverb that runs something like 'You tell me who you love and I'll tell you who you are'; I was finding it tough to maintain who I was without having someone to love.

So, around the end of 1992, I did what a lot of twenty-something gay women and men were doing: I put on some Doc Martens, a pair of aviator sunglasses, and one of those tight black-and-white plain print slogan T-shirts (mine said 'I can't even think straight' – I still have it somewhere) and strutted. Talk to the T-shirt, honey, the ears ain't listening. I marched in my first couple of parades and demonstrations (something about equal families or spousal benefits, I think), yelled my first slogan in front of gathered and mildly scandalised throngs ('We're here, we're queer, we're fabulous, don't fuck with us'), and entertained the possibility of straight-bashing as a valid form of grassroots social action.[3] I came out to everyone instantly and figured if they couldn't handle it instantly they could fuck themselves, and their little dogs, too. I lost a few old friends (obviously), made a bunch of new ones, and generally set about entrenching what I figured was a long-overdue sexual identity. I read Michelangelo Signorile's *Queer in America* when it came out in 1993 and teared up with righteous anger as his capital letters spelled out the wrongs that had been done, the wrongs that were being done, and the wrongs that always would be done if we didn't stand up, come out, and march. I went and saw Derek Jarman's *Edward II* for the second time and loved it (I'd seen it when I was in Dublin and thought it was more tantrum than film). Jarman and Signorile were giving me, and an entire generation of gay men and women, critical and cultural contexts for the anger and reaction that was becoming part of our increasingly collective self-image.

I was meanwhile becoming a lot more sexually adventurous. I'd only ever had sex with Mark, and figured it was about time to start using my twenties the way I figured one's twenties ought to be used. And as I started meeting other guys and having sex with a few of them, I started noticing two things. First, that sex could be a lot of fun in all sorts of different ways. And second, that I was having sex with a remarkable number of straight guys.

Now, I'm fully aware of the unreconstructed lust a lot of gay men feel for the mere fact of straightness. All you've got to do is take a look through the personals, or listen in on a cruiseline for a few minutes, and you'll see and hear the deluge of 'straight-acting, straight-lookings' and mostly (upon closer inspection) fantastical 'straight man looking for same or bi for first-time encounters'. And then there's that sub-subgenre of picture books with titles like *Straight Boys*. I do admit to a certain general attraction to that which ought to be, or is at least considered, unattainable. But, being the coy boy I was, in none of these straight-guy incidents did I even come close to initiating things. They all knew I had sex with boys and did the maths themselves. The first time it happened, I figured I was helping some poor soul out of the closet (and felt quite evangelical about it all, frankly). The second time, too. By the third, I started to wonder – two of the three continued to be completely happy, practising straight guys. And by the fourth, when fully half the men I'd had some form of sexual intercourse with identified as straight, I simply had no idea what was going on.

Take Josh (as we'll call him, to protect the unfaithful), for instance. He was a little younger than me, nineteen or twenty to my twenty-five when I knew him, introduced by mutual friends. I thought he was pretty attractive, but since he was seeing a woman at the time, and talked a lot about the great sex he had with her, and with several previous girlfriends, I didn't consider him a fuckable option. Still thought he was cute, though. And it had come out early in our conversations that I'd had sex with men.

After we'd known each other for six months or so, I helped him move. When we finished lugging boxes up stairs, we stopped by my place for drinks or something. He was all sweaty so he took a shower, came out wrapped in a towel, sat down beside me on the couch, and out of nowhere put his hand on my leg. Hesitating for only as long as it took to figure out this wasn't some thanks-for-the-help-with-the-boxes-my-good-man hand on a leg, I ran mine up his. The towel came away, giving me my first glimpse of two silky and leanly muscled thighs corded up in anticipation as one of them pressed itself tentatively against me. He leaned in first, to kiss my throat; my hand moved up his thigh to his torso. Et cetera. Very *Penthouse Letters*, I'm realising as I write it out for the first time here. He'd never done anything like it before, he told me later, and all the way through the sex we had over the next two days, he'd talk, saying how he'd never had sex with anyone who was stronger than him before, about how odd it felt for the roles to be so completely up in the air. And when it came to cocks, he'd never seen another erect one in real life, and had lots of completely unselfconscious fun figuring out how to handle a mirror image of his own, translating what he liked being done to him into something he could do to someone else. He was so light-hearted – 'Just let me obsess on this for a minute,' he'd say, just staring at my cock, licking it, putting it in his mouth, looking at it some more, asking if he was doing stuff right, laughing every once in a while at how weird it was to have two cocks in his hands. It turned out to be some of the best, most purely fun sex I've had.

Now of course I'd heard about straight people getting together and jerking each other off. And I'd heard about situational homosexuality, too – the stuff that goes on in prisons, convents, public schools, the navy, Magdalen. But as those experiences are inevitably described, they're substitutes – inmates or inductees or novices doing each other because there aren't opposite-sex options, boys or girls experimenting with each other because they're more accessible, and less scary, than members of the opposite sex. Or maybe they've just read *The Symposium* for the first time and figured they're being philosophically forward.

Josh was something different. He was sexually experienced and had a sexually compatible girlfriend. He wasn't any kind of a swinger, didn't consider himself bisexual. He did like me – we'd developed a pretty close friendship over the months we'd known each other and I had, unwittingly I guess, created an atmosphere in which he felt comfortable doing what he did. There was no surreptitiousness, no no-kissing rule or averted eyes, no shameful post-coital retreat – in fact we did it all again a couple of weeks later. He was doing something new sexually and figuring out whether he liked it. Which, clearly, he did. Later, he told me he'd mentioned it to a few friends at school, who'd asked him all about it, and he said he noticed hot guys on the street and in class now, which he never had before. He never, as long as I stayed in touch with him, considered himself gay or bisexual. Those terms both meant something to him, and described a kind of person he was not, with boundaries and expectations he didn't feel. He did ask me not to tell our mutual friends – both of whom were gay – because he didn't want them gloating over his 'conversion'. He'd been in enough conversations with them, he said, in which they would talk about guys at work, guys at school, who they figured were gay but didn't know it, and were always wondering if this or that celebrity were gay. It took up a lot of the chat time, actually, and Josh found it a little obsessive, a little reductive. I figured he was just ashamed, or just didn't want to get into it with these guys.

But the way he talked about these friends, and the reasoning behind his not wanting me to mention anything to them, got me thinking. He had no problem with their being gay. He just didn't like where they put sexual habits in their list of priorities and character assessments, didn't want to get swirled into a pre-set world of In and Out, Gay, Bi and Straight, in which every sexual act is seen as a denial or affirmation of identity. As it was happening, from that first moment he touched my leg, I figured Josh was closeted and was starting, right there beside me, a natural process of coming out, that I, through my shining example of outitude and pride, had helped him see the real, gay Josh. It wasn't until months later that I started to admit the possibility that maybe this guy was something different.

Looking back to the era of situational homosexuality – the sort that existed before there was a general awareness of the possible diversity of homosexuality, when as long as you were a real man it was pretty much taken for granted that you couldn't be a fag – current common sense would indicate that there was a good deal of repression going on, a good deal of denial, of cognitive dissonance – 'I'm doing it, but I'm not that way.'

That Way. That Sort. The whole modern gay movement, from mid- to late-Mattachine[4]-style homophilia to Gay Is Good to Queer Nation and OutRage! to *Ellen, Queer as Folk* and beyond, has been a struggle first to define, then to justify and/or celebrate and/or revel in, then to normalise what was still thought of by many as being That Way. And there have been wild successes, genuine victories resulting in real progress being made in very short spans of time in thinking and acting on sexuality and human relationships. But there's a forgotten, ignored, or perhaps never acknowledged baby splashing about in all that bath water the Movement's been sumping: the possibility of a sexual attraction that is neither primarily nor exclusively based in anatomy nor especially relevant to your sense of self. It's an idea that lesbian communities have been dealing with for some time, something about which they have a lot to teach the rest of us.

It's also precisely this idea that was eventually brought home to me by Vince and friends in a what's-old-is-new-again sort of way.

So in my own drawn-out process of trying to figure out what sex was all about, I added the Josh Encounter to what I'd stored away from the Vince Incident and came up with . . . not much. Just a lot of confusion that I was happy to set aside for the time being as I tried to find some sex, and maybe a boyfriend.

What I found instead was my first girlfriend since high school.

I had been thinking about all this stuff, somewhere in the back of my head where most of my really entertaining thinking goes on, and then this woman appeared who was so thoroughly bright and attractive and funny and *interested*. I hesitated briefly, and then dove in. Well, I suppose waded would be an apter metaphor. I liked her, and I liked it (the relationship, the sex, the social possibilities), though I was always at a remove or two when I was with her. Should I be doing this? I wondered as I kissed her. I'm gay, I'd say to myself as I unhooked her bra. Man, I'm fucked up, I'd tentatively conclude as my tongue slid down her stomach.

The relationship didn't last long. And it probably would have been even shorter had she not lived in another city, allowing me to put off what I was quickly concluding was the inevitable. I liked her, I could even foresee loving her, but I figured I was fooling myself, and her. The sex was . . . distant, and I guessed it probably wouldn't get any better. I was gay and she wasn't a guy.

About three months after I ended it I was reading a book – *A Suitable Boy*, I think it was – when it struck me. I lowered the book to my lap and said out loud, 'Man, that was stupid,' and then raised it again and continued reading. What had struck me fully formed and in a flash was that it didn't matter. Girl, boy – it just didn't matter. The sex wasn't bad because she was a girl, it was bad because I couldn't stop thinking about it, chastising myself for it.[5] Though I hadn't gone looking for it, and though I was not instantly turned on by her the way I was instantly turned on by any number of bike couriers zipping past on any given day, I had been genuinely interested in her physically once we got down to it. Though it seemed counter-intuitive at the time, I really dug the whole vagina thing and got totally turned on by mucking around with it. It was, I discovered, innately sexual, just like a cock, just like an anus (we have just got to find a better word for that). I enjoyed the different ways we positioned ourselves for different aspects of sex, enjoyed how different they were from the ones I used when I was with guys. I noticed some real engineering advantages.

A major factor in my decision to break it off was the reaction of my gay male friends when I told them about her. Without exception (I think I told three or four of them), the first look I got was guarded, the second vaguely angry or frustrated, and the third tutelary.

'You sure you wanna be doing that?' I'd get from one. 'You *are* still gay, right?' from another. 'Man, are you fucked up or what?' from a third. 'You trying to run back into the closet or something? C'mon – are you trying to tell me you're as turned on by her as you are by' – zip – 'him? You know as well as I do the pressures that come to bear on us from all corners, and the temptation to recidivism is...' (you get the idea).

There'd be supportive, even curious noises in there too from time to time ('So...um...what's it...like?'), and even, as I brought the subject up in more general terms with others, the occasional 'Oh, yeah, I've done that. It was fine,' but they were always underpinned by a barely contained mixture of offence and defensiveness. In our early twenties many of us were still too close to the then common high-school cover-date experience, that smothering feeling of being forced to date a member of the opposite sex, to pull a pretty comprehensive and usually long-term scam on your date, your peers, and your family to belay fears and suspicions of sexual difference. The whole late eighties and early nineties Signorile-led come-out-come-out-wherever-you-are movement was a reaction against that very thing. We'd all read it, and we were all, to a greater or lesser extent, living it. We certainly all believed it. We were in the middle of a stridently and necessarily monolithic time in the creation of the basic modern homosexual, and challenges to that monolith were met, from within ourselves and without, with condescending and evangelical anger usually reserved for free thinkers during times of war. I didn't, significantly, take these questions and problems to any of my straight friends (whose numbers were on the wane). I saw myself as a member of a group that had definite image problems it was vigorously trying to resolve, and dissension among the ranks could only vindicate the homophobic presuppositions of the mainstream. One of the most insidious was that gay was a phase in the young, a case of arrested development in the old, and I did not want to give any straight person the impression that I was wavering, that I was coming to the end of my gay phase, which I never really figured I was.

Another question I was asked by most I mentioned this girlfriend quandary to was, did she mean I was bisexual? I assured them I wasn't, as immediately as I'd said I was the first time Mark asked me if I thought I might be gay. I wondered from time to time whether I'd have to reconfigure all this lavish identity construction I'd done over the past couple of years and start looking for a bisexual community to become a part of. New friends, new vocab, a confusing club scene – way too much to handle so soon after such major personal upheavals. And besides, the more I thought about it, the more I was pretty certain that, empirical evidence to the contrary, I wasn't bisexual. I had liked my girlfriend, I was attracted to her on any number of levels – and I liked the sex and in retrospect figured I would have liked it even more as time went on, if I let it (which is how it happens with most of my sex). But I was still gay. I still paid way more attention to Hugh Grant's butt and lips than I did to Elizabeth Hurley's. I still knew Ryan Phillippe's filmography by heart. I still bought underwear for the pretty pictures on the box.

All this of course caused some fissures in my understanding of the terms involved, but I figured I had more important things to worry about and banished them to the back of my head. Well, almost to the back. Those couple of years when I could unabashedly declare myself to be gay were over. I still told people I was, but there was now a nagging little pull inside that kept prompting me to add, 'Well, actually, to be perfectly honest . . . ,' but there was no word for it as far as I could tell, and it would only come out sounding like I was embarrassed to be gay, which wasn't it at all. So I shut that nagging little pulling part of me up; the offending relationship was over and done with, and I doubted, given all the agitation it caused me, that it would be repeated. So I continued having a mostly gay old time.

In late 1994 – a year that was, I would realise later, a bad, bad year for gay and, consequently, for straight – I started working at a literary magazine as an editorial assistant, and over the next two years worked my way up to review editor and then right out of the job over some teapottedly tempestuous publishing controversy. I had been spending those two years, my head finally freed up from the one of my two great concerns that had been pressing down on me more and more urgently (finding a job that didn't make my heart sink), reading and thinking an awful lot about sex and me and sexuality and identity and acceptability and social essentialism versus social constructionism. You know, the sorts of things you talk about with a good friend on a cool summer patio over a half dozen tequila and sevens. I'd begun reviewing a lot of gay non-fiction for *Publishers Weekly* magazine in New York, a lot of big hefty bricks on the history of gay men in New York, gay men in the American South, Latino gay men and HIV, Cuban homophobia, prison rape, the battle between the gay movement and the religious right in the United States, that sort of thing. And when I added these detailed pictures of gay life in other decades, other centuries, other cultures, and just generally in other lives to my own once again nagging little pulls, a different picture started developing in my head. And as it did, I started finding more and more context and corroboration for it among friends, in e-mail correspondence with people about a decade younger than me, and in brief and tentative references in the introductions and prefaces to some of those bricks I continued to read. I started to wonder about how essential sexual identity was to one's overall identity, to wonder whether in fact gay had always been with us, or whether it was one of them newfangled things like the metric system or kiwi fruits that just seem to have always been there. And once I started actively looking for books and essays that would help me with this still coalescing picture in my head, I found there were plenty, often pretty heavy lingo-ridden academic things, but substantial and interesting once you got past all that.

And then, after I'd finished with the magazine job and begun to think and write on my own full time, when I started really grilling my friends (whose numbers by this time turned to a roughly 70–30 straight-gay split), I found that they, especially the straight women, were right on-side, that it had, in fact, been something a lot of them had thought about but never talked about – not with a guy, anyway. I found many of them either had had some sort of adult sex with another woman or looked forward to someday doing it or didn't rule out the possibility if the right girl and the right circumstances were to present themselves. It was another case of that Starbucks-tramway syndrome. But this time, I just walked right in and ordered a latte to stay.

## The End of Gay

The end of gay comes like the end of most things – from the inside. It is almost never through direct, even prolonged, external attack that systems of thought and, more important, belief, are taken down. Only Christians could ever have defeated something as enormous, as all-encompassing, as Christianity. And they have, despite some rather noisy holdouts – one by one, family by family, generation by generation – by noticing that it doesn't make our lives better. It did once. It doesn't now. And that's what it – and everything else – comes down to. What makes our lives better survives as long as it continues to do so, and when it stops, it begins to die. And within a year, a generation, a century, it's gone. Feudalism's done it, communism's done it, Freudianism's done it, the Spice Girls have done it. Now gay's doing it.

Gay is not dead yet, of course. It is, in fact, trying to evolve into something that can survive, going, coincidentally, in much the same direction as Christianity has gone in the past couple of decades, trying to appeal to ever-broader audiences and in the process obviating whatever special attraction and use it once had. It is mortally wounded. To take an analogy perhaps a little too close to home, it's not a question of if, when you come home from the doctor who's just crossed your HIV '−' into a '+', it's a question of when, and how.

But unlike the death of most people, the death of a movement, of a way of thinking and being, is usually a good thing, though it often doesn't seem so at the time. At the time it seems very much like what it is, at first − a cataclysm, a destabilisation, a big shaggy rug being pulled out from underneath us. And though the vast majority of those who consider themselves members of the international gay communities are too concerned with current struggles − marriage, adoption, spousal benefits − to see what's coming up behind them, scoffing or lightly chiding when they do hear catchphrases like queer, anti-gay, post-gay, ungay, it's quite obviously here, and it quite obviously makes sense. It means we're getting on with things, it means we're not being bound by what's no longer good for us. It means we're taking care of ourselves.

In the closing moments of a pretty active millennium and the opening days of a new unwritten one, the gay community has become stronger and, for white folks, more integrated than anyone two decades ago ever seriously imagined. However, the first cracks, predicted by queer theorists as much as ten years ago, and by Gore Vidal longer ago than that, are starting to appear.[6] People, generally younger people brought up on the notion that not only was there such a thing as sexuality but that sexuality of all sorts was pretty much okay (as long as there was some latex involved somewhere), are starting to notice that their hearts and loins are not described very well by these only now solidifying sexual designations. Though there has always been a fair amount of sexual experimentation among adolescents and young adults, in the past few years they've been not only having sex with members of their sex as well as its opposite, but consciously not acknowledging – in light of extensive familiarity with the concept of sexual identity – the significance of their actions on definitions of their own identity. Whatever their current or eventual sexual habits, more and more of them are chafing at definition, not only at gay and straight but at bi, too.

Some have called it queer, some post-gay or anti-gay, others call it immature, still others seditious. Michelangelo Signorile, once a useful activist but now little more than a calcified memory of an exciting age now over who refuses to crumble and be swept away, has described it, in a column in *The Advocate*, as a claim to 'intellectual underpinnings for what [is] nothing but political complacency'. I see it as a natural and wholly salutary step in a sexual evolution, one that we should not only accept and understand but foster as well.

The gay movements are a stage of sexual evolution, perhaps the most important stage it's been through since the adoption of Mosaic and Mohammadan law, but a stage, nonetheless, a means to an eventual sexual end, rather than an end in itself, something that will ultimately and, I predict and hope, imminently be superseded. We are enriched, straight and gay (and bi and transgendered and two-spirited), for having gone through gay, and we'll be much better off when we're out the other side.

So though it will undoubtedly seem in poor taste to many, let me offer an obituary, a eulogy, a thanatology, for sexual identity – because it's not just gay that's dying here – while the patient is still around to enjoy it.

## Sexual Identity

Sexual identity – like gender, race, and class – is generally spoken of in either exceedingly measured or exceedingly strident tones; either in academic, theoretical journals and treatises or through megaphones from makeshift podiums in front of government buildings and crowds of unusually dressed (or worse yet, self-consciously normally dressed) people. As a result, and entirely reasonably as far as I'm concerned, most people just tend to turn off when the term comes up. Sexual identity, oppression, rights, blahblahblah – anything else on?

Never has something so big been talked about by so many, so often, to such little intellectual effect. Listen in any local gay café or restaurant and you'll hear, in the background noise, the words 'sex', 'gay', 'out', 'sexuality', 'orientation', 'Ricky Martin and Enrique Iglesias', all indications of conversations on the subject of themselves, of this defining aspect of themselves. But as has been the case with many of the transsexuals I've spoken to, despite the fact of their self-definition, little progress has been made in the understanding of the issues around which they've centred their lives.

But also like gender, race, and class, sexual identity, and our understanding of it, has a lot to do with our everyday lives and how much happiness we can squeeze out of them. You'd just never know it to listen to the people who tend to talk the most about it.

Dropping sexual identity from our collective psychic wardrobe might at first seem like a big, complicated thing. It certainly seemed that way to many of the sex radicals of the sixties and seventies who figured it was one part of an inexorable path to socialism, or anarchy (of whom, more later), as it did to the queer theorists who stumbled on the notion again in the eighties (of whom, not so much more later). But these days dropping it seems a lot more straightforward. Though it can be explained and bolstered with the use of any number of philosophical and theoretical exoskeletons, when it comes right down to it, it's a simple and – apologies to the poststructuralists – natural thing. Leaving sexual identity behind is simply what happens when our natural instincts to love and to fuck come together with a culture that has brought sexuality in general, not just homosexuality, out of the closet, that has taken it out from under the ever-frowning gaze of religion and removed it from its place as a grim, grey cornerstone of the social order in the formalised shape of marriage.

In a society that has pretty successfully separated sex from reproduction and even, to a large extent, from its role as a stable basis of social propagation, the door's been left open for sex to be a lot more fun than it has been in millennia.

It's in the name of fun that I want to talk about sexuality. And it's tough to talk about sexuality without starting out with gay. Just as there is no nationalism without at least one nation feeling impinged upon by another, no notion of race without at least two races, there is no sexual identity without one group identifying itself as sexually different, making itself heard, and thereby impinging on the rest of us, throwing up this notion that is every bit as amorphous and every bit as enervating as nationalism and race.

Before people came up with the notion that there was such a thing as gay, people were seen, and saw themselves, as pretty much of a piece. And as a result they were. Despite what the nascent gay studies departments tell us, Edward II wasn't gay; he was just a man who seems to have loved Piers more than Isabella. And neither were Michelangelo, Goethe, nor, for that matter, Oscar Wilde. For most of the Christian era in Western Europe and North America, there were those who got married and those who entered religious life. And in both categories, men fell in love with and had sex with men, and women with women, and this said not a thing about what sorts of people they were.

It's pretty clear by now though that sexual identity is a reality. Every time you rebuff a potentially sexual advance by someone of the same sex by saying 'Sorry, I'm not gay' instead of 'Sorry, not interested', you are negatively defining yourself as straight, just as every time you rebuff a potentially sexual advance by someone of the opposite sex by saying 'Sorry, I'm gay' or 'You got a sister?', you're positively identifying as gay. Every time you see a movie on gay themes and think to yourself, 'Well, that's all well and good, but it's not really got much to do with *my* life', you're just as implicated in sexual identity as the person who goes to see that movie expressly because it's about gayness. Gay, in this not so roundabout way, far from involving the 10 percent of us we usually figure (or, if we believe the more recent and no more reliable studies, 1 to 2 percent), actually affects approximately 100 percent of us.

So we're all implicated. So what?

It all comes down to identity, that thing we carry around with us tucked away somewhere near the middle of our brains that enables us to distinguish ourselves from other people. It's part of the same mechanism, the same way we have of understanding ourselves, that allows us to read headlines like 'Crazed Killer on the Loose' and understand it to mean that there are people in this world who are crazed killers and then there are people like us, allowing us in the process a certain degree of comfort in the knowledge that no matter how poorly things go at work, no matter how loudly that sweet little child screams at us about the mess she's made in her diaper, we will not use this knife gleaming up at us from the counter to do anything about either. It allows us, in short, to imagine there's a connection between action and identity, to imagine an equal sign between the verb 'kill' and the noun 'killer'.

Sexual identity is a new addition to the identity portfolio, and we can see in recent history, and to a large extent even within living memory, the process of its accretion. That's just plain interesting, I think, like being able to watch a pearl form in front of our eyes. Why not take a look, since we're able. It can't help but give us a better, perhaps even a more profound, view of ourselves.

But I'd say it's most important because sexual identity, like that equal sign between verb and noun, is in the end a house built on sand, the living in which makes us, through omission rather than commission, more anxious, less happy people than we might otherwise be.

## Identity Politics

'I am human, and nothing human is alien to me.'

When I first read this, maybe twelve years ago, my first impulse was to look up who the writer, Terence, was – I'd never heard of him. Once I did (he was a Carthaginian comic playwright writing in Rome of the second-century BCE), that was pretty much it. I didn't think too much about it again until, for no real reason – chalk it up to temporary mental vacuity – I began a couple of years ago to think about its implications. Which are pretty vast. James Baldwin said it another way just before he died: 'There's nothing in me that is not in everybody else, and nothing in everybody else which is not in me.'[7]

If you agree with it, if it sounds to you like a reasonable way to see yourself in the world, then it becomes an eloquent argument, in the realm of literature, for example, against the constrictive implications of Ezra Pound and T. S. Eliot's 'write what you know' (easy for them to say, they knew everything), and its more recent incarnation, the appropriation-of-voice debate (now thankfully mostly dormant). And in that part of the world where the personal is political, it bungs up the basic premises of identity politics pretty badly.

The effect of sticking to writing what you know has been quietly disastrous. Journalists regularly step gingerly around observations of those unlike themselves, making for often eggshell-thin reporting, and over the past several decades we have been deluged with novels that deal only with the precise raw material of the author's own life, novels whose narrators' names bear striking resemblances to their authors', novels that are less acts of creation than exercises in self-mythologisation. We've decided to follow Jane Austen, who never wrote scenes involving men in rooms without women because she had no idea how they acted or what they said, instead of, say, Henry Fielding, who had no qualms about writing in the voices of men, women, slaves, courtiers, courtesans, and statesmen in situations of which he could have had no experience. In matters of journalism and literature, the effects of identity politics have been deleterious. In matters of actual identity, they're getting to be cataclysmic.

As far as I can make out, the roots of identity politics – that realm of human understanding that holds that there are many discrete human experiences that are incomprehensible in any significant way by anyone but members of the core group in question (women, blacks, gays, Kurds) – are to be found in a fundamental mistrust of the human imagination. At the base of Terence's words is not only the assumption that we can imagine what it is like being someone else but the further, more profound corollary to that assumption, which is that imagination is not some childish, frivolous thing to occupy a student's mind while the teacher talks about prairie weather patterns, not just something artists and other entertainers make use of to prettify the margins of the real world. They lead one to the utter realness of the imagination and its fundamentality to the most basic human interactions. It's the cable we can use to follow E. M. Forster's absolutely practical, absolutely necessary injunction to 'only connect'.

Two examples of this innate interconnectedness can be found in two movies of the past couple of decades, one a semi-spoof of the other. Both movies, since imagination and understanding are nefariously internal and difficult to film, use the handy-dandy catch-all metaphor of the undercover cop to do the job. The films are William Friedkin's *Cruising* and James Burrows's *Partners*.[8] Both have macho young police officers go undercover into gay life to catch a gay killer. Both baulk, both chafe, and both, eventually, are profoundly affected by what a thin line separates Them from Us.

In *Cruising*, Steve Burns, played by Al Pacino, on poppers and in the New York leather clubs of the late 70s, starts getting turned on and confused by all the sex around him, actually has to have sex at least once with a man in the line of duty, and goes off from time to time to fuck his girlfriend and re-establish his sense of self.[9] In *Partners*, Benson (played by Ryan O'Neal), set up in an undercover household with a gay cop named Kerwin (John Hurt), starts the assignment homophobic and abusive, but slips into a kind of accidental domestic partnership with his temporary partner, who's begun to act like a wife and shows obvious affection for Benson. All of which culminates in Benson absent-mindedly kissing Kerwin goodbye as he leaves for work one morning. Shocked by the materialisation of what we've seen brewing over the past few scenes, Benson, too, goes off to fuck a chick and set his bearings straight, and becomes abusive with Kerwin again, only to be turned around in a final scene in which Benson, cradling Kerwin (who's been shot), makes what seem to be genuine assurances of future domesticity, turning the familiar scene of one buddy dying in another's arms into something subtly different.

Burns and Benson take physical journeys, like Odysseus and Dante and Dorothy before them, into worlds that help them better understand and deal with their own. Odysseus learns to love life from Achilles' ghost, Dante to read his love for the prepubescent Beatrice as a metaphor for a love of perfection, and Dorothy not to overlook or underestimate untraditionally expressed inner qualities. They, being characters, make physical journeys so that we, being people, might make imaginative ones. And so it is with Burns and Benson, who discover that the boundaries of their own sexuality are not so thickly drawn as they'd thought. And of course, since both characters are made out to be about as macho and heterosexual as any man could be, the implicit message is, if it could happen to them, then what about the rest of us?

Of course we don't at the moment tend to take American films made since about 1974 that seriously, and so we baulk a bit at taking anything more than homophobia from *Cruising* and the typical tragic dead or dying fag from *Partners*. Both films were made from a heterosexual vantage point – as any commercial film that intended to be anything other than an issue film (like *Philadelphia*) would have to be, given the structure of the market – and so throughout both, 'gay' remains 'other'. And neither film steps through the final door separating Us from Them the way *Kiss of the Spider Woman* was to several years later.[10] But both show us that in the proper circumstances, we're capable of redirecting our lusts (*Cruising*) as well as our loves (*Partners*). Which does not mean that we would be just as likely to go gay (or straight) if we were immersed in the sorts of things these characters were. All we have to do, being people rather than characters, is see the films, or read the books (*Cruising* was based on a book of the same name by Gerald Walker, *Kiss of the Spider Woman* on a play by Manuel Puig), and do a little thinking.

But identity is much bigger than gay, as any gay black woman knows. And you can't really open a discussion of the gay aspects of identity politics without opening the door to the whole schlemiel.

When you get right down to it, in fact, gay is only one facet of a much larger problem. This was made abundantly clear at a staged debate I had not so long ago. The question of the debate was 'Is gay passé?' Flyers were posted, ads placed, and about a hundred people showed up in a little bar to hear and, during the second half, take part in what I and three others had to say on the subject. Colour-coded American-style, the panel quickly fell into the multi-mirrored infinite regress of identity, and as a result, after the opening remarks, we really had nothing to discuss but discussion itself.

The debate's primary inspiration came from an article playwright and columnist Sky Gilbert had written called 'Everybody in Leather' in the January/February 2000 issue of *This* magazine. In addition to Sky and I, the panel consisted of Rinaldo Walcott, a professor of various things queer and black at Toronto's York University, and T. J. Bryan (also known as Tenacious; not without reason as it turned out). As far as I can tell, based on how much she seemed to know about the subject, Tenacious was there because she was black and a woman (and tenacious), an example of the fallacy of identity as inherent knowledge.

But both she and Walcott decided that nothing about gay – ended, passé, or otherwise – could be discussed until the issue of race and class was resolved. And since this was not going to happen any time soon, gay got left behind. Walcott derailed the debate early on in his opening remarks, calling the entire question of the end of gay and the death of heterosexuality a 'white middle-class male identity crisis'. The crowd of mostly late-twenties and early-thirties activist types actually cheered.

The assumption Walcott was making here was that sex and sexuality are inherently different among different classes and racial groups. That assumption is based on the idea that the major differences that divide us as people are group differences. I don't blame the highly invested Walcott for buying into it – he not only is gay and black, he teaches gay and black. But I, admittedly a white man, could not agree with him.

The fundamental principle of identity politics, as of racism, misogyny, anti-Semitism and homophobia, is that the differences among groups outweigh the differences among individuals. It is a profound elision of individuality. 'Individuality', as privileged white male Michael Ignatieff has pointed out, 'only complicates the picture, indeed, makes prejudice more difficult to sustain, as it is at the individual level that identification and affection can subvert the primal opposition of "them" and "us". Intolerance... is a willed refusal to focus on individual difference and a perverse insistence that individual identity be subsumed by the group.'

Everything, in Walcott and Tenacious's interpretation, changes when you cross gender, race and class boundaries. Nothing can be seen except through these filters, and anything that does not acknowledge this fact ends up being, by default, a white, middle class, and probably male analysis. Especially, of course, if the analyst happens to be white, middle class, and probably male.

I thought we'd figured out how stupid all this was.

Those of us who were in university in the late eighties and early nineties and had something to do either with student politics or campus journalism recall the golden age of identity politics. I remember the first time I noticed identity politics for what it really was, the first time I figured it was something I was going to have to pay attention to. It was at my first national student journalism conference. A good portion of the resolutions debated and passed at that conference's plenary sessions involved issues with their roots in notions of identity, of representation, of de-stereotypification. Righting Wrongs. A lot of time was spent expanding acronyms, fitting a B in there with the G's and the L's, going through old documents and changing every reference to specific non-white races to phrases like Person of Colour, making sure Gay and Bi and Asian and Woman had equal face-time, not only in the documents but on the floor, speakers recognised boy-girl, boy-girl and, whenever possible, white-non-white, white-non-white. Identity politics was never anywhere but centre stage. It was exciting. My first taste of hard-nosed political activism. So this was what the sixties must have been like. Cool. Rock the vote. Fuck the Man. Change the World.

Cultural assumptions of course had to be challenged. They still do. But man, did we sell ourselves short. We had fallen victim to what Robert Hughes has called the central myth of the traditional avant-garde – the misconception that by changing the order of language or the method of representation, we – through advertising, through journalism – could change the order of experience and so alter the conditions of social life. As the adoption of words like sodomy, homosexual, heterosexual and gay show, it is possible for the appearance and apprehension of things to change with a change in vocabulary. But the things themselves, in this case the basic structures of human sexuality, are not, however long we might like to think that they are, ever altered.

&gt; We were in university. We were learning about stuff like that. Things like language and text was all there was. No objective reality; you change text, you change the world. I believe it's called nominalism.

So what ought to have been a concise preamble to a cultural manifesto of change turned into not only the major but the *only* battlefield of an entire generation of student activists. Debates were fought between the Left, who thought we should smash the patriarchy by forcing it to acknowledge difference, and the Right, who were caught arguing that white men got where they were because they were generally better at what they did. Both utterly untenable, pathetically puerile positions.

The quickest way to figure out what a failure these times and attitudes were is to look back and realise that almost every major battle the Left waged, the Left won, and won quickly – and nothing changed.

If you look back at the age we were modelling ourselves after – the mythical sixties – and if you take the two major by-words – 'peace' and 'love' – you'll see they got those, and the world did change. Especially on the love front: we got the seventies. Sexual attitudes and practices changed quickly and radically and, as a result, so did the Western world, and even with AIDS, very much for the better.

But with identity politics, all we asked for, and all we got, was representation. We got inclusion in human rights codes. We got funding for organisations, for studies, for books. We got some Dead White Males – mostly Kipling, it seems, which is just as well – taken off the course lists and got Toni Morrison and James Baldwin and Adrienne Rich put on them. Within a space of no more than five years from the beginning of this eighties' onslaught, Benetton, Calvin Klein and just about every major corporate advertiser in the Western world had said, Yeah, sure, why not? and included in their ads black and gay and Asian and the differently abled. This was undoubtedly a good thing; but it was just as certainly not an especially big thing. And as soon as it happened, quite naturally, it was business as usual. For of course business quickly realised that acceding to these sorts of activist demands would not only be easy, but in their best corporate interest. They wouldn't have to change anything about the way they did things, other than sign different models and re-arrange their language and – sometimes – their hiring practices. Like all good systems without ethical standards, corporations were able to digest all this without even a hint of heartburn, never mind soul-searching. And nothing changed. But the tail still got excited, figuring it had finally, in the face of all better (and likely patriarchal) wisdom, found a way to wag the dog. Neat trick.

And so, these days, I'd been hoping that activist folk had learned something from this, that we'd now be more concerned with the fundamentals of corporatism instead of simply trying to dictate the terms and images they use to sell us things.

But judging from the crowd gathered to participate in the Gay Passé debate, I'd have to say not so much has changed in the minds of the politically activated over the past decade. There is still a disconnection between them and their times. Just as they were briefly ahead of the curve in the late sixties and early seventies, they now lag behind it. The problem of identity politics is the problem of external versus internal, surface versus substance. And we go wrong, we become autistic, when we forget there's a distinction. Politics is a simple business; people are not, as a quick look at the respective lengths of *The Prince* and *Remembrance of Things Past* will show. So, in order to win political victories in anything like a decent amount of time, we need slogans. Black is Beautiful. Gay is Good. Make Love Not War. Equal Pay for Equal Work. All good and effective. But we go off the rails when we start to believe that these phrases are the beginning and end of truth.

Which is what gay communities, bringing up the rear in this and other regards, have started to do over the last decade.

What Walcott and Tenacious and almost every one of the members of the audience who got up to speak that night were saying fell directly in line with those principles I'd run into ten years earlier at that student conference. Nothing seemed to have changed. I was being derided for thinking like a middle-class white male under the misapprehension that middle-class white males – or upper-class black females or lower-class Asian males – cannot think beyond the boundaries of these newly confabulated and now utterly hardened identities. These folks, in their different ways, are in a rut. They've got into their rhetorical groove and are unable to see the changes wrought by people before them saying much the same things.

Sky Gilbert provided a couple of excellent examples of this in that essay of his. As a result of being the sort of gay person he is, he wrote, 'many personal and professional doors are closed to me'. This from one of Canada's best known playwrights, from a man who's had columns in wide-circulation arts weeklies, in national newspapers, who's written regularly for the country's highest circulation newspaper on any number of subjects close to his radical heart, who founded his own successful theatre in Canada's largest city, who's even been a cast member of a children's TV series. What doors, exactly, have been closed to Sky because of his sexual behaviour and gender performance? (he's a little femmy, our Sky, and doesn't always dress in men's clothing).

He went on to say, quite poignantly I thought, that 'until faggot boys are no longer left for dead tied to Wyoming fenceposts – call me crazy – but I'll have a weird affection for labels'. Poor Matthew Shepard. Yes. His death was directly related to his sexual tastes and his sexual behaviour. Just as James Byrd Jr's death by dragging was to his race, and the thirteen women in Montreal's were to their sex. Does this mean that we should be eternally vigilant? Yes, of course it does. Does it mean we should be treating race the same way Martin Luther King Jr treated it, or gender the way Gloria Steinem did when she started out? Or gay the way Larry Kramer or Peter Tatchell have? Of course not. The stream of discussion and understanding evolves, and balances shift, and it is absolutely necessary, if progress is to continue, that people recognise these shifts when they occur, and take advantage of them to press ever further on.


## Sex

It would take a set of encyclopedias to address the concerns and chart the missteps of all the various identities out there. But as Northrop Frye used to say, drilling deeply into one subject can often get you down into the groundwater that feeds everything else. So let's get back to the sexual aspect of identity and now, more precisely, to the creature that lies behind it.

Though it's not always been this way, it's become a cliché that whenever we're not actually doing it, we're talking about it. And if we're ever caught off guard thinking about, say, terrorism, or the rapacious price of hot-house tomatoes on the vine, we're sure to pass under an enormous underwear or cologne billboard that yanks us back into it, reminding us of and strengthening the ties between sex and commerce, and in so doing, insinuating sex into absolutely everything.

But we've heard all this before, even though we still haven't figured out too much about sex, haven't really been able to work sex into our lives in any smooth or coherent way. We still feel guilty or geeky about masturbation and, for the most part, about lust unalloyed with anything more emotionally complex. Talking about sex, about sex in advertising, about sex in movies or on TV, about sex in the workplace, has become trite – a problem of getting most of our information, of engaging in most of our discussion, through television, magazines, and newspapers, all of them digest media not suited to handling big, profound, or fundamental issues. They are also media that rely, in increasingly frantic marketplaces, on attracting viewers and readers in the most immediate, the most abrupt ways possible. Which, given the sorts of people people generally are, more often than not involves sex. Which further complicates these media's relationships to this particular subject. We get overloaded by surface-skimming discussions of sex, as we do of race and gender and youth and age and capitalism and war, and long before we ever get to a real understanding of any of these issues, or are even able to work our way back to their roots, we get bored with them, sick of hearing about it all over and over again, everywhere we turn.

And so sex gets hit with a double whammy. Not only do we get bored and self-conscious talking and thinking about it in any form other than the purely anecdotal or fantastic, we also feel guilty about it, odd about thinking too seriously, or at any great length, about something that's considered alternately puerile or sinful, simple or ineffable.

And yet sex remains a pretty big deal. How else could it sell us milk and underwear, cologne and cars? It's arguable that all our relationships, in fact, are based in varying forms of essentially sexual attraction. That we choose not only our lovers and spouses because of it but our friends and our employees, too. That there is, in short, less of a difference between social and romantic attraction than we might think. Think about how your various relationships have started, the ones that began in the context of a large pool of people, in places like offices and classrooms and parties. Sometimes there are obvious common interests that bring people together, a T-shirt with the name of a mutually admired band, or someone might be carrying *The Rainbow* and you just love Lawrence. But if you think back over these various comings together, you'll almost certainly find a part of them, with both men and women, with their roots in nothing more than pleasant looks. If they're the wrong gender, you'll likely not have thought to yourself, 'Ooh, he's hot, I'll go talk to him'. It'll more likely have been something unarticulated, even to yourself, precisely because you will not have been used to articulating your reactions to the looks of incorrectly gendered people in ways that hook these looks up to anything remotely related to attraction.

This is not to say we really, in some amorphously Freudian way, sub- or unconsciously want to have sex with all our friends and employees. It actually means something a step beyond that. It means that there is more of a division between sexual attraction and sexual compulsion than we generally admit, that there exists a more generalised force, which for lack of a better term we could call eros, and that will and intellect can play a much larger role in sex and eros than we generally figure they can. It means there are different kinds of sex, that the kind of sex that's had between two loving and committed people is only one of many possibilities. It means that sex can be had for fun, without leaving any film of meaning, any traces of identity compromise or construction on the participants beyond the act itself. It means that sex, though far more pervasive than we generally assume it to be, is also far less necessarily profound, far less universally significant, and far more open to incidental enjoyment than our current monolithic treatment of it would imply.

## Gender

There is a discussion of gender that could run parallel to our discussion of sexuality, a notion of gender that would have it be as much a continuum, as much a spectrum, as sexuality. The issues are remarkably similar, as are the arguments for its rejigging, and the benefits to be gained from rejigging. I can't help but think, however, that though the two are closely linked, and changing one's thoughts on one means radically changing one's notions of the other, gender will, in society, always come after sex. Though there are, it has been forcefully and persuasively argued in many places, definite and easily imaginable benefits to expanding one's concept of gender, as I am suggesting here that we expand our ideas of sexuality, the pleasure, satisfaction, and happiness derivable from sex and sexual behaviour will, at least at first, be more readily comprehensible.

There is also the simple matter of naming. Though sex and, increasingly, sexuality and sexual identity are concepts that have been bandied about with a fair degree of regularity in the media and over dinners in the past few decades, with heightened enthusiasm and understanding in the decade we've just seen the end of, gender – when it refers to something other, or greater, than women's issues

– is still for the most part ignored as a topic of current concern among those not forced to think about it out of some more or less obvious gender dysphoria (as the medical experts are for the time being calling behaviour that does not fit into current ideas about the binary nature of gender).

The most compelling arguments realise that gender is a category, a fundamental one that we base an awful lot of our social, political, and personal interactions on, one that we subconsciously, unconsciously, and sometimes consciously define for ourselves and others as far more than possession of one of two possible sets of primary and secondary sexual characteristics; a category, in other words, constructed for various social and cultural reasons that have changed over the course of history, that differ, sometimes subtly, sometimes egregiously, from one culture to the next, and, most important, that are subject to change in our own time and in our own culture.

Though there are few enough instances of complete gender confusion – anatomical women being taken for men and vice versa – to open the discussion of any of them to charges that they are anomalous, there is a wealth of examples of people who are taken as lesser forms of their gender, women who are not real women, men who are not real men.

An easy way to work your way into this one is to ask yourself, what is womanly, and what is manly? Make a mental list of a few qualities for each. And as soon as you do, you'll notice men and women falling off the cart, getting Bs and Cs in manliness and womanliness. Are men strong? What about Stephen Hawking? Are women nurturing? What about Margaret Thatcher? And to get a little further afield, do men have testicles? What about castrati? Penises, then, at least? Are you willing to go so far as to say that George Jorgensen actually, fully, completely became a woman when he had his cut off and started calling himself Christine? Or how about the young future porn-opportunist John Wayne Bobbitt in those awkward moments before he had his sewn back on? Even when you get down to the nittiest of the gritty, chromosomes, you get tripped up with stories like the woman who was told upon getting her urine tests back before competing in the Commonwealth Games that she was disqualified on the grounds that she was a man. No secrets had been kept from her – the news was as startling to her parents and doctor as it was to her. It seems that despite outward appearances, she was an XY. Go figure.

None of these gender quibbles is meant to be a keystone that when pulled makes your whole idea of gender instantly topple into a gelatinous androgynous mush. They're meant only to call attention to the fact that, despite what one may at first think, not only do we regularly define manhood and womanhood as something more than recognisable collections of anatomical bits and pieces, but rarely do all the characteristics we do use to define these qualities to ourselves come together in any single person, or are not at the very least undermined by some other aspect of their past or present behaviour or physical-mental make-up. In each of the instances above, we'd probably say, if pressed, that any one of those things made the person in question somewhat less of a man, less of a woman (less, that is, than the ideal, than the various Platonic forms of the gender I think we all walk around with in our heads). And as soon as you admit to there being greater and lesser degrees of gender, the whole dichotomy starts to dissolve. Which merely means that gender is a continuum, and not the static, binary system most of us automatically presume it to be.

## Kiss Me, Kate

In *My Gender Workbook*, Kate Bornstein, who's far and away the most interesting and entertaining person to speak and write on gender issues, outlines her ideas on exploding or conflating gender:

> They're vital concepts because nearly everyone believes there is such a thing as a real man or a real woman. Many people think they themselves are one or the other, or awfully close. They're meaningless, useless terms because of the nearly universal disagreement about what those terms actually mean. Step across a generation line and you'll get a shade of different meaning for "real man" or "real woman". Step across cultures

and those terms could shift radically in definition.

Now to this one could say, But we're not living in any of those different times, and we're not living in Africa or New Guinea or wherever the hell else men think they're women or whatever. Just because other notions exist does not mean our own are any the less stable.

Except that we live, in North America and Western Europe, in a vigorously multicultural society and are continuously, sometimes quietly, sometimes noisily, adopting and adapting other cultural norms, culinary, vestiary, architectural, and sexual. And except also that we do, underneath it all, rely on our unconscious belief that there are men and there are women and we've got the dichotomy more or less right, just like the Talmud/Bible/Qu'ran/April issue of *Cosmo* says.

And to this 'it's obvious everybody knows it's this way' attitude that most people have towards gender – and sexuality – Bornstein has this to say

> If the world's greatest thinkers have taught us anything, it's that we rarely achieve personal fulfilment by mindlessly wandering through life, taking the path of least resistance and little or no responsibility for our actions. We need to question our assumptions, and that includes our assumptions about sex and gender, if we're going to understand those aspects of ourselves and others.

She continues:

> I think most people need to create for themselves the illusion of an identity: a self-identity that matches up with others in the world. I think that's sadly silly. We are so unique, each of us, that each time we try to say, 'hey, I'm just like you, let me join your club', we lose a little of our individuality. People have known that for a long time, but what hasn't been talked about is the stunning fact of our doing that with gender (identity), sex (the

act) and desire (the longing). We dim down our desire, so we can say 'Oh, I'm heterosexual', or 'Oh, I'm gay'. We dim down the act of sex because we don't want to be perceived as kinky. We filter down our self-expressions to fit into someone's idea of MAN or WOMAN. We do all this stuff, I think, because we're so afraid of not belonging, so afraid of being alone. And we institutionalise all of these dumbing-downs of ourselves, and we call the result society or culture. At least that's the way we've done it to date, I think. The oppression of love, sex, and desire are built into the very nature of the kinds of communities in which we huddle.

I met Kate Bornstein in a hotel room while she was touring with *My Gender Workbook,* the follow-up to her category-begetting *Gender Outlaw.* She lounged on her bed while I sat on a bedside easy chair and asked her all the questions I'd only just started asking myself about gender. It's not something I'd thought that much about before reading her introduction to a collection of writing called *PoMoSexuals,* and my questions were pretty basic. But as we got into the territory blurring the boundaries between gender and sexuality, she stood up and asked me to do the same. It was a very small room, and we were pretty much pressed up against each other. She pressed harder, wrapped one leg around the back of mine, pressed her pelvis ever so slightly against my own, and with the combination of gentleness and forcefulness that all seductresses worthy of the name can juggle, put both her hands to my face and brought her face close enough to mine to almost be touching it. 'You like this?' she whispered, a bit of a sexy-nasty grin on her face. I cleared my throat and managed a 'Uh-huh,' feeling precisely like one of those boys in that eighties film subgenre, milky spin-offs of *The Graduate* in which the buff and unaccountably still virginal young man is introduced to the wonderful world of sex by an older, preferably foreign woman. I'd always wanted to feel like that. 'My name used to be Al,' she purred. 'So just what is it,' she said, glancing downward to make sure she'd made her point, 'that you're attracted to now?'

Then she wiped the seductive look off her face as quickly as she'd painted it on, plopped down on the bed, and started playing with her *Sailor Moon* action figure.

Sometimes it just takes a date with a transsexual to really get you thinking about the sort of basics we generally never feel compelled to think about. Like why do most of us figure we're straight, some of us consider ourselves gay, and a very few of us hover somewhere in between? I think it's probably a notion, nothing more. A compelling notion, mind you, and often a situationally useful one. Not a gene, not a biological tendency, not an evolutionary imperative, not a law of god or a law of nature; at best, it's a law of society. And we've always been pretty adept at flouting those at the least provocation, when we think we can get away with it. Why, then, do we persist in defining ourselves by these behaviours?

I think it's because getting away with this particular flout has been a problem. We don't think we can get away with it. I don't mean that we don't think we could keep the secret – we can and we do. I mean we don't think we can escape the experience, or even, in many cases, the proposition, with our sense of our selves intact. Because of this notion of identity, because we have over the past quarter millennium developed the idea that sexual orientation is as much a part of who we are as our height and our shoe size – more so, even – we have grown to feel as a matter not even worthy of a second thought, or a first thought, that to have sex with a member of the same sex (if we're straight) or the opposite sex (if we're gay), with a buddy, for example, a best friend, would destroy not only that relationship but our social circles, our view of the world, our very selves.

Guys who think nothing of getting clobbered on the field or punched out in a bar get all tense and defensive when it comes to being around guys who could be expected to be sexually attracted to them. 'Just don't make any moves on me, okay?' they'll say. 'I'd just freak, I don't know what I'd do, so just don't, okay?' You don't, you may have noticed, see these same guys going into rough bars making pre-emptive pleas like, 'Just don't hit me, okay?'[11] The stereotypical – and occasionally actual – man-hating lesbian is an incarnation of the same thing, just like the fairly common misogynist fag.

Why is that? The defensiveness issue, another one of those trite-before-its-time discussions,[12] remains an enormously pregnant one. So let that one sit for the time being, and let's just talk for the moment about why it is that sex between friends or acquaintances of the same sex who are not gay identified, or among friends of the opposite sex for those who are, is, especially for men, considered so completely out of the question.

'Just because' is the answer I most often hear. 'I've just never felt like it. Sorry. Some of my best friends are gay, and I think that's great, but I just don't get, you know, a hard-on for guys. Not even Brad Pitt or whatever. I mean, I can see he's beautiful,' they sometimes go so far as to say, 'but he just doesn't do it for me.'

That is where the conversation usually ends. It's where I'd like ours to begin.

I can hear people who've been around the block a couple of times – people who remember Dennis Altman's 1971 essay 'The End of the Homosexual?' for example – saying to themselves, 'I've heard this before. Everyone's gay, there's a dyke lurking inside all of us, a gay man waiting to get out. We're all really bisexual. Yadda yadda yadda.' That was the talk of the late-sixties and early-seventies sex radicals, many in the then-young modern gay rights movement. And it sounded good to many of the people who listened to or read it. For about ten minutes. It fizzled because it was a first blast. People had to get used to the notion of publicly expressed same-sex sexuality before they could be expected to consider the various possibilities of its more extended meanings, which of course include the death of heterosexuality.

Which we are now just on the cusp of having had enough time to do. And it's happening. People – Western European people, North American people – who have hit puberty since the early part of the last decade, since, say, Madonna started flirting with Sandra Bernhard, since Sandra Bernhard became *Roseanne*'s lesbian, since *Ellen* in '97, *Will & Grace* in '98, since Ian McKellen became a big gay wizard and no one seemed to mind, have been thinking and acting differently than those who grew up with Little Richard and Liberace or David Bowie and Elton John. And it's this notion that

Madonna and Roseanne and, in a roundabout way, Ellen (despite her sometimes quite defensive and conservatively reactionary sexual statements and behaviour) have given people – this idea that whatever human beings may be, categorisable is not one of them – that I find so interesting. Madonna in her prime was every bit as much of a sex symbol as any of her predecessors, every bit as much as Betty Grable, Marilyn Monroe, and the late, great Farrah Fawcett-Majors. Roseanne's big and fat and as white and as trashy as they come, and not only is she cool with her best friend's same-sex girlfriend, she goes off and has a big ol' same-sex kiss herself. But both Madonna and Roseanne found a space to play with gay. (Ellen, much more a product of latter-day notions of gay – rushing with the rest of the contemporary gay vanguard to forge an identity and lifestyle as close to the heterosexual model of their parents as they can – has a more complex relationship to the current argument, and we'll deal with her, and the difference between queer TV and gay TV, later.)

It is a playfulness with precedents. Like Marlowe, Shakespeare, Beau Brummel, Oscar Wilde (the man who married for love and fathered two beloved children and whom Marjorie Garber, author of the 1995 book *Vice Versa: Bisexuality and the Eroticism of Everyday Life*, describes as 'the bisexual inventor of modern homosexuality'), a good portion of the members of the Harlem Renaissance (Zora Neale Hurston, Ma Rainey, Bessie Smith, Langston Hughes, Wallace Thurman, Countee Cullen), and of course those Bunburying Bloomsburians Virginia Woolf, John Maynard Keynes, Vita Sackville-West, Dora Carrington, Lytton Strachey, and the rest of their overwrought bedhopping posse.

Though every one of the above-mentioned names has been claimed at some point by gay – Marlowe for his *Edward II*, Shakespeare for his sonnets, Wilde for Bosie and his trial, etc – they are at least as interesting for the way in which they saw love and beauty as unfettered by gender as they were for the courage it took them to flout convention and to speak and act more or less openly in the transgressive parts of their love affairs. Of these, it happens that Shakespeare's is the primary voice of a watershed era like our own. His world had become sufficiently secularised and sufficiently sophisticated to allow many of the more uncomfortable or complicated human truths out to play. The build-up of London's literature to the fevered sexual pitch it reached just before the Puritans hit town is pretty similar to what was happening in North America and Western Europe just before AIDS.

He's also a touchstone. We like Shakespeare, figure he's a genius. He's hit enough home truths, convinced us that he has a firm enough grasp on what the more romantic among us call the human soul, that we are more than usually willing to take his word on things. If he says the quality of mercy is not strain'd, well, then it may very well not be. If he remarks on what a piece of work is man, we're more likely to look upon man as maybe being a piece of work. And if Shakespeare judges male beauty to be as love- and passion-worthy for men as female beauty in the poems that many, including Wordsworth and Auden, consider his private musings, then perhaps we'd be more likely to do so as well.

It has been said of 'myriad-minded' Shakespeare that he unravelled the human heart, that he was 'the man who of all modern, and perhaps ancient poets has the largest and most comprehensive soul.' I think a look at these sonnets that seeks to label him neither straight nor gay might prove Coleridge and Dryden right in ways they didn't suspect.

The first couple of dozen sonnets in Shakespeare's cycle, with their addresses to the 'master-mistress of my passion', are a beautiful, seamless weaving of appreciation and passion for male beauty and male love, as well as for the beauties and joys of female love. While praising his young man effusively, he orders him to father children, to deny himself none of what the world has to offer a beautiful young man. There is no hint that the man should marry or sire out of onerous social duty, or because of the constraints of heterosexual hegemony; he should marry because women can be beautiful and children wonderful (and, to further underscore the transcendent nature of beauty, admiration, and passion, the child is envisioned as the young man's 'beauty's use', a product and extension of his father's qualities).

The appreciation of male beauty, and the passion evoked by it, are unmistakable, as they were in the *Phaedrus* and *The Symposium*, in Catullus and even Virgil. Repeated loving references, in sonnets addressed to a young man, to 'thy beauty', 'thine own bright eyes', 'Make thee another self for love of me', 'Dear my love', should not be written off in any facile way to the fact that they spoke differently back then. Of course they did, and it was a reflection of the fact that they felt differently, too. Shall I compare these sonnets to a Calvin Klein billboard? They are more lovely and more literate. But they reflect the same world view, a world view that may have been fairly common in Elizabethan England, at least in literary and courtly circles, and one that is gaining ground in our world today, in a very general way. The sonnets and the billboards worship beauty in a thoroughly ambivalent way. With the close connection Shakespeare makes between human beauty and love and passion, I'm not sure sex can be eliminated from the equation here unless one figures sex is bad, or eroticism inappropriate between men. Though it is not clear through any of these sonnets that the poet and the young man ever had sex, it is equally clear that the poet would have liked to very much. It's all quite innocent, and quite sexual. It lacks its apparent innocence in this reading only if one assumes that the highest, most noble form of love excludes sex. Which, I am here to say, along with Shakespeare and Plato and the artist formerly and then once again known as Prince, it does not.

There is a passion in the advertising images of today, as good a reflection of our evolving tendencies and desires as any contemporary cultural product, that is every bit as free as Shakespeare is in these sonnets. And it's as ill-advised to label Shakespeare gay for admiring the beauty of a young man over the course of at least 17 and as many as 126 sonnets as it is to label the same-sex admirers of billboards of Mark Wahlberg and Kate Moss and any number of the other beautiful and underclad. Responding sexually to human beauty is a natural reaction. Acknowledging that response is for many people today a learned one.

The end of gay and the death of heterosexuality we're now approaching is in some ways a return to these less hemmed-in times, an acknowledgement of the lost possibility of intimacy among members of the same sex, and of the sexual possibilities, tensions, and desires that all true intimacies among human beings necessarily entail. But in a significant way, the end of gay and the death of heterosexuality is a big hop, skip and a jump forward as well. The days before the modicum of sexual liberation we've achieved were not by any means halcyon days. Though there was a greater internal freedom evident, in poetry, correspondence and other personal communication and expression, there were very few if any external freedoms. If Shakespeare had wanted to publicly express his physical affection for his master-mistress, he would have been open to a whole host of socially acceptable indignities. The intervening periods, with their high and low points, have been absolutely necessary to get us where we are, a place that is starting to bear a striking resemblance to certain times past, with certain crucial differences.

Take Prince, for instance. From his very first album, which he recorded when he was still a teen, he was all about sex. Now, there's nothing new in a pop star being totally concerned with sex. Elvis seems to have been in his early days, the Beatles were for a time. Guns 'N' Roses and those naked Red Hot Chili Peppers were. Even the boy bands seem to be getting closer to admitting they are, as well, with songs about wet dreams and whatnot leaking into the repertoire. But there was something radically different in Prince from the standard cock rock. Prince didn't swagger – he wiggled.

He was little, wore stuff that looked an awful lot like lingerie, and even wore stiletto heels. And the music he wrote about sex was utterly orgasmic, and tantrically so, more like a woman's swells and waves than cock rock's explosions and splatters.[13]

I still remember the first time I ever heard his early single 'International Lover', at the house of a couple of cousins of mine. They were both big Prince fans – they introduced me to his stuff – and the younger one, who was about twelve, really loved it. Especially 'International Lover'. But every time the album got round to that single, she'd shudder and get up and leave the room, saying she couldn't listen to it, it made her feel funny. Her older sister (about fifteen) was embarrassed and called her stupid. I (seventeen, I think) thought it was great. I'd say any artist who could give a prepubescent girl proto-body-orgasms has really got something going for him. It hooked me.

But one of the most interesting things about Prince is that despite his obvious feminine co-optations, he's managed to mostly escape gay, in gossip and in practice,[14] and in the process, challenge it and even subvert it, without ever dissing it. Early in his recording career, as early as 1981, the title track to his fourth album, *Controversy*, had lines like 'Am I black or white? Am I straight or gay?...life is just a game, we're all just the same.'

Here's a thoroughly sexual, completely unimposing little man, a profound, spiritualised woman-lover who sings songs with titles like 'i love u in me' and 'if i was your girlfriend,'[15] songs with lyrics like 'I'm not your woman, I'm not your man, I am something that you'll never understand' and 'I'm not your lover, I'm not your friend, I am something that you'll never comprehend'. Madonna may have got all the press for being such a thoroughly and unapologetically sexualised, self-eroticised woman, at least in part because the notion of the sexualised man seemed a cliché, especially in rock. But Prince showed us, if we were watching, that a man can be sexualised in radically different ways from Gene Simmons or Axl Rose.[16] Prince is an excellent example of what gay can teach straight on the way to the disappearance of both, of what women can teach men on the way to realising that they've got plenty of tricks to swap.

Sandra Bernhard is another one. But people have had more problems with Sandra Bernhard. Gay women especially. Elspeth Probyn, in a 1993 book called *Sexing the Self*, talks a bit about Bernhard's brilliant, even groundbreaking 1990 film, *Without You I'm Nothing*: 'One of the obvious things the film forgets to mention is lesbian desire. For all her right-on rhetoric, Sandra never says anything directly about wanting the black woman [who mysteriously and provocatively appears and reappears throughout the film], or for that matter any woman at all. Sure, she turns "Me and Mrs Jones" against itself into a lesbian torch song...but, in actual fact, in actual words, she never quite comes out.' And Rose Collis, in the March, 1994 edition of the *Gay Times*, concluded her review of a documentary, *Sandra Bernhard – Confessions of a Pretty Lady*, with: 'Bernhard says she doesn't really see herself as an idol for dykes, but more for straight women for whom the word "sexuality" could be the name of a new perfume. "I'm a spokesperson for the modern woman," she declares – and an old quote about idols with feet of clay comes to mind.'

Bernhard was one of the first, along with Madonna, to leapfrog gay, to go not only past the Elizabeth Taylor some-of-my-best-friends-are-gay routine but right on past gay itself. In *Without You I'm Nothing*, Bernhard's monologue about the seventies straight dude stepping into a bar, getting poppers shoved under his nose, and seeing an apparition of a big black man with a blond afro and gold lamé muumuu is not about coming out of the closet or discovering your true, hidden homosexuality but about shortcircuiting both your inner straight guy and your inner fag. Her implicit criticism is not of the by-1990 already recognisable motif of the overcompensating homophobe. As Probyn recognised, Bernhard never calls herself a dyke, and never calls her disco-guy a fag. As his cries of 'But I'm straight, I'm straight' are overcome by the disco and the poppers and the lamé, the identity vacuum is replaced not by a road-to-Damascus revelation of faggotry but by nothing at all, his actions beginning to be governed by circumstances, by the moment and the context, rather than by an identity. Both the structure and the content of the rest of Bernhard's film are extensions of this basic theme: that second-guessing behaviour based on premises stemming from identity is inherently absurd.

I spoke to Bernhard a couple of years ago about where she is on the subject of sexual identity these days, a decade later. 'I think that it was a lot of years ago that this was an issue,' she said. 'Times have caught up with me, I think, enough to know that it's a lot more sophisticated and interesting not to be dead-on. It's not really an issue any more in my circles.'

It's these examples of uncategorisability that the people who were establishing their ideas about sex and sexuality and sexual identity as all these cultural forces stormed around them have in increasing numbers glommed on to. More of them have begun sleeping with their friends, whatever their gender. Fewer of them are happy with the status quo, whether it be the mainstream or the gay community.

Todd Klinck's a friend of mine. Born in 1974, he is an excellent example in crystalline form of what we are getting at here. A writer and webmaster, sexual admirer of men, women and the transgendered, Todd came to the big city from a small town, and after doing some messing around with girls and some messing around with guys, became convinced, as he began moving in urban gay circles, that his experiences were common (which they were), and that they meant he was gay (which he wasn't). After a few years of thinking and having all sorts of sex and then thinking some more, when he's asked these days what he is, he replies, as he did to me when I started working on this book, 'I don't call myself anything. I just am.'

## Bisexuality

None of which means that we are all turning bisexual. In fact I think the current popular definition of bisexual is as misguided as definitions of homosexual and heterosexual. All infer that infernal Kinsey scale: 0 = straight, 6 = gay, with varying degrees of bisexuality roaming around in between. But the notion I and a few others have been mumbling about to ourselves for the past few years, the notion that Bernhard's circle of friends now seems to simply takes for granted, is that there's no such thing as those two poles, no Kinsey zeroes or Kinsey sixes, that they're more asymptotes than facts. And without the poles, without absolute gay and absolute straight, the term bisexual loses much of its traditional and popular meaning.

The idea of bisexuality is complicated. After decades of investigating the subject, Freud said of the matter in his posthumous book, *An Outline of Psycho-Analysis*, published in 1938, 'This fact of psychological bisexuality... embarrasses all our enquiries into the subject and makes them harder to describe.' Complex enough, too, to inspire Marjorie Garber's *Vice Versa*. And unlike Thomas Moore's *The Soul of Sex*, which sets out to investigate the eroticism of everyday life, but gets horribly gnarled along the way (more on that a little later), Garber actually manages it. In the face of any number of enormous problems with the issue – not least among them gay's enthusiastic and often self-righteous appropriation of historical figures from Socrates to Shakespeare to Woolf who were clearly interested in the opposite sex as well as their own – Garber suggests that bisexuality is more narrative than label, more process than state, that it is, to use as she does Poe's image from *The Purloined Letter*, written so large on the map of the human condition that it is difficult to see. The book is a monument to the subject. Yet it takes more than one book to teach, more than one to learn, more than a dozen to get any real number of people to change the way they think or act. So consider this section of my book a buttress to *Vice Versa*, a variation on a theme.

If one defines bisexuality – and it's all about definition – as the practice of having sex with both men and women, its history is a long and almost entirely inclusive one. Every era in every culture of which we have records provides examples of it, and many – ancient Greece, ancient Rome, medieval Arabia, Renaissance and Regency England, late-nineteenth-century Northern Europe as a whole, Bloomsbury, North American and English urban centres of the late sixties and seventies – have either explicitly condoned or idealised it. It was, though now often obscured by gay discourse, famously the norm for at least a century in Athens and Sparta, where, in a similar but not identical fashion to Rome, the medieval Muslim world, and feudal Japan, sexuality was lodged firmly in the subject rather than the object. Which is to say that beauty, sexual attractiveness or sexual utility were not being seen as affected in any exclusive fashion by gender. Because of recent gay experience with bisexuality – its use as a cover for a half-in/half-out phase of homosexuality, the mid-eighties scapegoating of the 'promiscuous bisexual male' as plague rats in the early days of AIDS – it is often assumed that figures who in the past expressed homosexual desire while married, or sequentially expressing hetero- and homosexual desire, were being forced by an unjust or narrow society into moulds. They're seen as having to be straight but wanting to be gay, straight to reproduce and abide by society's various rules and structures, gay to follow their hearts. This is one of the most egregious of many elisions of the modern gay sensibility. Before what we know as organised religion became the overarching cultural structure, differences in sexual pleasure and forms of human beauty were recognised, appreciated, and, most importantly, acted on. And though there were always any number of rules and taboos – don't be penetrated by a slave, only fuck the camel boy (or the camel) when you're on the road – they were the result of extra- rather than intra-sexual concerns: class, propriety, politics, rather than sexual morality. Not being penetrated by the slave was wrong for the same reason you shouldn't be taking orders from him or letting him use your best horse.

## Lola and Dil

In 1970, Ray Davies and the Kinks released 'Lola'. Big hit, everybody loved it. And it had staying power. I remember it was the first thing that popped into my head when Joel met Jackie at the door the first time I saw *Risky Business* fourteen or so years later (probably because of the song's dark-brown-voice lyric). It's a story song, as you'll recall, about a young man who's only just moved away from home and never ever kissed a woman before he meets up with Lola.

Lola is queerness pure and simple, if somewhat *avant la lettre*, and an indication, in her presence in the early work of this self-consciously anti-establishment band, of the place sexuality had at that point in a more general alternative ideological landscape (the same album on which 'Lola' was originally included also has songs criticising the music industry, organised labour and capitalism in general).

Our narrator gives no indication of same-sex sexual interest; he falls for someone he thinks is a woman, if perhaps a slightly odd one (one who picks him up and sits him on her knee, for instance). And when he finds out Lola's a man, after a short (four-line) crisis, he looks at her, she at him, and in the space between stanzas six and seven, our narrator's world view changes. From not understanding how someone can look like a woman but talk like a man, the narrator ends up singing that boys will be girls and girls will be boys and happily jumps right in.

Contrast this to a similar moment in Neil Jordan's *The Crying Game*, the moment around which the film revolves and on which it built its reputation, the moment (warning: spoiler ahead) when the androgynously named Dil (played by the equally androgynously named Jaye Davidson) takes off her clothes to reveal a penis. Stephen Rea's character, Fergus, has been hot for Dil for some time, he's had sex with her once (she gave him a blow job), but now, as they're heading to the bed, he spots the offending member, hits Dil, and in a scene whose substance is only moderately less ludicrous than its parodies the following year (*Ace Ventura*, *Naked Gun 33¹/₃*) runs off to the toilet to throw up. It's a scene that was presented and received as the realisation of the worst nightmare of any good, upstanding straight man who'd ever been tripped up by the androgynous and often outright feminine looks young men had been sporting on and off since the mid-sixties.

It's clear in 'Lola' that the fact of attraction precedes and precludes other considerations. If the narrator was mistaken, or even fooled, concerning some of the particulars of his beloved, the emotional and sexual connection is not broken by the revelation of an unsuspected gender. He fell for a person, and, in the end, it's the basic connection that matters. In Jordan's version, the question, framed by the recitation of a parable of the frog and the scorpion towards the beginning and in the final scene of the film, is one of identity. 'It's in my nature,' the scorpion explains to the frog it's talked into carrying him across a river once he's stung him and they're both drowning. Scorpions sting, the IRA kills its hostages, straight men like women, and gay men like men. It's the question of who likes transvestites that's the centre of this movie – a question especially threatening to the stability of gender and sexuality. That, and whether a man can change, and whether an attraction is nullified by a little gender-play. The tension's maintained, and the question's never answered (though the two begin to act just a little like a couple in the final scene). And although the tension being maintained throughout the film provides a good impetus for the audience to consider the issues and how they might react themselves, that it is a sticking point that identity could be such an obstacle, and that this reaction is really the only one imaginable in 1992, marks a striking change from decades (and centuries) past.

It was definitely a sign of the times. Only a year before, Neil Banerjee, a college residence friend of mine, had been told by a grinning Johnny Carson that the singer we'd just seen in full Gauthier-garb, whose sexier than average performance elicited a greater than average number of wolf whistles and catcalls from the men in the common room, was in fact a male Madonna impersonator. Neil fell into the seat from which the performance had actually raised him and said in a cracked voice, 'I feel like I've just been raped with a broken bottle.'

A year after *The Crying Game*, Cronenberg's *M. Butterfly* relied heavily (though slightly more complexly) on the same zeitgeist, and both Jaye Davidson and John Lone (who played the androgyne in *M. Butterfly*) were popular on the talk-show circuit and in stand-up and sitcom routines for months.

Extreme responses all around, created by a newly created but fully evolved fissure in the fundamentals of identity and attraction. Only a small minority, whether it be old-time tricksters or new-time queers, have ever especially enjoyed being fooled by sex and gender. But I can't imagine someone even as late as Archie Bunker reacting with anything more than a judgmental scowl and an 'ah jeez'; and though there is little reliable evidence one way or the other, my guess is that the transvestite being beat up by a not-so-observant trick or john when the truth is revealed is a pretty modern development (previous tricks mightn't have been overjoyed, but my guess is, once again, that they'd either get right into it or at the very most close their eyes, get their blow job, and think of the queen).

There is, however, some evidence that outside this especially American and Northern European context, even those brought up in it act and react differently. Frank Browning, author of the extraordinary *The Culture of Desire* and the slightly more ordinary *A Queer Geography*, travelled to Naples researching the latter book and fell into conversation with one of the feminielli, or transvestite prostitutes, for which that city is famed in certain circles. She told him:

> If an American boy comes now, and he's alone, he's the best
> homosexual in the world...If he's in a group, though, they
> won't respect you at all. They sneer and poke fun at us and say
> nasty things. Then the next day, one by one, they come back on
> their own and want to fuck. And they want to touch you and
> wank you.' 'Don't the Italians want to play with your dick, too?'
> I ask. 'Not so much. Maybe two out of ten. It's not a big
> question.' 'And the Americans? How many of them want it,
> want to get fucked in the ass?' 'The Americans, they all want to
> play with your dick, and maybe three or four [out of ten] want
> it up the ass.

On the surface, this feminielli experience could be seen as a
variation on the situational homosexuality theme that also covers
such anomalies as prison sex. Looked at more carefully, however, it
shows up the shortcomings of that particularly fragile way of seeing
things. There is no shortage of women in Naples, nor of female
prostitutes. What these American boys see in the feminielli is
excitement and difference and transgression and all sorts of things
that are inherent to the heightened sexual experience. And what
they also notice is that they are, to use Hugh Kenner's shading of the
term, 'elsewhere', outside the confines of their own cultural
narrative, just as prisoners are, just as, Lord-of-the-Flies-like,
boarding school residents are.

Have you ever felt, going to a new school, moving to a new city,
or starting a new job where nobody knows you, that you could
make yourself up again? I remember moving to a new school in a
new city and deciding that I'd erase some of the nasty bits of my
personality that had stuck to me at my old school in my old city. I
wouldn't be shy anymore, I told myself, I'd just walk right up to
people and say hi for no reason at all, something that would have
given the old me cold sweats. With no one at the new school from
my past – my previous narrative, if you will – I could get away with
this alternative me with no fear of embarrassment or accusations of

inconsistency. And it worked. Just as it did for those Americans in Naples who hadn't necessarily always dreamed of doing it, or had secret yearnings for cock; these guys were not, that is to say, necessarily gay and in the closet. The closet is part of the (fading) Northern and American story, not the Neapolitan one.

It's a corroboration of a late notion of Freud's, expressed in 'Homosexuality in a Woman', that attractions may never be erased or replaced, only concatenated. And it's this concatenation towards which I hold our culture is moving, a concatenation captured effectively in tone and often reception of Blur's speedy 1994 Britpop hit 'Girls and Boys' about 'love in the nineties' and looking for girls who are boys who like boys to be girls who do boys like they're girls who do girls like they're boys.

The Blur lyrics, and their popularity, are indications of something post-*Crying Game*. *The Crying Game* can in fact be seen as a cultural representation of something that had by 1992 already begun to pass, to be superseded, or at least joined, by another stream of which Madonna had been an early eddy. An ethos informed and represented, though not defined or initiated, by raves, those neo-sock-hops in which the spiked punch was replaced by Ecstasy, a drug that in its increasingly rare pure form creates very generalised feelings of love, irrespective of gender or even usual sexual attraction.

'Girls and Boys' is not radical in the way 'Lola' was and is. In its tone, its ease of acceptance, the relative silence with which the extremely popular lyrics were received, the song showed itself to be much more of a reflection than a prescription, and its own narrative approval of the suggested sex and gender blending comes in the refrain's final line, 'always should be someone you really love,' a line that validates feelings over boundaries, feelings that by definition overtake boundaries. The song's jumble and context also suggest the sex-gender circus is a universal one, not a collection of various groups, one representing boys who are girls, another of those who do girls like they're boys, etc.[17]

I choose Blur simply because I liked the song when it came out; it does not stand alone but in a broader context of popular music and culture in general. It was around the same time that Kurt Cobain put himself on the cover of the world's largest-circulation gay magazine, *The Advocate*, and declared himself to be a bisexual who hadn't had sex with a man yet;[18] Brett Anderson of Suede said something similar at about the same time, as did Sharon Stone. And though it seems to have always been marginally easier for women to make such declarations, especially if they're as hedgy as Stone's was, the fact that Cobain and Anderson and others were making such statements (in gay magazines, significantly, not straight ones, the way Bowie and Jagger had), even if they weren't backing them up with same-sex anecdotes or photo-ops, marks yet another major change since the days of Lola.[19]

I recently came across someone who's a bit of a modern-day Lola who made me think that perhaps we are in fact recapturing some of what we'd lost in the identity wars. Let's say his name was Rafe, though he sometimes went by Renée.

I'd been working on this book for some time already, and whenever people asked me what it was about, I'd say sex, and they'd say something about the research being a lot of fun, and I'd come up with some reasonable approximation of a nudge and a wink while thinking about library due dates and trying to remember which cafés had electrical outlets for the laptop.

After a few of these conversations I figured, well, yeah, why not have a little more fun. How many more books on sex did I think I was going to write? I remembered those first couple of sex books I bought when I was in grade seven and eight, making excuses to clerks as they rang them through that I was doing a paper or something. Well, now I really was doing a paper or something, and I realised it would be a shame not to take advantage of it. It could even help me out, to boot, with a specific sexual anecdote or case study or something that might make good copy. And as any culturally literate urbanite knows, the best way to order up sexual specifics is to call up the phone lines. So, for a few weeks, I did, going through a list of things I'd never done, having the sort of randomised sex I'd heard about in other eras, talking to people post-coitally about sex and learning a thing or two.

Which is how I met Rafe. He was Latino, small, cute, and probably somewhere around 20. And after some efficient sex, we lounged around and talked for a couple of hours. He showed me pictures of himself as Renée and told me about going out to bars and clubs, as a woman, to pick up men. I'd already determined he was definitely a surgically and hormonally unaltered male. Yet he didn't seem to have much trouble getting guys in bars and clubs – mostly in their early to mid-twenties – to buy him drinks, proceeding to get a few interested in him, picking his favourite, getting serious, and when sexual interest was definitively expressed and arrangements were being made, retiring to the most convenient apartment. Only then, Rafe told me, would Renée let them know that she was a he and ask them if that mattered.

I'd seen the movies, so I assumed he'd probably nabbed a few dates this way but not many. I also figured he'd probably got hit a lot. But Rafe told me he'd only ever been turned down twice out of dozens of such pick-ups – and even one of those was hesitating. And no violence or serious unpleasantness at all. With the exception of those two, they went home and had sex. Though he was enormously charming, and had the ingénue flirting thing totally down, I still found that remarkable.

But what was even more unexpected was that Rafe had a vaguely neurotic opposition to sexual passivity. If there was penetrative sex to be had – and there often was – the straight boy would be the one giving it up. He went into a little more detail, describing how the boys had reacted, their residual confusion being overcome by an attraction that was firmly established in the bar (Renée was pretty hot). They'd talk about it – Rafe was a big talker – and he said they were mostly good experiences; several repeat performances and a number of ongoing casual relationships. And at no point during the sex was Rafe pretending to be a girl.

Which makes it different from what one assumes happened between the verses in 'Lola'. What the guys Renée picked up were discovering and acting on was not only the permeability of gender-based attraction but the possibilities of entirely different, genderfucked sexual dynamics, similar to, but I'd say even more radical than, the sort of dynamic that comes into play with the surprisingly busy population of she-male prostitutes many large cities now support.[20] The presence of tits can make many men accept and even relish most anything else, even the presence of a cock.[21] Paying for it also changes things considerably. No matter what happens in bed, there's never any real doubt about who's calling the shots. But Rafe was something much more familiar, much more straightforward. He was a guy combing the bars to get laid, using, as guys often will, whatever means necessary to get some hottie into bed. He was, at every point in the negotiations as well as during the sex, in charge. At the point at which the evening's date was told Renée was also Rafe, any notion they might have had about being the one doing the pick-up evaporated.

Though Rafe/Renée is one of the more remarkable people I ran into during this little sex run of mine, it's all those guys he went home with who are of real interest to us here. Unlike Rafe, who'd done a lot of thinking about gender and sexuality and figured out just what he liked and how he wanted to get it, once confronted with the Rafe part of Renée, the guys he picked up were making snap decisions. Would they go or wouldn't they? Though there's loads to take into consideration – am I still attracted? interested? what exactly am I going to do when the penis pops out of the skirt? what if someone sees me? who am I? I don't do this sort of thing, I'm straight – snap decisions, like reflexes, are made with raw materials, the more fundamental bits of your make-up. And what these dozens of guys who ended up going home to Rafe's little downtown ground-floor apartment had in that make-up, these young men born mostly between 1973 and 1979, the same age as Vince, allowed them to take sex over identity, pleasure over principle. I'd say Rafe's dozens, having been picked up in non-gay bars, the only thing in common being Rafe's attraction to them and theirs to him, though they wouldn't stand up in a court of science, were a pretty good random sample of the *fin de siècle* sexual state of things. After two hundred and fifty years of lashing sexual behaviour to personal identity, the ties were starting to come loose.

# Part Two

ALL THIS TALK OF GAY AND STRAIGHT and bi and transgendered, all these labels, does not mean that this is in any way a semantic argument. I'm not just arguing labels, I'm arguing ontology – Being itself. But in the case of sexual labelling, perhaps more than in any other intersection of words and life, there's a symbiotic, maybe even a parasitic, relationship that exists. In the beginning was the word, and that word was homosexual. And the word was made flesh, and that flesh was the gay community. Ever since Karl Maria Kertbeny (1824–1882) came up with a word to define a state of being that hadn't been pinned down before this word was invented, people have been heading in this one direction.

The French philosopher and leather-enthusiast Michel Foucault has become rather famous for pointing out this very thing. And he's been volubly and effectively argued against in the couple of decades since he published his *History of Sexuality*. Ample evidence has been unearthed pointing to the existence of something very like our current notion of homosexuality in the couple of centuries prior to his watershed nineteenth. And what about those Greeks? And the Romans? Catullus certainly seemed to have some notion of something or other in those naughty pastorals of his. John Boswell came up with the idea that there were homosexual marriages in the Middle Ages, which he goes into in his book, *Same-Sex Unions in Premodern Europe*. Surely there had to be an idea that there was such a thing as a homosexual for there to have been same-sex marriages. Then there's the neoplatonism of the Italian Renaissance, and all those affectionate shepherds of the English Renaissance. It certainly looks, on the surface, as if homosexuals have always been with us. And so various activists and professors of gay studies (as opposed to queer theory) would have us believe, with the best intentions in the world. In a battle that was once against the threat of torture and death, and that is now mostly against things like insensitivity and relatively mild social exclusion, gay folks can take some in seeing themselves as heirs to a line that now includes Socrates, Alexander the Great, and Michelangelo.[22] But now that they are progressing from life-and-death struggles to one that's a little calmer, and one that's frankly being won (despite occasional setbacks, as painful and outrageous as they often are, especially in the States), and though there will no doubt be many defeats before some sort of final, quiet victory can be realised and we move on to other things, it may be time to take off the T-shirts proclaiming and reclaiming the lists of gay forefathers and mothers and take a look at our past, recent and distant, square in the face.

Once upon a time, about a century and a third before I met Rafe/Renée – in 1868 to be precise – sexual identity was born in a modest house in Germany.

Its father, Kertbeny, was a scientist and professor. Its mother, an era already somewhat long in the tooth at the time of birth, often known by her English name, Victoria, was famous then as now for her penchant for collecting, cataloguing, categorising, naming, pinning butterflies to cork and measuring people's noses and craniums to figure out whether they were Jews or criminals or both. Though quite popular at parties at the time, she's been refigured since as something of a dowdy puss.

By the time she went looking for love in the German countryside, she had already divided humanity into several distinct races, the globe into three basic segments (mine, almost mine, and not worth the effort), given birth to several political ideologies, including communism (in a rather questionable conjugal arrangement with Karl Marx and Friedrich Engels), as well as several thousand species of insects, mammals, fish, birds, and shrubberies. She had the bases pretty much covered, actually, when late in her childbearing years she noticed a bothersome empty spot in the nursery where Sex should be. So round she goes to Karl Maria Kertbeny's place – Germany being much better for that sort of thing at the time than England or even France – and wham-bam-thank-you-Karl, two more bouncing baby species were born. Karl immediately and proudly (and somewhat coldly, it seems in retrospect, given the names we've been able to come up with since) named the Siamese twins Homosexuality and Heterosexuality.

Of course, people had been sleeping around with all manner of person, beast, and shrubbery ever since they made the sex-pleasure connection several eons before. But until Karl came along, very few people outside the church hierarchy or, when it suited them, their law-enforcing secular equivalents, Victorian or pre-Victorian, had thought that what you did sexually had much bearing at all on who or what you were. There were precedents but they were localised, and if they were spreading, they had been doing it very slowly. Who you were, quite self-evidently to contemporaries, rested on any number of more important factors, like which earl you paid your tithes to, who your grandmother had married, and how much land you either owned or worked. Later, when such things became possible, what political views you held went a long way towards defining who you were and which pubs or parlours you were welcomed into. And, naturally, obvious things like the colour of your skin and whether you had internal or external secondary sexual characteristics (or both) pretty much pegged you as well.

But who you had sex with? Never. Certainly, there'd been a good bit of name-calling and stake-burning over men and, at certain times, women who made a point of fraternising or sororising exclusively with members of their own sex, who eschewed various fundamental social principles and contracts such as marriage and worker- or heir-production. They even had names for them: sodomites and, sometimes, witches.

The witch question I won't be dealing with in these pages, involving as it does all sorts of things quite distinct from sexuality. But sodomites were something else.

There have been arguments about just what the sin of Sodom was in Chapter 19 of the Book of Genesis. Here's the pertinent passage (19: 4–9) from the King James version, describing Lot and his family, visitors to Sodom, gathered in a house:

> . . . the men of the city, even the men of Sodom, compassed the house round, both old and young, all the people from every quarter.
>
> And they called unto Lot, and said unto him, Where are the men which came in to thee this night? Bring them out unto us, that we may know them.

And Lot went out at the door unto them, and shut the door after him.

And said, I pray you, brethren, do not so wickedly.

Behold now, I have two daughters which have not known man; let me, I pray you, bring them out unto you, and do ye to them as is good in your eyes: only unto these men do nothing; for therefore came they under the shadow of my roof.

And they said, Stand back. And they said again, This one fellow came in to sojourn, and he will needs be a judge: now will we deal worse with thee, than with them. And they pressed sore upon the man, even Lot and came near to break the door.

A lot, obviously, rests on how you choose to define 'know'. But as early interpreters of the Bible, and of this passage in particular, show, the 'knowing', however it's defined, was not the only, or even primary, issue.

Jerome, the Bible's first Latin translator, wrote 'The Sodomitic sin is pride, bloatedness, the abundance of all things, leisure and delicacies.' Others have since argued that the chief wrong committed in Genesis 19 is the sin of inhospitableness.

In *The Invention of Sodomy in Christian Theology*, Mark Jordan writes that he was able to find no reference to sodomy, no trace of the term, before the eleventh century. No one, apparently, had thought to attach the sorts of things the folks in Sodom did with a basic element of the human condition. Before the eleventh century, he traces references to Sodom and Sodomites through Jerome (342–420 CE), Ambrose (339–397 CE), Augustine (354–430 CE) and Gregory the Great (540–604 CE). But during these centuries, the concept was a more general kind of sinfulness, roughly equivalent in its use to 'communist' as a synonym for 'bad' in the US, Canada and UK of the fifties, or 'Christian' as a synonym in many circles still for 'good'. The terms, while having bases in some particularities, were used to cover far more.

Jordan figures it was Peter Damian, a monk who wrote a treatise addressed to Pope Leo IX called *The Book of Gomorrah*, who coined the abstract noun 'sodomy' around 1050 and he makes a case that from here on out, through Thomas Aquinas (1225–1274 CE) and beyond, the Church began, haltingly, to see sodomy as 'a pure essence of the erotic without connection to reproduction'. Jordan makes the argument that this sodomy was, in fact, the invention that Foucault ascribed to the nineteenth century. But though the Church may have started thinking of sodomy in the eleventh century the way the scientists began thinking about it in the nineteenth, from the wide range of non-clerical references to it in the years between the eleventh century and at the very earliest the beginning of the eighteenth (see below) as being something much more related to act than essence, it seems that the general population did not.

By late medieval times, sodomites were men who indiscreetly had sex, chiefly receptive sex, with other men. What is important to note about the distinction between the ages-old sodomite and the later homosexual is that with the former, at least outside the various church definitions, it was the indiscretion and receptivity that were the key issues, not the sex with men. Also key is that the definition was based in action, not being. There was no clearly defined sort of person who did this sort of thing. There were effeminate men and masculine women, of course, but this had little to do with presumed sexual practice, and nothing at all to do with sexuality.

By the time the concept had filtered through the church, and then the state, the secularised world handed the ball over to science, which came up with its much more specific term. And the moment people – chiefly writers and intellectuals – got wind of Kertbeny's new word from Germany, things started clicking into place. It took a while before an English translation of Kertbeny's writing appeared. It even took a while before Germany itself heard much of what he'd had to say – about thirty years in fact before Magnus Hirschfeld (1865–1935) republished Kertbeny's original pamphlet, and it got its first relatively wide distribution and discussion. But winds will waft, and of course had been wafting for some time already, at least since some gay purges of the first half of the eighteenth century.

Which is, as it happens, about the firmest ground I know of for

The Absolute Beginning of Gay.

The boy brothels and molly houses of eighteenth-century London – and their equivalents in Copenhagen, Amsterdam, and elsewhere – are now the generally academically accepted locus of the beginning of the formation of gay identity. As urban authorities started becoming less and less enthusiastic about strangling, burning, and drowning people caught in acts of various sorts of non-marital sex, the occasional entrepreneurial innkeeper let it be known that the neighbourhood boy prostitutes, of which there always seem to have been a number wherever there have been prostitutes at all, would not be actively discouraged from hanging out in his tavern. Clients followed, and what had been entirely surreptitious and private transactions became more social and public enough for word to get around.[23]

At the time, this sort of congregation was a new phenomenon (at least as far as current historical research indicates), and as with any new movement, technology, or practice, new words sprout up as ways to communicate new things are needed. This is not necessarily an indication that people were at the time thinking of the *vlaggemänner* and *nichtjen* as any more different than we currently think johns or tricks are. There's some evidence for this. A few years after these inns and meeting places started flourishing, Dutch authorities began a brutal series of prosecutions of sexual criminals. In January 1730, several former soldiers were arrested for their involvement in sodomitic acts. One of them, twenty-two-year-old Zacharias Wilsma, a Catholic with all sorts of guilt and it seems more than a little vicious self-importance, gave out the names of dozens of men he knew to have committed similar acts around the countryside. It was his testimony, for which he was kept alive for years, that first gave Dutch authorities the idea that there was some sort of transprovincial sodomitic subculture.

For the next two years, courts were set up in Amsterdam, Delft, Haarlem, The Hague, Utrecht, and in various smaller towns and villages throughout the Netherlands to root out this sudden evil in a pogrom that may represent the first national scapegoating of sodomy. In order to focus their vengeance, the authorities began speaking of the people they were rooting out as a breed, of a generally lower moral character than average – in much the same way as courts of the American South would come to portray blacks, or the courts of colonial Massachusetts their witches. In fact, the story of what happened in the Netherlands with their sodomites between 1730 and 1732 reads a lot like *The Crucible*, with makeshift courtrooms filled to capacity to hear the lurid details of sex (court testimony being at the time the only generally accessible form of pornography).

Though many people were made to feel guilty by this new designation, and many turned themselves and others in to cleanse themselves of the judicially fomented taint, those not implicated, unlike in Miller's tale, took offence at the presumptuousness of the prosecutions. In the village of Faan in the province of Groningen, for example, the flurry of trials had been set off in April 1731 by a blind thirteen-year-old boy who accused his thirteen-year-old cousin of attempted sodomy. The local magistrate, Rudolph De Mepsche, who would have heard about the big-city prosecutions of the past year, hopped on the bandwagon and brought in as many as thirty-six suspects on the heels of the young cousins and got many of them to confess to all sorts of things under torture. By September, twenty-four of them had been found guilty and were strangled and then burned at the stake.

But instead of feeling cleansed of the evil De Mepsche thought he'd found, the population of Faan turned against the judge and his staff. According to the late L. J. Boon, upon whose research I'm partially relying here, 'De Mepsche became known in popular legend as a brute and a scourge and as an executioner of innocent people. The families of the condemned voiced their indignation about what the judges implied about their relatives; namely that they had not been obedient fathers and sons who occasionally 'sinned', but instead a band of 'dogs and dirty swine'... To my knowledge,' Boon adds, 'this was the first time in history that the general public had become acquainted, not with the actual life of sodomites, but with the concept that sodomites were neither isolated individuals, nor lapsed "heterosexuals", but people with their own subversive ways.'

Within two years of the end of the trials, we have a record of one Justus van Effen in the Dutch counterpart of Addison and Steele's London *Spectator, De Hollandsche Spectator*, writing of 'effeminate weaklings' and 'hermaphrodites in their minds', which are significantly different beings from the occasionally, even habitually, sinful individuals of the years before 1730. And since labelling is a natural and practical way for people to deal with the world around them, this new labelling, which shifted emphasis from act to a state of being, and was established for purely judicial and vengeful purposes, began to catch on. Judging from Dutch newspapers of the time, the media had already signed up and had started writing about the people being tried and executed as a distinct and pernicious breed.

It seems to have been a matter of zeitgeist. Within a couple of decades, we also have the Danish judge C. D. Hedegard commenting that 'it has been noticed that the persons most devoted to this [sodomitical acts], as to other kinds of filthyness, are misers', an example of the sort of division between word and fact that was exhibited as early as the eleventh century when Rome declared the Balkan Bulgars (from which the word *bugger* is thought to have evolved) were guilty of treason, sodomy, and heresy, any one of which was supposed to imply and perhaps cause the others, and each of which warranted burning. There is in this designation, as there is in the persistent modern predilection for associating gay with serial killing (*Cruising, Basic Instinct, Silence of the Lambs*, rumours of Toronto sex-murderer Paul Bernardo's days as a male prostitute, and later, of the sex he was getting in prison) or spying (Guy Burgess and McCarthy's communism-inspired gay-baiting) or any other association of sexual sin with non-sexual sin, a perhaps thoughtless but nonetheless useful lumping together of undesirable qualities that allows one to more completely dissociate oneself from the criminally perverse.

The legal and social imperative to categorise in order to organise and administer was creeping across Europe as the loose and idiosyncratic feudal systems slowly converted themselves to early bureaucracies. The process was slow, and had a tendency to work in fits and starts, advancing, regressing, and advancing again. But the overall trend seems to have been two steps forward, one step back, and slowly but surely, the associations made with sodomites became more and more exclusively sexual, more and more clearly identity-based, less linked with extraneous nasties like heresy or miserliness, and more closely linked with sexual deviance, most prominently, and most lastingly, with sexual abduction and paedophilia. And as this process evolved, as the old sins were separated from sodomy, and new perceptions of general sexual evil began to stick to it, the ground was being prepared for the notion of a strictly sexually transgressive being to be born. And over the next century and a half general perceptions slowly changed, until Kertbeny and Richard von Krafft-Ebing (1840–1902) and others came along to crystallise them, as Foucault noted, in the late nineteenth century.

But the pre-1868 world is filled with familiar examples of the radically different ways in which we used to see our relationships to each other. We've already seen a Shakespearean example. And a fairly recent controversy over an interpretation of some correspondence between Goethe and a close friend provides another fine case in point.[24]

A Goethe biography published in Germany in 1997 purports to prove its subject's gayness. In a public stance that could be the template for such historical reclamations,[25] author Karl Hugo Pruys told Reuters, 'I am firmly convinced that Goethe was gay... The legend that Goethe was a lady's man is pure invention. The only woman in his life was his wife, Christiane Vulpius. They had children but slept in separate bedrooms and she drank herself to death... Goethe has been fundamentally misunderstood. We must pull him down from this marble pedestal and destroy the false myths created about him by a stiff academia.' Like other seekers after surety and celebrity before him, Pruys bases his assertions on such evidence as Goethe's letters to a friend, in this case the man he holds was Goethe's first love, a philosopher named Friedrich Heinrich Jacobi.

Pruys quotes a letter the twenty-four-year-old Goethe wrote to his buddy Fritz in 1774 that reads, in part, 'You have felt that it was rapture to me to be the object of your love – O it is splendid that each one believes he receives more from the other than he gives. O Love, Love! The poverty of wealth!' etc, and ends, 'Do not let my letters be seen! Do you understand!' Of the same relationship Pruys points out that Goethe wrote of Fritz in his memoirs about forty years later, 'At midnight you still sought me in the darkness – I felt my soul was reborn. From that moment on I could never leave you again.'

Reuters quotes a member of the German literary establishment, which is being accused of missing the boat on the whole Goethe thing, as saying, in effect, that guys talked to and about each other differently back then, and throws in for good measure that he and the rest of the establishment figure Goethe's first sexual liaison was with an Italian woman in Rome when he was thirty-eight.

As usual they both have a point, and they're both probably wrong. Snippets like these found in your presumed-heterosexual brother's e-mail today might raise an eyebrow or two. But should they with Goethe?

I don't think so – at least, not the same eyebrow.

But where the (older) establishment goes wrong and people like Pruys go too far is with the relationship between language and sentiment. Language, though heavily dependent upon convention for its form and structure, nevertheless bears a constant relationship to the mind and worldview of the speaker, and though it is cavalier to call this husband and father gay, it is just as irresponsible, or at least sloppy, to imagine that the enthusiasm of the correspondence of the eighteenth century and of centuries before it did not reflect a drastically different concept of the boundaries of relationships between members of the same sex. The notion that all those exclamation marks and professions of love and despair and jealousy were mere literary or epistolary convention – commonly held until members of gay studies departments started questioning them – shortchanges the very shapers of our notions of ourselves and love and all the other ineffables writers like Shakespeare and Goethe have devoted their careers to. It is also the product of an unquestioned assumption that people, despite some different approaches to language, have always seen themselves and behaved in essentially the same way.

It seems far more reasonable, and at least as probable, that before our churches, courts, governments and then we ourselves made the link between sex and identity, a great many people, perhaps the majority of people, perhaps everybody, felt less constrained in giving rein to their emotions and their physical extensions. Perhaps it's some more of Poe's really big print across the map of our collective history that we can't for the life of us see.

We can see this sort of language and the sentiment it expressed being stamped down on the road to gay before our very eyes in familiar circumstances, also in Germany, about a century and a quarter after Goethe, in the decades immediately following Kertbeny's coining of his terms.

In 1907, Kaiser Wilhelm II's closest friend, Philip zu Eulenburg, whom the Kaiser had once described as 'my bosom friend, the only one I have', was condemned in the anti-establishment press as being the leader of an 'effeminate camarilla,' fuelled perhaps by the success of the Krupp scandal five years previous, in which the richest man in Germany, Alfred Krupp (whose company would build Germany's war machine), was revealed to have had sex with young men in Capri. (Krupp killed himself and the Kaiser eulogised him at his funeral, saying that he had come 'to raise the shield of the German emperor over the house and memory of Krupp'.)

The paper *Die Zukunft* (appropriately enough, for the scandal the report caused would prove to be the harbinger of our own age, the paper's name means 'the future') had romantically linked Eulenburg with General Kuno Count von Moltke. The story, written by one Maximillian Harden at the suggestion of a disgruntled, recently fired court counsellor, also accused several other men, in league with Eulenburg and Moltke, of softening the Kaiser's opinion of the French (whom Harden and *Die Zukunft* hated). The charges, bolstered by several other attacks, a pro-homosexual testimony from sexologist Magnus Hirschfeld and one of the first modern-style outings (of Germany's chancellor, Prince von Bülow, by early gay activist Adolf Brand), soon ballooned into a full-scale scandal, the biggest in Germany that year once it led to a series of libel cases, which all ended ambiguously. But before they did, there was embarrassing testimony from the wives of the allegedly libelled men, which included Moltke's wife relating an instance of her husband coming across a dropped handkerchief of Eulenburg's, pressing it to his lips, and whispering, 'Phili, my Phili,' and referring to Eulenburg as 'my soulmate, my old boy, and my one and only cuddly bear'.

Though Moltke eventually won on appeal, and Harden was sent to prison for libel, and though Eulenburg fell ill coincident with his trial, preventing it from ever reaching a conclusion, the language and sentiment of intense male feeling was exposed to the radioactive light of public scrutiny. And of course, as always happens when intimacies are made public, they are seen as either laughable, perverse, or both (the Prince of Wales' tampon conversation with Camilla Parker-Bowles comes to mind), almost inevitably forcing the participants into denial or silence. But not only were these intimacies made public, they were associated, through accusations of effeminacy and unpatriotic pro-French sympathies, with a type. The *Zukunft* report was meant to foster the impression that these men, though they might seem to be one sort, were another. It was not necessary to specify what sort they might be; it was sufficient to imply surreptitiousness, duplicity, and vague offences against popular notions of Prussian machismo. The men were made a laughing stock, not because the sentiments they expressed to each other were necessarily uncommon ones (you may not have ever wished to be your lover's tampon, but it is likely that you've said something about wishing you were a beauty mark on her chest, or that you were his boxer shorts, or her pantyhose), but because those sentiments were made to look ridiculous when bandied about in public. We all regularly say things to each other that would look horrible in print. This does not mean those things are perverse, or even irregular.

From that point on, in Germany and, as such zeitgeisty things go, elsewhere (the Eulenburg Affair was media fodder across Europe; in France, it gave rise to same-sex sexual activity being referred to as *le vice allemand*), men would become more guarded in their expressions of mutual affection, both verbal and otherwise, for such expressions were fast coming to mean, in a post-Wilde, post-Eulenburg world, that one might not be what one (and one's peers) figured one was. As Moltke wrote in a letter at the time: 'At the moment when the freshest example of the modern age, a Harden, criticized our nature, stripped our ideal friendship, laid bare the form of our thinking and feeling which we had justifiably regarded all our lives as something obvious and natural, in that moment, the modern age, laughing cold-bloodedly, broke our necks.'

After the furore over the Krupp and Eulenburg scandals had been squelched by the pan-European calamity of World War One, the new, fairly liberal Weimar Republic became one of the breeding grounds of the modern homosexual – much of the groundwork for which had been laid by Magnus Hirschfeld.

Bavaria had abolished its laws against same-sex sexual activity in 1813 under the influence of the Napoleonic Code,[26] and Hanover likewise in 1840, but in 1871, various German states united into a single Germany under a Prussian monarchy. And since the militaristic Prussians, Spartans to Berlin's Athenians, never legalised 'unnatural sexual acts between men and men, and men and beasts', this law became part of the unified German legal code. It was in opposition to this Paragraph 175 that the first gay movement recognisable to modern activists, in fact the precursor to what have become truths held self-evident by the international gay communities, was founded by Hirschfeld, a neurologist specialising in nervous and psychic disorders. Based on principles quietly discussed and thinly distributed around the time of Hirschfeld's birth by Kertbeny and Karl Heinrich Ulrichs (1825–1895), the Scientific Humanitarian Committee was founded in 1897, the year Oscar Wilde was released from prison.

The committee was established on the assumption, which Hirschfeld took from his sexological predecessors, that homosexuality is biological, the homosexual a type. In Hirschfeld's mind, the homosexual was a third sex, intermediate between the other two.[27] He would eventually petition the government, with some degree of success (though he never managed to get rid of Paragraph 175, he would collect thousands of signatures on his petitions, including Einstein's, Rilke's, Thomas Mann's, Hermann Hesse's). But Hirschfeld's first major media hit was his polling. In 1903, he sent out three thousand questionnaires to high-school boys asking them whether they were primarily attracted to boys, girls, or both, providing them all with anonymous blank postcards on which they could write their coded responses. In 1904, he did the same with five thousand male factory metal workers. Though his findings were greatly overshadowed by a lawsuit brought by six students who charged him with obscenity (he was found guilty and made to pay a fine and costs), he had managed to conduct the first large-scale gay survey, the scientific technique upon which the entire gay movement was to continually re-establish its credentials with increasing frequency and specialisation over the next century.[28] Hirschfeld's two ultimate justifications for his organisation and his activist tactics and pursuits also bore a striking resemblance to those used in continuing the fight he started. The first was to establish as scientific fact that the homosexual was born, not made, and so was beyond the scope of a legal system that could punish people for what they did, not for who they were. The second was to prevent teenage suicide.

During his trial, Hirschfeld told the court:

At the beginning of this very week, a well-known homosexual student at the School of Technology poisoned himself because of his homosexuality. In my medical practice, I have at present a student in the same school who shot himself in the heart. Just a few weeks ago, in this very room, I attended a case against two blackmailers who had driven a homosexual gentleman – one of the most honourable men I knew – to suicide . . . I could present hundreds of cases like this, and others similar to it. I felt it was necessary to bring about this inquiry in order to free humanity of a blemish [Paragraph 175] that it will someday think back on with the deepest sense of shame.[29]

Throughout this century, at least from this point forward, we have required there to be respectable, non-sexual reasons for the defence of various forms of sexuality, most obviously homosexuality. Feeling awkward making public arguments in favour of pleasure and the happiness that derives from it, activists have felt the need to hitch their cause to recognisable social causes, such as suicide prevention, causes it would be difficult for people not to get behind. Pleasure has never been conceived as a right in the Western tradition and only rarely as even a worthwhile pursuit, and the pursuit of happiness, in American mythology, is only valid when happiness is born of struggle or odds overcome to the greater glory of the state or some corporate subsidiary thereof and not as the outcrop of purely personal, especially sensual, pleasure (unless the pleasure is simple, the sort you might get from a nice slice of pie).

It didn't work for Hirschfeld, and if it's sexual freedom we're looking for, rather than ensconced, static rights for an imperfectly defined group, it's not going to work for us, either.

The Eulenburg trial got everyone talking about homosexual behaviour, and helped put an end in Europe to the masculine habit of expressing love for other men. This widened the gulf between what was increasingly coming to be seen as two distinct sexual camps, making necessary the gay movements to come. But the scandalous tone of the trial and the media attention to it did in fact break the neck of the burgeoning gay rights movement, taking its basic precepts and turning them against it. Indeed, almost all future anti-gay movements and sentiment (with the exception of the American religious right and their healing ways) would use the ammunition provided by Kertbeny, Karl Heinrich Ulrichs, Krupp, Eulenburg and Hirschfeld.

## The End of the Beginning

It is just as important to civilisation that Literary England should be cleansed of sex-mongers and peddlers of the perverse, as that Flanders should be cleared of Germans.
– Alfred Lord Douglas

## The Big Gay War

In the middle of Hirschfeld's career, an archduke was killed in Sarajevo. Hirschfeld continued his work, but public attention shifted.

When I began this book, my impression was that the First World War was ever so much more important in the history of homosexuality than the Second. I read Paul Fussell, among others, saying in one form or another, 'No one turning from the poetry of the Second War back to that of the First can fail to notice there the unique physical tenderness, the readiness to admire openly the bodily beauty of young men, the unapologetic recognition that men may be in love with each other,'[30] and interpreted it as meaning that World War One was singularly important to the study of sexuality.

I was wrong. It is chiefly in its contrast to the next war that this first one becomes interesting, for all its Wilfred-Owen, Sigfried-Sassoon, Rupert-Brooke homoeroticism had almost precise antecedents in pre-war literature. The dead boy and the naked (and probably bathing) boy were around long before Sassoon fell in love with his dead German soldier or Brooke noticed his 'swimmers into cleanness leaping.' They were there in Whitman and Houseman and any number of more minor poets with such names as Gillett, Gurney and Rodd.

> He had the poet's eyes,
> – Sing to him sleeping –
> Sweet grace of low replies,
> – Why are we weeping?
> He had the gentle ways,
> – Fair dreams befall him! –
> Beauty through all his days,
> – Then why recall him? –
> That which in his was fair
> Still shall be ours:
> Yet, yet my heart lies there
> Under the flowers.

That unfortunate poem was written by Rennell Rodd in 1881. Which is simply to say that it is not so remarkable to find poems like Owen's 'Arms and the Boy' or 'To Eros' thirty-five years later. Nor is it remarkable that they were as popular as they were, what with the poetic tradition already intact, and a war on. No, it is the history since this war that is remarkable.

World War One was chiefly notable in this respect for the last blast of publicly possible old-style homoeroticism it occasioned, the sort the death of which was presaged by Moltke during the Eulenburg Affair. It could have been, were it not for certain unfortunate circumstances to follow, a balm for the blow the Wilde affair had delivered to the possibility of male-male affection and sexuality.

But on January 26, 1918, eleven months before the war ended, English impresario and member of Parliament Noel Pemberton Billing printed, in a newspaper he owned called *The Imperialist*, the following screedlet:

There exists in the Cabinet Noir of a certain German Prince a book compiled by the Secret Service from reports of German agents who have infested this country for the past 20 years ... In the beginning of the book is a précis of general instructions regarding the propagation of evils which all decent men thought had perished in Sodom and Lesbia. The blasphemous compilers even speak of the Groves and High Places mentioned in the Bible ... There are the names of 47,000 English men and women ... Privy Councillors, wives of cabinet ministers, even Cabinet Ministers themselves, diplomats, poets, bankers, editors, newspaper proprietors, and members of His Majesty's Household ... prevented from putting their full strength into the war by corruption and blackmail and fear of exposure ... the stamina of British sailors was undermined ... Even to loiter in the streets was not immune ... agents of the Kaiser were stationed at such places as Marble Arch and Hyde Park corner ... Wives of men in supreme positions were entangled. In Lesbian ecstasy the most sacred secrets of State were betrayed.

The sexual peculiarities of members of the peerage were used as leverage to open fruitful fields for espionage.

Already in danger for some time of lapsing into desuetude, the Wilde affair of twenty years earlier was resurrected in a most spectacular way in another libel trial that stemmed from Billing's same paper, as a result of the same campaign of sensational purification launched in that January issue. The next month, Billing's paper, renamed *The Vigilante*, ran a snippet about a dancer of some popularity and notoriety named Maud Allan who was to perform in a production of Wilde's *Salome* in London. The mini-headline read 'The Cult of the Clitoris' and the fifty-three-word story suggested that if Scotland Yard were to monitor the audience, they would be sure to find some of the already infamous 47,000. Although, according to Philip Hoare's account of the trial and scandal, many readers had no idea what a clitoris was (Billing had had to consult a physician friend when he decided he needed a suitably provocative yet still somewhat hooded term), the item caused enough of a ruckus to prompt Allan to sue for libel. The case was to run in close parallel to Wilde's. Robbie Ross, the Canadian who was Wilde's first male lover and who had warned Wilde not to proceed with his libel action against the Marquess of Queensberry, warned Allan not to proceed with hers against Billing. Allan's counsel was the son of the man who first prosecuted on behalf of Wilde and then defended him in the preliminary trial that followed against him. And the producer of Allan's *Salome*, Jack Grein, had represented the man who'd supplied the long line of young men who testified against Wilde at the trial that sent him to Reading Gaol. There was more than enough to bring back all the bile that had risen against Wilde.

The trial itself is barely believable in its details (for a blow-by-blow accounting of which you can pick up Hoare's book *Oscar Wilde's Last Stand*). In short, Billing made it a trial about the 47,000, calling witnesses to testify to the particulars of the black book that was said to contain the names, and spending a good deal of time actually naming names, which ended up including not only the prime minister and his wife but the presiding judge as well. Despite an absolute lack of evidence (the black book, after all, did not exist), the trial became big news, temporarily knocking even the war off the front pages. Everyone wanted to know whose names were in that book, which the witnesses continually assured the judge could be produced at a moment's notice. Allan lost her case against the now very popular Billing, who took his victory as a mandate to continue his fight against the sodomites and lesbians who were betraying their country to its enemies.[31] But once the spectacle of the trial was over, the public lost its consuming interest, the fight became increasingly sad and pathetic, and Billing and his cause fell from the limelight.

## Meanwhile, Back in Germany...

Though Hirschfeld was never able to achieve the goals he set for the various committees and organisations and institutes he founded and inspired, he did manage to get the machine moving. In 1911, the same year a coalition Hirschfeld formed with the women's movement succeeded in preventing Paragraph 175 from expanding to include women, Jacob Schorer founded the Nederlandsch Wetenschappelijk Humanitair Komitee, a Dutch equivalent of Hirschfeld's committee, and by 1914, the British Society for the Study of Sex Psychology was established in London, with Edward Carpenter its first president and with Shaw, Forster, and Vyvyan Holland (Wilde's son) among its early members. Of course, this was also the age of Freud, and sex was becoming more a topic of conversation, seen as more important, at least among the intelligentsia, in all sorts of aspects of life with which it had never before been associated. The same-sex force of this newly sexualised age was felt the most in Germany – in Berlin and Hamburg in particular – and it was to these cities that Auden and Spender and Isherwood were attracted, and which they would later eulogise, spreading the news of the glories of gay subculture, the possibility of which was only slowly evolving in other urban centres, and creating a permanent foundation for twentieth-century urban gay mythology (and later a touchstone for 1970s Studio 54 American equivalents in the film of Isherwood's *Berlin Stories*, *Cabaret*).

In writing about the Weimar years (1918–1933) in the introduction to his resurrected novel, *The Temple* (written in 1929, published in 1988), Stephen Spender said, 'For many of my friends and for myself, Germany seemed a paradise where there was no censorship and young Germans enjoyed extraordinary freedom in their lives. By contrast England was the country where James Joyce's *Ulysses* was banned, as was also Radclyffe Hall's *The Well of Loneliness*...England was where the police...took down from the walls of the Warren Gallery pictures from an exhibition of D. H. Lawrence's paintings.'

In the United States, there was Prohibition; in France, books about same-sex sexuality were being written by prominent writers, like *Corydon* by Gide and *Le livre blanc* by Cocteau, but were being published anonymously.[32] 'Prohibition,' Spender continued, 'resulted in young Americans like Hemingway and Scott Fitzgerald leaving America and going to France or Spain. For them, drink; for us, sex.'

Something else Spender wrote in that introduction gives a hint of something else going on at the same time:

Another result of censorship was to make us wish to write precisely about those subjects which were most likely to result in our books being banned. There was almost an obsession among young English writers at this time to write about things which were, as subjects of literature that could be published, forbidden by law...Writing *The Temple*, I felt that I was very much one of my generation, exploring new territory of living identified with a new literature. This was the time when the title of almost every anthology or literary magazine incorporated the epithet 'new'.

A subject that had been brought up by Wilde, turned into a cause célèbre by his martyrdom, and strengthened by the singular form of poetically expressed male passion in the First World War, but which had never gained any sort of genuine public support, was in the late

1920s, becoming a part of the 'new', part of the rebellion against the old. And since it was writers like these taking up the cause, very good writers, writers who were quickly gaining an international audience, writers able to argue compellingly, to create a mood, a scene, a world, word spread, and seeds that had been planted around the American and European world, on New York's Bowery and in London's Soho, began to sprout and pools to crystallise into self-conscious and increasingly public communities. Spender was very much a part of his generation. With Wilde, the War, Freud, Sassoon, Owen and Proust, as well as the whole raft of nineteenth-century sexologists as primary materials, Spender, Auden, Isherwood, Cocteau, Gide, and Thomas Mann were building the very thing we're now in the process of taking apart.

So by the time respectable, and even man-loving, men started cocktail chatting about the breed, well, it was just an idea whose time had come, wasn't it? 'Of course!' these writers and intellectuals and trendsetters started saying to each other in cafés and letters and essays and books. It all made sense now. A lot of these people given to spending big wads of time thinking about themselves and each other did in fact have sex with members of the same sex, though of course most were also married. Many had far more intimate and far more complex relationships with these other members of the same sex than they'd seen represented in any of the media available to them. And they already thought of themselves as a set apart, bohemians, intellectuals, artists, free thinkers. Now a subgroup of them, the ones who had, perhaps, had particularly intense, particularly earth-moving same-sex relationships (for, in the context of European single-sex residential schools of the time – and rural and communal urban life in general – a great many of them had had some form of same-sex sexual relationships), could rally around a new concept, a new identity.

For it was, conveniently, also the great age of identity construction, and since sex, of whatever variety, is such a powerful force in people's lives, an identity based in it, especially with the new concomitant notion of there being such a thing as sexuality (as distinct from sex), found particularly fertile ground for cultivation.

Here's the artist F. O. Matthiessen writing to his boyfriend, Russell Cheney, in 1925, smack dab in the middle of all this: 'Of course this lie of ours is entirely new – neither of us know of a parallel case. We stand in the middle of an uncharted, uninhabited country. That there have been other unions like ours is obvious, but we are unable to draw on their experience. We must create everything for ourselves. And creation is never easy.'

Now the straightish men among you may be saying to yourselves, Sure, I'll go along with this whole lack of emotional constraint thing. Yeah, maybe modern notions of machismo and convention, when mixed with neo-puritanism, do make us, men especially, a little less likely to let each other know how much we really care about each other, and maybe, if we were able to admit it, maybe we really do love each other, we men and our best friends, in some way or other. But come on, there's absolutely no proof at all that that would necessarily or even possibly extend to sex. And sex is what we're talking about here, isn't it? There's nothing that hard to swallow about the possibility of greater emotional closeness between buddies of the same sex.

Yes, well, that is a tough one, and one I thought a lot about after I intuited what I intuited from the various primary and secondary texts I've been digging through these past few years. And when I realised that we as a general population have only been able to write publicly and explicitly about sex – about the sex we have, that is – for a few decades (and before that, in Western literature in any case, there's a big black hole back to round about the sacking of Rome), I also realised that if we're talking actual sex, well, there's simply never going to be any proof that *anybody* did much of anything for most of the centuries of our collective history, except for Chaucer and court records of some especially imprudent or unlucky people (and of course the fact that we're here, which means some people must have been having some heterosexual sex, at least).

And then I started thinking about polls and surveys and how unreliable they are, about history, and how academics in history departments all over the world are beginning to take apart their own discipline, figuring everything's constructed, everything's unreliable, everything's up for grabs. And then I remembered how Descartes set about proving the unprovable – the existence of God. He took things back, step by step, until he got to the most basic, unquestionable fact in the universe: his perception of himself (I think, therefore I am). His proof may have gone off the rails somewhere along the way between himself and God, but his method was sound: induction and extrapolation from the self, instead of deduction and generalisation from facts, figures and documents.

If we hold that as humans nothing human is alien to us, and if we look at how we acted before various social constraints were placed upon us, if we look at children, especially very young children, and recognise, if we don't flinch (and most of us do flinch around the very young in such matters), that Freud was right in his observation that they are polymorphously perverse, and see the close analogy to the very young and sex with the very young and language (babies are born with the ability to make every sound used by any human language; it's only with straightened practice in a single language that the propensity is lost), then we might just see how we are made into the sexual beings we are, and how eminently, and imminently, changeable that is.

## Harlem

Round about the time Weimar was conducting its grand experiment, something similar was happening on the island of Manhattan in the blocks just above Central Park, as well as down towards the bottom in the Ninth Ward, which the people who'd recently begun to displace the Italians there had started calling the Village.

It was a time in the United States when one still needed a doctor's certificate to be able to buy a copy of Krafft-Ebing's *Psychopathia Sexualis*, a fin-de-siècle book of sexual case studies.[33] And though there were bars where men interested in sex with men congregated in New York, in Philadelphia, in St. Louis, San Francisco,

Milwaukee, New Orleans, Chicago, Boston, and most of the other large cities, it was in Harlem that same-sexiness was incorporated into a cultural movement, the Harlem Renaissance, where the players, like their rough contemporaries huddled around Russell Square in London, succeeded in having the sort of practical, catalytic effect artists, especially in groups and movements, are able to exercise. Male writers like Countee Cullen, Wallace Thurman, and Langston Hughes, though not producing much explicitly same-sexy writing,[34] lived their lives in the heart of Harlem, according to the rules of what Bruce Benderson has called in a similar context the culture of poverty from which they came,[35] the Black South. Female Harlem performers, like Ma Rainey, Bessie Smith, and Gladys Bentley, singing songs like the one about a husband running off with a man named Miss Kate, and male blues singers singing songs with titles like 'Sissy Man Blues' ('If you can't bring me a woman, bring me a sissy man') and, in Bentley's case, wearing tuxedoes and top hats and conducting very public affairs with a string of women,[36] did a lot to cement Harlem's reputation as a 'jungle' where anything went, the sort of place the knowledge of which led to the winking success of popular lyrics of the time, in the vein of, say, 1934's 'When ev'ry night the set that's smart is/Indulging in nudist parties/In studios,/Anything goes!'[37]

What we have, in the case of Harlem in the twenties and thirties, is a case of essentially poor, rural, and unselfconscious, uncentralised culture transplanting itself to a wealthier, urban, very self-conscious, and very centralised setting, transforming both itself and its new home. The sexual behaviours of many of the main players in the Harlem Renaissance represent a transitional phase, a testing of the waters, seeing how old took to new and new to old. So, for a while, Gladys Bentley was able to carry on as she did. For a while, anything did go in this part of town, where the black locals were figuring out how they could and would act in their new surroundings, and where whites, from middle-class to upper-class, were able to behave differently – mixing race and gender in all sorts of unaccustomed ways – protected by the distance, both physical and cultural, from Park Avenue or Murray Hill or even Broadway.[38]

## Nineteen-Thirty-Three

Nineteen-thirty-three was a bad year for sex. In 1933, the fifteen-year-old Weimar Republic collapsed and created a void into which Germany's future fell. And in 1933, the thirteen years of American Prohibition ended, and with it much of the draw of the lawlessness of 'darkest uptown' New York City. People could drink closer to home now, no need to venture north, and the adventurousness of much of the middle class was knocked out of them (as was their ability to act on any they might have retained by the '29 crash). Harlem's day as a cultural centre with direct influence on mainstream urban America was, at least for the time being, done. The comparison of the two events may seem bathetic, but in terms of sex, the two had strikingly similar effects. In Germany, it came in the form of a striving to reclaim the country's glorious, and mostly mythical, past, a calling on Nietzsche, on Wagner, (and, soon enough, on Donner and Blitzen) to whip up a population in definite doldrums after years of post-Versailles-treaty blues. No more time for messing around with personal fulfilment – Hirschfeld's books and his institute were burned, an effigy of his head impaled on a stick in protests. Then there was the storming of the cabarets, the night of the long knives, the rainbow of triangles . . . [39]

In Harlem, the effects were less dramatic. Things just started drying up. The Depression hit everyone, of course, but, as with many things in the States, the blacks were hit harder. No more stompin' at the Savoy, and the Cotton Club, whose audience had always been an enforced cotton-white, became more and more exclusive, with less and less cultural impact. Both it and Smalls' Paradise (which with the Savoy made up Harlem's big three night spots) were making a quick transition, as David Levering Lewis describes it in his book *When Harlem Was in Vogue*, from being Harlem nightclubs to nightclubs in Harlem. Johns Hopkins political scientist Broadus Mitchell, addressing a civil rights meeting in 1933, predicted the 'end of the era of individualism'. Several of the most prominent characters behind the Renaissance moved away, and Harlem began a transition from ghetto to slum.

But what had burned brightly and short up in Harlem had

glowed slightly less but lasted considerably longer down in the Village, where the wealthier, more socially stable white middle-class bohemians had more of a cushion to fall onto when the Depression hit. Already in the thirties residents were complaining that mere poseurs were beginning to buy up flats in the Village, turning it from the truly bohemian to the merely apparently bohemian. And they were probably right (enclaves like the Village last much longer in legend and student travel guides than they do in fact), though a truly bohemian element did persist, at least through to the Beats of the fifties.

The gays stayed even longer than that. It was from the teens onwards that the Village gave birth to the settled homosexual. Though they moved in at the same time as the bohemians, and were in large part bohemians themselves, as the Village got a wider and wider reputation for being free and easy and non-judgmental, as *Variety* and *Vanity Fair* and other leisure periodicals spoke more and more alluringly of the Village and its wonders, men and women from all over the country started showing up looking for action. Behaviour that elsewhere would have been considered quirky or even just normal, when conducted in the Village began to be tinged with something else. Stephen Graham, in *New York Nights* (1927), commented that two women dancing together in Times Square and seen as fun-loving friends would, if they decided to take it downtown, be automatically assumed to be lesbians. A circular, self-perpetuating process had begun. What had started out as a place open enough to allow people to behave as they liked sexually was becoming a gay place. Two women dancing together in the Village now meant only one thing, much as it did in the rest of the country. It had been simply inverted instead of subverted. The openness, the lack of assumptions, the freedom to follow one's attractions and one's sexual whims was being boiled down to standards.

It was about this time, too, and in about this place, that the family jargon was adopted by the burgeoning gay male community, an unconscious prelude to today's unsavoury gay family-values contingent. There were sisters, husbands and wives, aunties and mothers, and soon, daddies and sons. Men, in this latter dichotomy, did not have sex with other men, only with fairies, wives, and sons or boys. Sisters never had anything sexually or romantically to do with one another (or if they did, it was referred to with terms like bumping pussies, denigrating both the experience and lesbians at the same time); neither did husbands and husbands, or wives and wives. And aunties or mothers, though respected for wisdom or seniority or merely longevity, were out of the sexual realm altogether (except when they hired boys).

Of the earlier days of Greenwich Village and Harlem, Harlemite Bruce Nugent said later, 'You just did what you wanted to. Nobody was in the closet. There wasn't any closet.' The Harlem and Greenwich Village of this time were transitional, and like all transitional times – the transition from the fourteenth to the fifteenth centuries in Western Europe, for example – all sorts of new and unstructured possibilities were glimpsed before a new structure was formed to contain them, transforming innovation into tradition. In this case, as Nugent suggests, it was a time when sexology and a more progressive literature and popular cultural scene allowed for open, or at least not entirely covert, sexual investigation, and before a powerful new structure – the closet – came along to rigidify paths into roads.

C. S. Lewis's Narnian wardrobe is not a perfect analogy, but it may be a useful one. The discovery of that closet in *The Lion, The Witch and the Wardrobe* changed everything. A whole new parallel world opened up when Lucy stepped through the wardrobe, felt the new turf beneath her feet, and said, 'This is very queer.' And though for the children, stepping into rather than out of the closet was the liberating move, the fact that Lewis's wardrobe bisected a single familiar and humdrum world into two very different yet parallel ones that had little effect on one another is very much of a piece with the early and middle history of our big gay closet. The closet demands that there be two possible states of existence for people who have same-sex sex, a dichotomy paralleling the one that separates gay and straight. You are either in the closet or you are out of the closet. There may be some intermediary stages – the process of stepping out may take you through being out to yourself, being out to your gay friends but not your straight friends, being out to your friends but not your family, being out to everyone but your mother (it would kill her) – but these are all more or less negligible, preferably quick steps on your way out. Being out is liberation, being in is oppression. In its baldest and most compelling terms, Michelangelo Signorile wrote in 1993:

> We must all tell our parents. We must tell our families. We must all tell our friends. We must all tell our co-workers . . . What was done to us when we were children was nothing less than child abuse . . . Liberate yourself and all others who are locked in the closet . . . Badger everyone you know who is closeted – your friends, your family members, your co-workers – to come out. Put pressure on those in power whom you know to be queer. Send them letters. Call them on the phone. Fax them. Confront them in the streets. Tell them they have a responsibility: to themselves, to you, to humanity.[40]

The closet was, by Signorile's heyday, taken wholly for granted. Signorile's subtitle for the book this was taken from is 'Sex, the Media, and the Closets of Power'. You are one thing or the other. If you are a woman and you have sex or have had sex with other women, and you are not out of the closet, you are in it. Two choices. Gay or straight; Narnia or England. By introducing the closet – a natural extension of Ulrichs and Hirschfeld's biomedical designation with which gay began – two worlds were created. Though our Narnia was outside the wardrobe rather than in it, we both – gays and Lewis's Pevensie children – had to pass through it to reach a more exciting world, a world where we could be truer to ourselves, where our inherent specialness and powers really shone through.

Perhaps the closet is a necessary thing. Perhaps absolute freedom, with no initiation process, is unworkable. It's proven to be in Western society, in any case. But does that mean the closet's a permanent part of our furniture? Must it always be with us, this dichotomising box, or could it be, like it was for Lewis, a feature of a room from our childhood, something to help us grow, to show us something we might never have been able to see without it, but something that, ultimately, must be transcended, relegated, along with the rest of our grandparents' things, to memory and rummage?

Lewis was a great fan of the neoplatonism that's been no friend to sex in the five centuries since Florentine scholar Marsilio Ficino started devising it at the behest of a pope who wanted the works of Plato and Aristotle reinterpreted and recontextualised as the natural harbingers of Christianity. But perhaps we can turn it to the good. In his Narnia books, Lewis uses the wardrobe as a Platonic device. The Narnia the children first visit, which appears to them so wonderful and so harrowing, turns out to be just one world within a world, a shadowland, as Mr Tumnus the faun points out towards the end of the story's final volume, just as the England they leave behind was – 'like an onion', the faun continues, 'except that as you continue to go in and in, each circle is larger than the last'. Their initial liberation through the wardrobe ends up being merely an initiation into a grander sort of liberation they would not have been able to grasp had they not first been through their Narnia adventure. Worlds within worlds and portals between them. What seemed like it had always been there, a place where time moved more quickly, giving the appearance of permanence, turned out to be not a place at all but a phase, just a doorway to someplace else.

Just like gay.

The years leading up to Stonewall saw a breach in the assimilationist attitudes of the docile homophiles of the previous generation in favour of more revolutionary ones of people who craved more purely sexual freedom.

In August 1968, at The Patch, a bar just south of L.A., a couple of undercover cops casually arrested a couple of men who'd been dancing together. It was illegal, this same-sex dancing and carrying on, and this sort of quiet reminder of authority and the status quo happened fairly regularly. But this was the summer of 1968. This was the summer those bras were burned outside the Miss America pageant in Atlantic City. The summer Ron Gabe, Jorge Saia, and Michael Tims got together to form General Idea.[41] The summer black athletes who made it to the podium at the Mexico City Olympics stood to the US national anthem with black-gloved fists raised in the air. This was also the summer that 'Gay is Good' was adopted as a motto by the North American Conference of Homophile Associations (NACHO) in Chicago just a few days before that Democratic National Convention during which Gore Vidal almost made William F. Buckley cry.

There was, you might say, a zeitgeist afoot. Something was happening here, and though what it was may not have been exactly clear, it prompted Lee Glaze, the manager of The Patch, to get up on stage and rally about two dozen men to march down to the police station, arms filled with flowers, and announce that they were there to wait for their imprisoned sisters. The Patch was never harassed again, and about one month later one of the two men arrested, Troy Perry, placed his first ad to see if anyone might be interested in starting a gay-positive Christian group.[42] A month later, *The Advocate*, a gay magazine that had been founded in 1967 by stapling together sheets surreptitiously photocopied on ABC TV copiers by an employee, ran a story on the Patch incident, saying that if the reaction of the customers 'is any indication, a new era of determined resistance may be dawning for L.A.'s gay community'.[43]

There were at least five more significant public demonstrations in the States – in Fort Belvoir, Virginia, in November, New Orleans in March of 1969, another one in L.A. the same month, in San Francisco in April, and in Columbus, Ohio, in May[44] – before the spark jumped over to New York and really ignited on the night of June 28–29, a little more than a month after Justice Minister Pierre Trudeau said, echoing a sentiment expressed in 1903 by Nabokov's father, the founder of the pre-Revolutionary Constitutional Democrat Party, that the state has no place in the bedrooms of the nation and his Bill C-150 decriminalised homosexuality in Canada (passed by a vote of 149 to 55).[45]

Though there was much gayness afoot, those doing most of the agitating and activating often had grander notions. In these pointedly and self-consciously politicised times, when the space between personal and political got so drastically shrunk in young people's minds, a fight for the acceptance of same-sex sexuality was seen as part of a larger pansexuality. These people were looking for a transformation of society, one that is based on a 'new human' who is able to accept the multi-faceted and varied nature of his/her sexual identity. That such a society can be founded is the gamble upon which gay and women's liberation is based . . . It has been said that a liberal is someone who wants to help others; a radical someone who knows that he/she needs help. The liberal sees homosexuals as a minority to be assisted into a full place in society. The radical sees homosexuality as a component of all people including him/herself.[46]

These radical years were born in part of the Beat generation (following Burroughs and Ginsberg), as well as the nascent student activist movement (primarily in Eastern Europe, Paris, and the United States), and the gay sexual revolutionaries of the sixties and early seventies became, as the revolutionary spirit of the age crested, an unpopular minority. They attempted, in the form of, among others, the Gay Liberation Front (an organisation that started in New York, then expanded to Los Angeles, and a few months later, to London), to align themselves with various other groups, including the Marxists, the women's movement, Abbie Hoffman's Yippies, and the Black Panthers, but though their aims were largely in sync with the rest of the age, the espousal and practice of same-sex sex – even though there was a significant proportion of them to begin with who were more interested in a generalised sexual liberation than a more restricted gay liberation – mostly excluded them.

In its early stages, this radicalism connected gay liberation with the general sexual liberation of everybody. As Rick Bébout, an old-time and unrepentant activist and sexual archivist extraordinaire, writes in his evolving Web history of sex and sexual identity from the seventies forward (www.rbebout.com), 'Gay Liberation didn't begin as a bid to win rights for a distinct minority. It didn't separate mind from body, men from women ('Gay liberation is a farce as long as we retain genital based identities,' an early activist wrote), adults from children – even homosexuals from heterosexuals . . . . People studied Herbert Marcuse (*Eros and Civilization*), Norman O. Brown (*Loves Body; Life Against Death*), anti-psychiatrist R. D. Laing (*The*

*Politics of Experience*), sexual repression, as they saw it, the root of everything from rabid aggression, violence against women, children, queers – anyone 'other' – to the poisoning of the globe with toxic waste.'

The ideas were all there, sometimes in remarkably radical and full form. Listen, for example, to one of the authors of the seminal (she would say ovular) 'The Woman-Identified Woman' manifesto put together by a group of 40 women members of New York City's Gay Liberation Front (women who would later call themselves the Lavender Menace) in April, 1970 as she describes the document which was to become an exemplar of this era's sexual thinking:

> In addition to desexualising lesbianism, the document declared that lesbianism is a socially constructed 'category of behaviour possible only in a sexist society characterised by rigid sex roles and dominated by male supremacy...In a society in which men do not oppress women, and sexual expression is allowed to follow feelings, the categories of homosexuality and heterosexuality would disappear'. This statement was not meant to be taken as a proclamation that sexual acts would disappear; rather, we believed people were forced to choose relationships with either men or women. Were gendered roles to disappear, we would each be free to relate to others as individuals. Every person would be a potential sex partner.[47]

In this early explosion of thought, belief, and action, Gay Libbers had much in common with the Harlem Renaissance: they were too much too early. And, also like that renaissance, which led directly to a mainstream interest in jazz and slumming, various elements of the gay mini-revolution made it through to the mainstream. Discos, for instance, and a return to male primping. But their underlying principles and aims were largely abandoned, first by the groups they tried to align themselves with, and not too much later by the revolutionaries themselves. This abandonment led to the separatist notions that reigned through the seventies, in which political and social aspirations were dropped, as they were in the rest of young society, in favour of general sensual indulgence.

This resulted in the gay world that still resonates in the minds of many, the one portrayed in contemporary prime-time news reports like Mike Wallace's 'The Homosexuals' (which aired for the first time on 7 March 1967), and films like *Cruising* (filmed and protested in 1979, released in 1980), the one that survives in the images selected from pride parades by most television coverage, as well as the continued niche popularity of moustaches like Tom Selleck's.

The sixties and the seventies are some of the most closely considered years of the twentieth century, the time the century's biggest American generation started becoming aware of the world and itself. Deep and extensive analysis of the age is available from any number of sources, and like World War Two for the previous generation, current generations have not been able to grow up without being deluged by the glory that was the sixties and the grandeur that was the seventies. We've heard about the pill that finally created a way to separate sex from reproduction that men wouldn't whine about, about the poetry, music and philosophy that erupted in things like making love not war and not trusting anyone over thirty, and about the subjects of sex and fun and dropping out. It took some getting used to, but before long we managed free love, which has since become known as 'healthy sexual behaviour'.

An excellent document exists and, as luck would have it, is even generally available that reflects the contemporary perception of sex and the individual in the seventies. *Looking for Mr Goodbar*, starring Diane Keaton and her very pretty tummy, tells the story of a young woman who decided to take advantage of all this great new sexual possibility, which had been open to men after a fashion for centuries. The story's told with a mixture of wonder at the sense of liberation and dread at the possible effects of so great a force as sex, so long curbed, so suddenly unleashed. It is sort of good that Diane Keaton and her stomach are able to do what they do, and have as much fun as they are having. But it also kind of makes her a slut, too, and she kinda gets what she deserves when Tom Berenger and his butt and chest hack Diane and her tummy to pieces at the end.

Sex being sex and people being people, of course, everyone who was in any way able was going to leap right into the big urban orgy the seventies turned into in North America and Western Europe.

But sex being sex and people being people, we couldn't really be expected not to worry about it all quite a lot, to chuck millennia of bad sex karma and be happy and free like bunnies.

## World War Two and the Great Decommissioning

A couple of years before Keaton and Berenger defined their heterosexual era, Thomas Pynchon's *Gravity's Rainbow*, a novel about, among other things, Second World War erections, looked back to the war that gave the Goodbar generation its start and noticed that sex and love had become something quite different from what they were in World War One:

> In the trenches of the First World War, English men came to love one another decently, without shame or make-believe, under the easy likelihoods of their sudden deaths, and to find in the faces of other young men evidence of otherworldly visits, some poor hope that may have helped redeem even mud, shit, the decaying pieces of human meat . . . While Europe died meanly in its own wastes, men loved . . . The life-cry of that love has long since hissed away into no more than this idle and bitchy faggotry.

Pynchon's narrator makes it easy to dismiss what he's saying as homophobic. And it is homophobic, no doubt about it. He's lamenting the appearance of the faggot in the place of the wistfully loving young men of the First World War who were manly and heroic and beautiful and not at all like the fags – *Gravity's* Sir Marcus Scammony for one – he's confronting in his war. He'd like this sort of same-sex sexuality to be contained by war, to be the effect of a cause that, once peace broke out, would disappear and the world could go back to normal, the men who'd buried their faces in each other's arms and crotches could marry and put both their masculine love and the war behind them.

But it oughtn't to be quite so easy to dismiss. Pynchon's put his finger on something else in this passage, something that's not as clearly cut, that points past the completely standard homophobia of the later sixties and early seventies when he was writing the book, something that becomes possible only after that homophobia is superseded. Part of what Pynchon is admiring here, and what he mourns the lack of in the 'bitchy faggotry' of his perception of the modern homosexual, is the sexual porosity that was still evident in the First World War, a sexuality that was not confined by identity, a sexuality that was expressive of passions in all sorts of directions, and for all sorts of reasons. There was an easy admiration of human beauty in the First World War that had disappeared by the end of the Second; it had been segmented and died on the table. Where a commanding officer of the first war could be seen and admired for loving his troops, collectively and individually 'with a love surpassing the love of women',[48] by the second, the possibility had been psychiatrically lumped and legislated away.

The difference between the wars was a result in large part of the degree to which the modern implications of homosexuality had been publicly discussed in the intervening years. In 1914, though the discussion had been brewing for some time in scientific and belletristic circles, there'd been very little trickle-down. So when the general English-reading public read the poetry of Sassoon and Brooke and Owen and the others (and the general public did read poetry back then, especially when it was seen to be patriotic), not an eyebrow need have been raised. After all, the poor boy was killed in the war, wasn't he? And it's Love he's addressing, not an actual boy, and everybody knows Love is Eros and Eros is Cupid and Cupid is a cute fat little angel boy and that's what poetry's all about, right?

But by 1939, we had Jean Cocteau's *Le livre blanc*, we had André Gide's *Corydon*, we had Berlin's cabarets and New York's Clam House and the American pansy craze of the thirties that George Chauncey outlined so well in his book *Gay New York*. Discussion of the subject of homosexuality was out of the salon and into the streets. New York's *Broadway Brevities*, a tabloid with the best of them, ran regular huge, clever-naughty headlines in the early thirties like 'FAG BALLS EXPOSED' and 'QUEERS SEEK SUCCOR!' The days of the clitoris scandal were already far behind us. There'd be no more boy-on-boy mooning and dreaminess in the trenches and the bunks after that. What had begun to be interpreted several decades earlier as indicative of innate homosexuality had now made it to the rest of us, the tabloid-reading masses, and though there would still be oodles of same-sex sex during the Second World War, and though many who engaged in it would continue to figure themselves straight, semantics had now entered the picture. Since homosexuality – pansydom, faggotry, bulldaggery – was a known quantity now, explanation, to oneself and others, would now be necessary to have same-sex sex and still maintain one's primary gender identity. So, he who was blown was fine, he who blew was not. He who fucked was just letting off a little steam, he who was fucked was fucked.

For women serving in World War Two, the case was not so simple. Sex never has been as simple for women as it's been for men. The combination of the masculine, and sometimes feminine, ignorance of womanly sexual matters and the longstanding social necessity for a woman to be married to have any rights at all – even if they were only vicarious or surreptitious – had conspired to thrust women's emotional and erotic interactions with each other into perennial obscurity. There were upsides to this, however.

Stemming, one suspects, from the same bit of the collective consciousness that inspired Queen Victoria's refusal to outlaw sapphism on the grounds that it could not possibly exist, at the same time men were being harassed, having their livelihoods crippled and their horizons shuttered, women were actually being encouraged, in the name of sisterly-love-in-arms, to develop the same sorts of unstatedly erotic camaraderie men had enjoyed in the literature and the trenches of the previous war.

Things did change eventually. By the end of 1944, as a result of the efforts of a Major Margaret Craighill, a wartime consultant for women's health and welfare – and a helpful complaint from the mother of a twenty-year-old female private at Fort Oglethorpe in Georgia who, after discovering some same-sex love letters among her daughter's things, contended that the Women's Army Corps was 'full of homosexuals and sex maniacs' – specific anti-lesbian screening guidelines were released that stated that 'without exception, they should be excluded at the time of examination'.

World War Two was different in many ways for women from the war that preceded it. World War One was, for all its destruction and loss of life, a far more geographically restricted war. World War Two was close to global and involved home fronts throughout much of Western and Eastern Europe and Asia. Women, as well as men, were being blown up in their living rooms. And in Canada, the United States, and much of Europe, women who were not actually being taken into military service were being conscripted into home service, taking over the essential jobs men had left behind when they were called up. It is safe to say that where women were passively involved in the first war, they were actively involved in the second. And as a result of the war and the military, the effect on identity and community among women was much the same as it was for men.

'Before the Second World War,' Charles Kaiser writes in his chatty and popular history of latter-twentieth-century American gayness, 'it was easy to grow up in America without ever seeing any public reference to gay people.' He interprets this absence as 'the sad product of society's toxic prejudice and a persistent self-hatred among homosexuals'.[49] Which may be defensible, but not absolutely true. I'd interpret the lack of discussion and visibility as a sign that homosexuality was still coalescing, the 'self-hatred' as tentativeness, the 'toxic prejudice' as an anachronistic nineties interpretation of what was disgust with the revelation of an act and its presumed disrespect for the social contract rather than what later, with the help of the US military, developed into actual homophobia. I'd say Kaiser's own reference to President Roosevelt's reaction to a scandal involving Senator David I. Walsh in 1942 corroborates this view of things.

When the president was told that Senator Walsh had been reported in the papers as having visited a male brothel, he told

Senator Alben Barkley that it was his impression that the army handled this sort of thing by allowing the offending party the discreet opportunity to kill himself. This is, in my opinion, the reaction not of a homophobe, not of someone who feels disgust at a thing called a homosexual, but of a man who perceives a loss of face, a dishonour, and who stoically feels that the man should do the right thing. Roosevelt, an old man at the time, and from a tradition older still, was a bit of a throwback in 1942, but amply representative of the state of things, pre-Weimar and pre-World War Two.

If the pansy craze had not been enough to crystallise the general public's notion of the modern homosexual, surely Wayne Lonergan was. Having in a very timely fashion for our purposes moved to New York City from Toronto in 1939, the 'tall, powerfully built and undeniably handsome youth'[50] hooked up with one William Burton, a forty-three-year-old playboy millionaire who took him in and made him his lover. Burton soon died, however, and, presumably at least in part to keep in touch with all that money, Lonergan fell in with Burton's daughter, and, conveniently once again as we attempt to mark historical shifts, just four months before Pearl Harbor the two eloped to Las Vegas. After fathering a child and then falling out of favour with the new Mrs. Lonergan in fairly short order, Lonergan returned to Canada, signed up with the RCAF, and on a weekend pass to New York, visited his estranged wife, who tried to bite his cock off while performing apparently consensual fellatio. Understandably miffed, Lonergan less understandably strangled her and then bludgeoned her to death with a candlestick.

The importance of the Lonergan scandal, which was huge news in the autumn of 1943, is the layer it added to the popular image of the homosexual. After the at least tolerant attention given to various bohemian and aesthetic notions of fairies and pansies over the previous couple of decades, during which time it was believed that gays and lesbians could more or less be spotted across a street – the men wore flouncy clothes and swished, the women wore big sensible shoes and stomped – Lonergan was not only masculine but extremely handsome, and physical, and violent. And he slept with women. And he was a father. And a killer. Although some reports, like the one that ran in William Randolph Hearst's *New York Journal-American* two days after Lonergan confessed, labelled him 'a bi-sexual or pervert', his profile reasonably entered the public consciousness as one of sexual difference, and since, in those days as in these, the major category of sexual difference in that public consciousness was the homosexual, that's where his image got dumped. He was a bad man who had sex with men.[51]

So, from the most popular image of the homosexual being the effeminate and mostly ineffectual fairy, Lonergan, together with the increasingly popular discussion of the biological (read: pathological) origins of homosexuality, swayed popular opinion in a different direction entirely. In that same *Journal-American* article on Lonergan, the sex pervert is portrayed as 'a monster whose growth always prefaces social collapse of one kind or another – whether in ancient Rome or pre-Hitler Germany'. Now, this image of the sex pervert, or homosexual for short, had existed for some time in one form or another. But it had not been the predominant one. Not since the furore over the Wilde trial and then again, briefly in the teens, in the furore over the Billing case. The States was, in adopting this view, just about exactly a decade behind Germany and its Hirschfeld-bashing protests against impurities and perversions. And though it is easy to talk about the extreme to which it went in Germany, with its thousands of presumed homosexuals interned and killed alongside the Jews and the Gypsies and the Catholics and the labour activists, it didn't take long for it to reach a similar, if not so efficiently deadly, pitch in both Canada and the US, under the auspices of the Royal Canadian Mounted Police and Senator McCarthy respectively.

Aiding and abetting Lonergan in this revaluation of the pansy, in a far less spectacular and entertaining way of course, was the US military.[52] Immediately upon his conscription bill being passed, Roosevelt received a memo from two psychiatrists who saw an opportunity to put their still languishing science at the nation's service. Harry Stack Sullivan and Winfred Overholser suggested to the president that in light of the enormous expense of not screening potential soldiers in the last war (more than half of the beds in American hospitals were still, in 1940, occupied by World War One psychiatric patients), perhaps he might think about doing it this time before things got too far along. Since they were going to have more than enough young men to call upon – somewhere between 16 and 18 million of them registered for the draft – Roosevelt thought it a fine idea and had the two draw up some guidelines to distribute to the 30,000 volunteer physicians (who had presumably little or no knowledge of psychiatry) at the country's 6,400 draft boards and 108 induction stations. Medical Circular Number One, as that first set of guidelines came to be known, started a process that neither Sullivan nor Overholser was too pleased about. Within a year, both the army and the navy had revised the plan, adding homosexuality to the list of 'deviations' Sullivan and Overholser had said should disqualify someone from service.[53] Both of the psychiatrists were, for their time, rather liberal on the whole sex issue. They thought that although there were some problems that men who engaged in homosexual activity were more heir to than others, they did not want to go so far as to call these men deviants, nor to exclude them a priori from service.[54] Sullivan, Overholser, and a good number of their colleagues were just making a transition in the psychiatric community from seeing mental illness as essentially neurological (with attendant theories proposing that homosexuality was caused by lesions in the brain, for example) to seeing various behavioural problems as a series of symptoms of a curable, non-biological illness. This was the working premise for Medical Circular Number One. But once it was handed over, a little reversion took place, and the military consistently, for the rest of the war and for decades thereafter, referred to men and women who engaged in or were prone to homosexual activity as sexual psychopaths. Shades of Lonergan. Doctors who showed up at seminars organised by the army, the navy, and the Selective Service were told that the homosexual came in three varieties: the psychopath, the paranoid, and the schizoid. As replacements for the language of 'degeneracy' that had been used previously, it was a step up. But as a result of all this talk of homosexuals and homosexuality in the bureaucracy and administration of the growing US war machine, a much fuller picture of this character, new on the landscape and quite different from the pansy or sissy or degenerate of decades past, was being drawn. In fact, according to Allan Bérubé (upon whose extraordinary primary research I am heavily relying), the administration went out of its way to convince the doctors and other military personnel and volunteers it briefed that the homosexual was not a sissy who could be butched up by a good stint in the service. The homosexual was sick in a way military home remedies would no longer cure.

Soon there was even more clashing, with the Selective Service's new director, Maj. Gen. Lewis B. Hershey, figuring all this psychiatric stuff was a bunch of hogwash and eliminating the screening from the Selective Service altogether, which prompted Sullivan to resign, and the screening duties were left in the hands of the army and navy at their induction offices. More than a year's work busily setting a definition of the homosexual – how he could be recognised, what his shortcomings were, and more generally establishing him as a type, like the Negro, say – came to an abrupt end on December 7, 1941, when Roosevelt informed the public that he'd declared war. Overnight the military went from going about recruiting what was to be a one-million-man service in waiting to a multimillion-man force needed for immediate active duty. Standards were lowered, and defects such as marginal intelligence and minor paralysis started to be overlooked.

But all that talk about homosexuality – and there had been a lot of it, more than there ever had been before, and more talk about that than any other single qualifying or disqualifying attribute – had done its job. By early 1942, the homosexual was considered enough of a type, and enough of a problem, to prompt the inclusion of a new paragraph in the military mobilisation regulations titled 'Sexual Perversions' that, according to Bérubé, 'set the tone for anti-homosexual screening procedures for the rest of the war'.[55] The new paragraph and its effects were an odd mixture of new and old. It listed, for example, three defining characteristics an examiner could use to spot a homosexual: 'feminine bodily characteristics', 'effeminacy in dress and manner' and a 'patulous rectum'. The feminine bodily characteristics were right out of the World War One regulations. The patulous (a carefully chosen botanical term used to describe flowers when they are just past full bloom and spread wide open) rectum assumed that the homosexual would be primarily a passive recipient of anal sex, that he'd do it enough to make himself patulous, and also represented a reliance on what were already becoming old-style notions of what it took to be a homosexual. The effeminacy, not a particularly new notion of a homosexual characteristic, was used in a newly odd way. A selectee was, somewhere between 1942 and 1943, deemed to be unacceptable by some drafting standards by singular virtue of his effeminacy, even if otherwise his sexual 'normalcy' was absolutely established. According to one psychiatrist's 1941 published paper on the subject, originally delivered as one of the military training seminars, 'effeminate' and 'sissy' men would be 'subject to ridicule and "joshing" which will harm the general morale and will incapacitate the individuals for Army duty'. The next year, a report on the screening system in Boston made the general recommendation that 'even the man who, without homosexuality, is so effeminate in appearance and mannerisms that he is inevitably destined to be the butt of all the jokes in the company, should be excluded'.

At this very moment old and new are being popularly accreted into something more layered. Before the sexologists and those who followed them, men and women were divided into what would now be called the gender-consistent and the gender-dysphoric. That is, men who acted or looked more like women than men were effeminate and called all sorts of names and treated in all sorts of unfortunate ways as a result; the same for women who looked or acted more like men than women. There are tomes and tomes and dissertation after dissertation on the vagaries and subtleties of gender politics in every conceivable age and place, and if you are interested in that as a subject on its own, I refer you to the bibliography at the back of this book, which will set you up with a primer or two. Suffice it for us here to say, however, that before the notion of gay and straight came up, there was masculine and feminine. And though there was from time to time some overlap between effeminacy in men, masculinity in women, and same-sex sexual activity, the two were not perceived to be inherently related because, as we've seen, people did not perceive sexual behaviour to be a result of particular character types. It was only when the sexologists came along and decided that since they knew that there were men who were sexually attracted to men, and since it was women who were supposed to be sexually attracted to men then it must be some woman inside the man that is being attracted, that a definite connection between male effeminacy and homosexual behaviour was made.

While the discussion of such things as the relationship of gender to sexuality was limited to scientific, literary, intellectual, and interested circles – as it was, mostly, from the nineteenth century through to the Second World War – the link was not firmly or especially popularly made. Many pieces of what would eventually be the popular conception of the early-modern homosexual (which let's say dates from the Second World War to about 1969) were floating about independently between the sexologists and psychiatrists. There was the effeminate man or pansy, there was the pervert and/or psychopath who could be expected to commit violent crimes of a sexual nature on any sort of person at all, and there was the man or woman, not much spoken of in polite company, who had a tendency to have sex with others of the same sex. When this was spoken of, it was in purely non-sexual terms, like the partners on ranches that *Front Runner* author Patricia Nell Warren remembers her father mentioning in Montana when she was a child in the late thirties and forties,[56] or those urban bachelors and the ubiquitous maiden aunts and their companions.

What the military did in its rough and ready way was to mush all these things together into one character type – the homosexual. The homosexual was now, for all the world to see, an effeminate man (and after the war, a masculine woman) who had sex with members of the same sex and was either passively or actively pathological.

## Start Spreading the News

In 1943 the US military introduced the Cornell Selectee Index, which in the context of a larger psychological examination asked potential soldiers about their occupational preferences in a multiple-choice format that included interior decorator, dancer, and window dresser. The link had been made and was now being strengthened. Anyone who checked off any of those boxes was a pretty likely candidate for rejection on the grounds of sexual psychopathy.

Which to some would sound like a good thing, not having to go to war and all. But that, according to the military, is the reasoning of a malingerer, and a malingerer was at least as bad as a sexual psychopath. And it's in its struggle to avoid malingering that the military's influence on the construction of international notions of homosexuality gets even more interesting.

Over the course of the 1940 build-up, all that backing and forthing between the military and the burgeoning psychiatric community, and then, once war was declared, all that psychiatric screening, in whatever its final form created in the mind of huge portions of the general public a picture of a character type known as 'the homosexual'. We've been talking up to now about the creation of the notion of the homosexual, of the first times men who wanted to have sex with other men congregated and created loose social units around molly houses and such, of the German sexologists who decided to swat as many of the problems men who wanted to have sex with men faced with one blow and decided that Urnings or Inverts or the intermediately sexed were a different species altogether, and of the literati and bohemians who took these ideas and applied them to themselves with various results. But for all that time, and for all that cultural and personal creative work going on, the circles we're talking about were pretty darn small, and the effect they had on the general population more passively informative than actively affecting. Whenever there was wide media coverage, as there was for those eighteenth-century Dutch pogroms, the various German sex scandals, or the Wilde and Billing cases, they were relatively brief flashes that became chatting fodder, and sure, lodged in the backs of people's minds and perhaps even in the collective sub- or unconscious, but the media at these pre-late-twentieth-century times were never powerful enough to be thoroughly pervasive, to effect real and lasting and, as they do now, immediate change. In fact, with telecommunications slowly developing over the course of the early twentieth century, and the taste for truly massive media consumption not established until television, and not even then until Vietnam (in the States) or the Charles-and-Diana Royal Wedding or Live Aid (in the UK), very little ever happened on massive instantaneous scales as almost everything we experience these days does. World War Two was an exception that ended up becoming the rule. With domestic and international communications and travel having reached a state equal to the task of moving and informing whole nations as large as the United States, and the urgent need, with the declaration of war, to do just that, the US military, in conjunction with its government, affected, with its actions over the years of the war, what an entire nation did and, to a large extent, what an entire nation thought. And, along with its nationalising of services and its designation of certain occupations necessary or unnecessary for the war effort, its mobilisation of a female workforce, and, eventually, its institution of the G. I. Bill, which effectively created the fifties boom, it submitted eighteen million young men to a more or less standard interview. And as a result of the work done by Sullivan and Overholser and others, each of these eighteen million young men, ranging in age roughly from eighteen to thirty, was asked about his sexuality.

Women experienced the screening somewhat differently. They were asked questions similar to those the men were, but where intimation of femininity in men was often cause enough to reject, masculinity in women was actually sought after – in the pre-Craighill and Oglethorpe years – since the jobs women in the services were expected to do were still seen as essentially masculine ones. As a group of Marine Corps examiners at Camp Lejeune in the States reported, 'Women showing a masculine manner may be perfectly normal sexually and excellent military material.'[57] In fact, the whole notion of femininity underwent enormous shifts during the war in Canada, the States, the UK and Australia. And as we've seen, what begins with the military in time of war doesn't take long to seep into popular consciousness, as a Fleishmann's yeast advertisement of the time, unearthed by Bérubé, indicates. Accompanying the picture of a uniformed woman on a motorcycle, the ad copy runs: 'This is No Time to be Frail!' and 'The dainty days are done for the duration'.

Now, we've talked a little bit about sexuality as a concept, and as we've seen, it's not innate. Its existence is something to which people's attention must be drawn. Which is exactly what the US military, through its Selective Service and its army and navy and Marine Corps and Coast Guard induction bureaus, was doing. It quickly became common knowledge, as the first thousands of young men who went through the screening told each of their two friends (and so on), that one of the things the draft board was looking out for was queers. And so, as each of these men filed through for their brief interviews and was asked if he liked girls, if he had ever masturbated with another boy or man, and later, if he had ever thought about being an interior decorator, it forced an association of all these things in all these young men's minds, mostly for the very first time. Though of course almost everyone said yes, they liked girls, no, they'd never masturbated or had sex with another boy or man and so therefore no, of course, they were not homosexual (or sexually psychopathic or interested in becoming interior decorators), they would all, as everyone does when first introduced to a new idea or forced to do some introspection into a part of yourself you'd never bothered to think about before, go away and wonder, maybe just a little bit, about themselves as sexual beings. Eighteen million. That's eighteen million out of an adult population of about ninety million. Through this rather simple process, induction became inculcation, and the US military planted a very specific idea of the homosexual in the minds of an entire nation. And not just any nation but a nation that would, after its role in winning that war, and after its adoption first of the role of one of two global superpowers and then one of one, come to have an inordinate, a still unestimated and inestimable influence – much of it cultural and ideological – on most of the European world. It's hard for people of my post-Vietnam generation to understand – or at least, it's hard for me to understand – the overwhelming role the military can play in people's daily lives when there's a war on. The US military affected everything, directly or indirectly, and whatever they did became news, including screening for and finding homosexuals.

So it became known around the nation that the military was not accepting homosexuals, and consequently, it is logical to assume that a good number of those who might not want to serve in the war, for whatever reasons, might avoid a lot of hassle, and even some expense,[58] by just saying they were a sexual psychopath and going home and spending a nice comfortable war. At least, that's what the military figured, and so, to avoid malingerers claiming to be homosexuals who weren't, they set about to make homosexuality as heinous a character trait as they could, so bad that no one, not even the most malingerous malingerers would want to cop to it, and in the process, hard on the heels of creating the first truly popular idea of the homosexual, created its antidote, truly popular homophobia.

According to Bérubé once again, 'hard-line military officials argued for the necessity of maintaining a widespread revulsion toward homosexuality both inside and outside the military to deter potential malingerers', and though certain psychiatrists thought this would cause more harm and suffering than was necessary, the military did see to it that, first, a widespread revulsion towards homosexuality was maintained within the military, and, second, that anyone who was rejected from the draft for reasons of homosexuality would have his draft record so annotated, so that future potential employers, who had the right under the 1940 Selective Service Act to demand an applicant's draft record as a condition of employment, would see that he had been designated a sexual psychopath. In addition to the obvious limitations to employment this would entail, as well as the rumours that were bound to spread in one's community as a result, these draft record annotations – along with the soon to be controversial blue or 'not honourable' discharges (between honourable and dishonourable) handed out to men who were discharged from the army for having been discovered to be alcoholics, liars, troublemakers, or homosexuals – would cause no end of trouble after the war when it became illegal for the employers of about one-fifth of the nation's workforce to hire homosexuals. The military first defined homosexuality as sexual psychopathy, conjuring up images of Wayne Lonergan, as reflected in a navy lecture on the subject given just after the war ('You read in the newspapers of fiendish and horrible sex crimes committed against men, women, and oft-times, small children. Sometimes the bodies of these victims are horribly mutilated,' the lecturer would say, adding that in most cases, this kind of behaviour 'can be related to homosexuality', and 'oft-times the person who commits such an act is found to be a homosexual').[59] It then made people's homosexual status a matter of public record, and the process concocted what amounted to the first large-scale oppression of homosexuals as a group.[60]

Of the post-war gay liberation movements, few people know anything at all. Few, for example, know much about the Mattachine Society, one of the first modern gay rights organisation. But even before Mattachine, there was the Veterans Benevolent Association, founded in 1945 by four honourably discharged veterans.[61]

Throughout the war, soldiers could be discharged in three ways, honourable, dishonourable, or 'not honourable.' A dishonourable discharge was most often the result of some offence committed while in active service that was either very serious or deemed by the military to have been within the soldier's conscious control. Not following orders, overt cowardice, theft, and various sorts of crimes would all result in a soldier's dishonourable discharge. But 'not honourable' discharges, handed down on blue forms, were given to soldiers who committed not-too-egregious offences that were a result of something the military perceived to be a character issue – alcoholism, troublemaking, lying, and sexual perversity among them. In 1946, the government estimated that the army had issued between 49,000 and 60,000 blue discharges and the navy tens of thousands more. The blue discharge was used during the war as a quick and easy way to get rid of soldiers whose commanding officers found them to be generally undesirable without having to go through the trouble of either conducting or justifying a court-martial. Perhaps predictably, those who were handed blue discharges were disproportionately black and/or same-sex sex offenders. As a result of the black part of this equation, the largest-circulation black newspaper of the time, the *Pittsburgh Courier*, began making the blue discharges an editorial cause as soon as the war ended, and in the process brought the various injustices related to the discharges to political and public notice.

As we've already seen, the blue discharges could cause no end of problems for the dischargees once they were released into civilian life, and until the *Courier* brought it up, most of these men (and they were almost all men) would presumably have been dealing with it on an individual level, which was, in the case of the self-identified homosexuals, the way things had been pretty much since they began self-identifying. And in June 1944, things became even worse for these nationally dispersed individuals. That was the month Congress passed the Servicemen's Readjustment Act, otherwise known as the G.I. Bill, which provided for generous reward packages for veterans, sending an entire generation to university and starting them off in small business and contributing greatly to what was shortly to become the economic and baby boom of the fifties. This bill did not apply to those with blue discharges. And as the prosperity of those with whom they had served became more and more evident, the injustice of labelling men who had sex with men as perverts and psychopaths became harder and harder to ignore for those on the short end of it. People who'd been caught or suspected of having sex with members of the same sex were being excluded from the greatest economic and social boom of the century. It was in reaction to this increasingly unifying sense of injustice, forged in the same fires that created the great sense of collectivity that fuelled the extraordinary proud and patriotic days that followed the end of the war, that the Veterans Benevolent Association was founded.

The association is, for our purposes, of more symbolic than practical value. Its membership, entirely local to the New York City area, never exceeded one hundred, and though at certain social functions this number swelled to four or five hundred with guests, the VBA is more a representation of the growing spirit of unity among those who considered themselves or had been labelled homosexual. Without anything specific or universal to rally round, this sort of burgeoning collectivity is very difficult – probably impossible. But as a result of this not so generous handling of certain of their veteran's post-war rights and privileges – in addition to the increased visibility of homosexuality because of the news spin-off value of the screening process, which provided the only media in-road to the subject (much as the *Kinsey Report* was soon to do, and as AIDS was to do even more effectively forty years later) – this national coming together, spearheaded of course by New York, Los Angeles, and San Francisco, where the right to assembly was most easily exploited, now became possible for the first time. And by 1950, when the Mattachine Society fired up, things really started moving.[62]

As San Francisco anthropologist and activist Will Roscoe points out in his introduction to a retrospective collection of Mattachine founder Harry Hay's writings, 'Before there could be a social movement of homosexuals, regardless of the presence of the necessary social conditions, someone had to think about homosexuals and homosexuality in a new way.' Roscoe also points out, 'Without the idea of Gays as a cultural minority, there would be no Gay identity and no Lesbian/Gay movement today.'[63]

The military and, increasingly once the war ended, the federal government provided the raw material; Harry Hay was one of the first to take it up and follow it to some of its gay-positive logical conclusions. In his pre-Mattachine days as a teacher of communist theory, Hay was fond of quoting Stalin to his students: 'A nation is a historically evolved, stable community of language, territory, economic life and psychological make-up manifested in a community of culture.' The underlying notion there, one that Hay stuck to, is that a community is made up of its collective memory and experience, from which it derives its identity, which in turn leads to a sense of commonality developing among people who recognise in each other this same sense of identity. It is a decidedly construction-heavy, essentialist-lite view of community.

I won't go into histories of the foundation and rather rocky and contradictory early history of the Mattachine Society, or of the less tumultuous Daughters of Bilitis; these exist elsewhere. The broad strokes are what matter here. And they are that as the war machine wound down, it was wound into the federal government. The fact that the supreme commander of the Allied forces would be elected president of the United States in 1952 was a symbol of just how extensive this rollover was. What had been the screening and hiring practices of the army and the navy were adopted by the Defence Department, which subsequently ordered the army, the navy, the Marine Corps, the air force, and the Coast Guard to submit standardised hiring practices that reflected this growing post-war intolerance of sexual difference.

As part of this process, on February 28, 1950, while testifying before a Senate committee on the loyalty of government employees in the wake of the nascent Communist scare, Secretary of State John Peurifoy mentioned that the majority of the State Department employees who had been determined security risks and dismissed were dismissed on suspicion or proof of same-sex sex offences. Republican senator Kenneth Wherry and Democratic senator Lister Hill immediately formed a subcommittee to look into the 'Infiltration of Subversives and Moral Perverts Into the Executive Branch of the United States Government'. This was followed by another subcommittee charged with investigating the 'Employment of Homosexuals and Other Sex Perverts in Government', headed by Senator Clyde Hoey. From here on in, the language gets pretty familiar. The Homo Scare was second only to the closely related Red Scare, and before long, the Hoey Committee had to decide what to do with lists the various arms of the military had accumulated through various investigations over the course of the war of all the 'known or alleged homosexuals', which included the names of not only those military personnel investigated but also all those mentioned by them – friends, lovers, tricks, colleagues, enemies. Though previous military and government studies into and comments on the issue had determined that homosexuals were not a security risk, as of now, with no further evidence, they were. So the

FBI, headed by J. Edgar Hoover, was given those lists and made into a sort of clearing house, providing information about who was and who wasn't to whatever government agency wanted to know. The security-risk issue was, it appears, entirely fabricated. Witnesses before the Hoey Committee were under no obligation to provide any factual evidence for allegations that formed the basis of committee recommendations and, later, government policy. There was testimony concerning names of international homosexuals accumulated by Hitler during the war that had since fallen into Communist hands when the Russians rolled into Germany in 1945. Pure Billing. As a 1957 government report pointed out, no factual evidence whatsoever was ever provided.[64]

As a result, upon assuming power in 1953, Eisenhower issued his executive order that made 'sexual perversion' grounds for not hiring as well as for firing federal employees. This policy extended not only to government agencies and departments but to all businesses with government contracts, affecting a total workforce of about six million. Within a couple of years, the policies were enforced on state and local levels, which meant that fully 20 percent of the American workforce had to sign oaths of moral purity and were subject to dismissal and disgrace should same-sex sexual activity be discovered.

What had been forged in a time of emergency was now crystallising into peacetime status quo. After years of instability, years in which it was entirely possible that everything that had been taken for granted at one moment could be erased in the next, people and their governments slid easily into a back-to-basics approach to life. In the UK and other European countries, this was a matter of material necessity. Rationing lasted years longer than the war did. Huge chunks of the continent had been turned to rubble and needed rebuilding. Germany had its very existence called into question with partition. And of course the list continues – Poland, Czechoslovakia, Hungary, Austria, Italy. In North America, it was more of an ideological imperative. The greatest insecurity the modern world at large had ever known had to be countered by as much security as the governments and families could muster. And since the issue of variant forms of sexuality had been brought up by the military during the war, it had to be dealt with the same way most other subtleties and nuances – personal, political, culinary, sartorial, architectural – were dealt with during this twenty-year decade we know as the American fifties: identified, simplified, vilified, nullified.

It would not be too much of a stretch to see the Mattachine's Harry Hay as a visionary, perhaps even a prophet. And unless one does believe in higher powers that are able to visit visions of the future upon a select number of Cassandras and Moseses, it is entirely reasonable to suspect that all fulfilled prophecies are, if not just blindly lucky, self-fulfilling prophecies. A vision of the possible, run through the lens of an intelligent and perhaps creative mind, becomes a vision of the probable, and if linked to an organising principle, a charismatic character, or both, actually becomes the future. And though gay has never really had the benefit of a true leader, Harry Hay has been one of the few (along with Larry Kramer in the eighties and nineties) to come close.

'The Homophile common psychological make-up,' Hay has written, 'manifests itself in a community so phenomenologically remarkable that it transcends the mechanical barriers of formal language by creating an international behavioural language all its own ... To be sure, the communities of culture differ in detail from one national community to another. But they are enough alike that no one need be a helpless stranger whatever the port of call.'[65]

We can see in these words the heavy influence of the sort of global optimism common among early-century Marxists, Leninists, and Stalinists, an optimism that is in effect a much more powerful version of America's manifest destiny of the previous century. Communism, being such a darned good idea, would eventually spread throughout the world. (Not, as it happens, a foolish notion in principle. Look what's happened with American capitalism.)

But as with most successful visionaries, the birth of the modern gay movement was not all Hay's doing. There was a certain conspiracy of circumstance that helped him along. A lot of the identity and minority groundwork had been laid by an obliging military, and that suppressed sexology from Kertbeny, Krafft-Ebing and Hirschfeld had by now had time to percolate.

Also, throughout the interwar years there had been an entomologist of some entomological renown who began feeling more and more dissatisfied with the general public's view of sex. He had tried to bring up rational discussions of it as often as he could with his own students at Indiana University, talking about methods of condom conservation and the best ways for men to masturbate, and he was also, apparently, frequently to be found naked in various untraditional circumstances, like receiving guests in his garden. As a result of his own irregular sexual interests and practices, including being married to one woman, having a long-term simultaneous affair with a man (upon whose death he took up with another), and a rather enthusiastic interest in the sado-masochistic sides of sex, he was not that fond of the sexual theorists of his day, not to mention popular opinion, all of which looked disparagingly for one reason or another on the things he enjoyed. So he began moving away from his casual discussions with friends and students into more extensively inquisitive ones, genuinely trying to find out what people did when no one was looking. He was sure he was not alone.

No one knew at the time, of course, that Alfred Kinsey's impetus for embarking on his monumental and epoch-shifting study of human sexuality came from a desire to justify his own sexual thoughts and practices. He was an entomologist, after all. When he asked his university president first to look into the possibility of setting up a marriage course for the students and then, once he'd designed one, to teach it himself, there were few objections, or even raised eyebrows. It was 1938, it was Bloomington, Indiana, and no department at the university claimed a natural interest in the non-anatomical, non-biological aspects of human sexuality. So why not an entomologist? At least they'd be sure he'd be dry and scientific about it all.

Within a year, Kinsey had begun handing out questionnaires to his students asking them basic questions about their sexual behaviour. Within another two years, he had begun collecting his data in face-to-face interviews, standardised by this time, and soon enough took his show on the road, visiting first Chicago and then St Louis to interview members of those two cities' nascently established homosexual communities. So, just as the war was beginning in Europe, Kinsey began finding out from a more purely statistical standpoint than had ever before been attempted what exactly self-identified homosexual men, in addition to men in general, were doing and thinking sexually.

Things were affected somewhat by the fact that Kinsey used these trips to have sex with men.[66] Now, no study, especially no study on sex, is utterly immune from the interests and preoccupations of the researcher. That Kinsey was a little more direct about things than many others have been since shouldn't cause us too many problems, and certainly should not discredit his work. In fact, the chief effect of his more libidinal interest in these trips to the big cities may in fact be the enthusiasm and full-hearted devotion to data gathering the study required, and got, from Kinsey. But the fact that the compiler of all this data (he eventually interviewed about twelve thousand white men) was out to make a point,[67] was out, in fact, to bring the world's view of human sexuality more in line with his own (which was of course based in intuition, formed as it was before he began his study), is of enormous significance.

Let's skip ahead a bit, to 1948, when *Sexual Behaviour in the Human Male*, which almost instantly came to be known simply as *The Kinsey Report*, co-authored by Kinsey, Wardell Pomeroy and Clyde Martin (a twenty-year-old undergraduate when the study began who became Kinsey's sometimes reluctant boyfriend and later his wife's lover as well), was published. The war was over, America had gone through all the psychological screening and discharges, and the precursors to McCarthy and Roy Cohn's anti-homosexual purges were already under way. America, along with the rest of the European world, was normalising after years of absolute uncertainty. W. B. Saunders, the publisher who'd agreed to bring out Kinsey's 804-page scientific study, filled with charts and graphs and tables and sex, conducted a market survey to figure out how many of these puppies they should print. Five thousand, it seemed, would allow them to get away with a decent profit. By Monday, January 5, 1948, the official publication date, there were orders for 180,000 copies of the three-pound, $6.50 hardcover. Within two months, it had sold more than 200,000 copies. 'Not since *Gone with the Wind* had booksellers seen anything like it,' *Time* magazine said in its March 1 issue. Even scientific journals were epochally enthusiastic, with an article published that summer in the *International Journal of Opinion and Attitude Research* calling Kinsey a 'man from whom an era would take its name'. And, perhaps most important on a popular level, the *New York Times Book Review* came out with a review on January 4 in that publication's typical mixture of prescience and a certain ability at prophetic self-fulfilment, that marked the book, as it had done to *Ulysses* twenty years earlier, as one of the most important of the century. The reviewer, Howard Rusk – a prominent physician, a prominent reviewer, a *Times* medical columnist, and founder of New York University's Howard A. Rusk Institute of Rehabilitation – was clearly in sympathy with what Kinsey was doing. It's an important and interesting first reaction to a book that would have extraordinary, and wholly unpredicted, effects on global society.

'It deals with man's basic drive to reproduce,' Rusk wrote. 'After decades of hush-hush, comes a book that is sure to create an explosion and to be bitterly controversial.' Rusk called it 'by far the most comprehensive study yet made of sex behaviour'. And realising that such things needed letters of introduction to polite *New York Times*-reading society, he gave Kinsey a good, honest, fatherly reason for writing what would surely be considered by some a lascivious, suspiciously motivated treatise. 'Kinsey began this study due to the frustrating experience of attempting to answer the sex queries of students when there were not adequate facts on which to base such answers', and, for good measure, to warn away the porn hunters he added that the *Kinsey Report* was 'cold, dispassionate fact'. Cold, dispassionate fact that served to reveal 'our ignorance and prejudices', though, and 'provide the knowledge with which we can rebuild our concepts with tolerance and understanding'.

'He decries the use of the noun,' Rusk says, 'and finds that there is often a mixture of both homo and heterosexual experience' and writes that people can 'become conditioned in any direction, even into activities which they now consider quite unacceptable. There is an abundance of evidence that most human sexual activities would become comprehensible to most individuals, if they could know the background of each other's individual behaviour.'

Rusk concludes that the *Report* offers the world 'material for sober thought, and a new basis for the personal understanding of our individual sex problems. It presents facts that indicate the necessity to review some of our legal and moral concepts. It gives new therapeutic tools to the psychiatrist and the practising physician. It offers a yardstick that will give invaluable aid in the study of our complex social problems. It offers data that would promote tolerance and understanding and make us better "world citizens"'.

The immediate mainstream effects of the *Report* were, as Rusk implied they ought to be, to allow people to think and speak more rationally about sex. Having undergone the social sanitisation of the Scientific Study, people were now able to refer to sexual matters, speak of their own practices, and inquire after the predilections and habits of others in the clean and tidy language of modern sexual science that Kinsey had provided for them. Cole Porter even worked some of it into 'It's Too Darn Hot'. Kinsey was serving as a one-man equivalent of the Victorian sexological movement, but managed to have a much greater, and a much more instantaneous, effect through the by now much-expanded media.[68]

People had been waiting for it. The interwar years had seen the birth of a good number of middle-class movements and working-class practices that looked into alternatives to the era's strict socio-sexual rules. The war put that evolution on hold while all other holds were barred. And now, though the era they were entering was shaping up to be an enormously conformist one, Kinsey's science allowed that evolution to continue in an orderly fashion. It pleased him immensely; it was just what he'd wanted. It could be said that the *Report*, followed within a decade or so by the birth-control pill, led the way to the transvaluation of all sexual values that was to take place beginning in the mid-fifties, continuing until people started noticing AIDS in the mid-eighties.

The chief value of the *Report* for the common reader – and as the sales figures indicate there were many common readers – was those numbers, which added up to one very big I'm OK, You're OK. 'Don't worry,' a five-word synopsis of the *Report* could read, 'everybody does it.' The *Report* pointed out, for example, and it needed pointing out to many people at the time, that almost everyone masturbated. By asking people who had been softened up a little by their war experiences about their sexual practices and desires in a most direct and very conscientiously and self-interestedly non-judgmental way, Kinsey was able to give his readers an indication that human sexuality was not at all the orderly thing it had for so long seemed on the surface to be. If one added up the numbers, for instance, one could see that more than 90 percent of Kinsey's respondents broke some American law or other on their way to an orgasm. *Ninety percent*. Laws would have to tumble. As would a lot (not nearly all, but a lot) of guilt and secret worries about perversity, and a lot of the behaviour that was a reaction to that guilt and those worries.

So, much of what Kinsey found became assimilated quite quickly and quite directly. But one of those early adoptions – co-optations would probably be a better word, as it turned out – that gay 10 percent figure, bears some looking at.

Let's start where it started. Pages 650 and 651 of the *Report*, towards the end of the chapter entitled 'Homosexual Outlet'. I think the primary document has been often enough overlooked and is of sufficient importance to warrant quoting it at length. Here are the total final homosexual findings of the *Report* as it summarised them (the bolds, as well as the more subtle emphases, are Kinsey's):

**37 per cent** of the total male population has **at least some overt homosexual experience** to the point of orgasm between adolescence and old age. This accounts for nearly two males out of every five that one may meet.

**50 per cent** of the males **who remain single until age 35** have had overt homosexual experience to the point of orgasm, since the onset of adolescence.

**58 per cent** of the males who belong to the group that goes into high school but not beyond, **50 per cent of the grade school level**, and **47 per cent of the college level** have had homosexual experience to the point of orgasm if they remain single to the age of 35.

**63 per cent** of all males **never have overt** homosexual experience to the point of orgasm after the onset of adolescence.

**50 per cent** of all males (approximately) **have neither overt nor psychic** experience in the homosexual after the onset of adolescence.

**13 per cent** of males (approximately) **react erotically** to other males **without having overt** homosexual contacts after the onset of adolescence.

**30 per cent** of all males **have at least incidental homosexual experience** or reactions (ie, rate 1–6) over at least a three-year period between the ages of 16 and 55. This accounts for one male out of every three in the population who is past the early years of adolescence.

**25 per cent** of the male population **has more than incidental homosexual experience** or reactions (ie, rates 2–6) for at least three years between the ages of 16 and 55. In terms of averages, one male out of approximately every four has had or will have such distinct and continued homosexual experience.

**18 per cent** of the males have at least **as much of the homosexual as the heterosexual** in their histories (ie, rate 3–6) for at least three years between the ages of 16 and 55. This is more than one in six of the white male population.

**13 per cent** of the population **has more of the homosexual than the heterosexual** (ie, rates 4–6) for at least three years between the ages of 16 and 55. This is one in eight of the white male population.

**10 per cent** of the males are more or less **exclusively homosexual** (ie, rate 5 or 6) for at least three years between the ages of 16 and 55. This is one male in ten of the white male population.

**8 per cent** of the males are **exclusively homosexual** (ie, rate a 6) for at least three years between the ages of 16 and 55. This is one male in every 13.

**4 per cent** of the white males are **exclusively homosexual throughout their lives**, after the onset of adolescence.

Depending on one's definition of a homosexual, these numbers will tell you that anything from 4 percent to 47 percent of the male population is one. And if you'll notice, that 10 percent is nothing like the 10 percent that's appeared on T-shirts, magazine covers and banners, or as a premise of more recent scientific studies. In the paragraph immediately following these numbers, referring to his now famous zero-to-six scale of sexual continuity, Kinsey writes, 'It should be emphasized again that there are persons who rate 2's and 3's who, in terms of the number of contacts they have made, may have had more homosexual experience than many persons who rate 6.' Which further complicates things.

Five years after their report on men, the same team came out with its *Sexual Behaviour in the Human Female*. For any number of reasons, though the volume was much anticipated, it never had as great an effect on the way people thought about sexual identity. One reason would have to be the same secondary position facts about female sexuality have always taken in public discourse. But more than that, the equivalent section to the one quoted above is just way more complicated, not nearly as pointed. For example, the description of the 5–6 rating, which in the report on men produced that 10 percent, reads in the women's book: 'Between 2 and 6 per cent of the unmarried females in the sample, but less than 1 per cent of the married females, had been more or less exclusively homosexual in their responses and/or overt experience – *ie*, rated 5 or 6 – in each of the years between twenty and thirty-five years of age. Among the previously married females, 1 to 6 per cent were in that category.'

There's no 'three women out of fifty' amplification; the bolding is limited in each section only to the rating number. There seems, generally, to have been more enthusiasm on the part of the authors in the report on men than in the one on women, and it comes across in the prose. So, though the emphasis on clitoral orgasms did do a lot for popular understanding of more general aspects of female sexuality – the popular notion before this report being that women had their orgasms as a result of labial and vulvar stimulation, letting men off pretty easily as far as their participation in women's orgasms was concerned – what we retain from Kinsey comes mostly from that first manly volume.

I think it worth noting two major points about the quoted section from the men's report. The first is that, as I've indicated, what Kinsey said and what we have come to believe Kinsey said are two different things. He did not say that 10 percent of the male population was homosexual. In fact, he said there was no such thing as a homosexual. He was quite explicit on the subject.

> Males do not represent two discrete populations, heterosexual and homosexual. The world is not to be divided into sheep and goats. Not all things are black nor all things white. It is a fundamental law of taxonomy that nature rarely deals with discrete categories. Only the human mind invents categories and tries to force facts into separated pigeonholes. The living world is a continuum in each and every one of its aspects. The sooner we learn this concerning human sexual behaviour the sooner we shall reach a sound understanding of the realities of sex . . . It would encourage clearer thinking on these matters if

persons were not characterized as heterosexual or homosexual, but as individuals who have had certain amounts of heterosexual experience and certain amounts of homosexual experience. Instead of using these terms as substantives which stand for persons, or even as adjectives to describe persons, they may better be used to describe the nature of the overtly sexual relations.

Over the course of the fifty-six pages he devotes exclusively to 'homosexual outlet', he tells us a story of male sexuality that's far more driven by plot than character. It's about what we do, he says, not who we are. Kinsey himself, as his biographer James Jones lets us know, was a complex sexual creature. Not only did he use his data-gathering trips to get sex, he and his wife, Clara, were active and creative lovers, and Kinsey was extraordinarily conscientious, and publicly so, regarding his wife's orgasmic life. He was not gay, and he was not straight. Over the course of talking to twelve thousand men about his favourite pet subject, he concluded that people in general weren't either.

The second, not unrelated point is that Kinsey was not merely presenting data in this first *Report* – he was making a point, a point he himself was clear about long before he handed out his first questionnaire. This colours things. Note his strategic use of bold, especially in the 30-percent and 25-percent citations, where he's bolded 'experience' but not the less specific, less compelling 'reactions'. Or his interpretation of the numbers, pointing out to readers that 8 percent means 'one male in every 13' or that the 37 percent of the male population that's had at least some homosexual experience 'accounts for nearly two males out of every five that one may meet'. He wants you to be absolutely certain of just how substantial these numbers he's compiled are, wants to make it as difficult as possible for you to discount these figures as mere statistics, forcing you to picture yourself walking down the street and checking off two out of every five of the men you see, forcing you to picture, as well, given the ways we think about people and sex, those two out of five having some sort of homosexual sex, and in the process, familiarising yourself with the notion, perhaps fundamentally changing the way you look at society and its sexual behaviour.

And he succeeded. But in a much more straightened way than he had hoped. Rock Hudson, to take one famous example, picked up a copy of the *Report* soon after it was published and looked for corroboration of the identity he was just then forming.[69] Of course he found it. As did tens of thousands of others. Numbers are good that way. They're much easier to pick up out of context and swing about than paragraphs are. And whichever percentage these early readers chose, the 4 percent, 37 percent, or, as the increasing majority did in the ensuing years, 10 percent, this meant millions upon millions of men who had sex with men. Aside from being probably titillating, this fact created a sense that each individual was part of a greater whole, a sense that built on the earlier, militarily induced one, and was one more reason to move further into this developing view that divided the world along lines drawn by choice of sexual object.

I lied – there's actually also a third, much broader point in addition to the discrepancy between Kinsey's cause and his effect and his teleological approach. *The Kinsey Report*, while being at the time far and away the most extensive taxonomic study of male sexuality, suffered from the precise quality that gave it its power. It was a numerical, standardised, thoroughly scientific and quantitative study of human sexuality. As cultural critic Lionel Trilling pointed out at the time, human sexuality, whatever it may be, is not a quantifiable thing. Which is not to say it's mystical and ought to be described in phrases beginning with 'Oh' and ending in sighs and fade-outs to warm hearths. It's merely to point out the fairly basic fact that science and surveys are one way to see the world. An effective way in certain realms. But only certain realms.

There have been many scientific studies of sex, of course, and they've all got their strengths and shortcomings. I'm concentrating in this book on Kinsey, and on some fairly recent projects looking into the possibility of there being biological roots to sexuality, because it strikes me that they're the most significant. Studies earlier than Kinsey mostly fell on dry ground. The timing of Kinsey's report, as I've said, was perfect. As Trilling said at the time, 'Freud, in all the years of his activity, never had the currency or authority with the public that the *Report* has achieved in a matter of weeks.'[70] And what was true of Freud was just as applicable to Hirschfeld, Havelock Ellis, and the others. Of those that have appeared since Kinsey, as they relate to same-sex matters, from Evelyn Hooker to Shere Hite, there have been none (until the harder science applied to the subject only recently) that have had as much of a lasting popular influence.[71] It's really only been in the last that serious, well-funded research has been done into areas that were, in times past, merely speculative. It's only recently that the obvious sort of genetic research, for example, has been possible at all. And it's only recently, in part because of AIDS and the general cultural openness engendered by it, that the issue of gay etiology has commanded enough public interest to warrant the number of polls and surveys that appear so frequently. The research and the polls have proved to be enormously influential in the way people are developing their thinking on the issue of human sexuality, playing as they do into people's reflexive desire for the certainty of numbers and scientific stamps of approval.

The struggle for identity is linked to the quest for certainty, and in the absence of religion it becomes for many the primary struggle. Without god or a great chain of being, there must, we figure, be something greater than ourselves to be a part of. But if there is in fact no gay gene, we have the chance to peek outside the identity envelope, as Nietzsche and many of his more thoughtful successors allowed us to do with religion. If there is no gay gene, sexual behaviour might simply be up to us, just like the fates and destinies we once figured were in the hands of God.

## Science and Surveys and Sex

> We do not even in the least know the final cause of sexuality. The whole subject is hidden in darkness.
>
> – Darwin, 1862

This fact of psychological bisexuality, too, embarrasses all our enquiries into the subject and makes them harder to describe.

– Freud, 1938

In the beginning science was all of a piece. One studied things like harmonics, which covered music and maths and the stars, or humours, which took in biology as well as weather and the environment. From there, over a few thousand years, science has very slowly splintered into scores of subgroups, while scientists look for a unified field theory to get back to where they started with the benefit of what they've investigated and learned through the splintering.

So with sex, where we started out all of a piece and have very quickly of late fractured into a dizzying number of groups. We should be looking for a unified field theory of our own – though, unlike science, which concerns itself with things outside ourselves and therefore relies on various forms of technology to enable us to observe phenomena, with sex it's all on the inside, and only requires of us a fairly high degree of introspection to discover the unified field within.

Which is why polling, the polar opposite of introspection, is just the wrong way to go.

A story that ran in the *New York Times* in August 1998 under the headline 'Chasing the Polls on Gay Rights' serves as a good example of the problem with polls and the categories they serve and create. In the wake of a national US campaign featuring ex-gays who offer help to others wanting to slough off their own gay turpitude, the story looked into general American attitudes towards the issue.

'In your view, is homosexuality something a person is born with or is homosexuality due to other factors such as upbringing or environment?'
- June 1977 – 13% born with; 56% environmental
- October 1989 – 19% born with; 48% environmental
- June 1998 – 31% born with; 47% environmental

'In general, do you think homosexuals should or should not have equal rights in terms of job opportunities?'
- June 1977 – 56% have equal rights; 33% not have equal rights
- October 1989 – 71% have equal rights; 18% not have equal rights
- June 1998 – 84% have equal rights; 12% not have equal rights

'Do you personally believe homosexual behaviour is morally wrong or is not morally wrong?'
- June 1998 – 35% not wrong; 59% wrong; 6% don't know/no answer

'Is it generally a good thing for our society or a bad thing for our society or doesn't it make much difference that more gay and lesbian couples are raising children?'
- June 1997 – 6% good thing; 56% bad thing; 31% no difference; 7% don't know/no answer

The problem with the first question goes to the heart of the problem with all poll questions. Responses have to be calculable, and preferably illustratable in the form of some sort of chart. And so not only do polls buy into the most often misleading dichotomies into which it is so easy to drop things, the fact that polls and those charts are so darn media-friendly is probably the prime buttress of this dichotomous world view. And so, in this first question, posed by Gallup, the possibility that sexual behaviour is a product of both nurture and nature, or neither, is utterly elided, relegated to a note at the bottom of a sidebar: 'Figures do not include replies indicating both causes, no cause or no opinion.' But it's the numbers, not the notes, that stick in people's heads, that are used by other media, by scientists forming their assumptions, it's numbers that seep into the cultural soil and grow into those mighty, unassailable oaks like the Kinsey 10 percent. The whole process becomes tautological.

The second and fourth questions are fairly egregious examples of the second biggest problem with polls: the phrasing. It's becoming common wisdom now that polls say what the pollsters want them to say, that pollsters, because they are always hired by an interested party, have dedicated themselves to the rhetorical art of the response-driven question: first, figure out what response you want, then phrase the question in such a way as to ensure you get that response more often than not. It's not that tough, as Gallup and Princeton Survey Research Associates show here. Gallup obviously wanted the sorts of results it got from their question number two. Stick the phrase 'equal rights' and 'opportunity' into any gently phrased poll question in most part of the United Kingdom, United States, Canada, or Europe, and you're sure to have people responding positively. It's a motherhood phrase, one that only the perverse could be expected to disagree with – everyone should have equal rights, doesn't it say so in the Constitution somewhere? So you ask even borderline gay-bashers whether homosexuals should have equal rights and many will say sure (unless you tack on a couple of scare-specifics, like 'teacher' or 'scout leader' or maybe 'minister'). Everyone should have equal (read: not special) rights to equal opportunities. It's abstract, and since these polls are generally taken with little or no notice, and the respondents given little or no time to reflect, there's little chance of them wondering about the various ramifications of their response to this or any other poll question. They respond reflexively to phrases that stick out at them from those questions. One can make people see larger issues, or at least synoptic versions of larger issues, by sticking other sorts of stock phrases into the questions, as Princeton did in question four here. Is it a good, bad, or indifferent thing 'for our society' that gays and lesbians should be raising children? 'For our society' will trigger a lot of people into thinking about family values, about societal decline, the various correspondences made by the American Republican Party and various religious organisations between societal decline and the rise of homosexuality, as well as the probability that since children are our future, putting that future in the hands of gays and lesbians is probably not an excellent idea. Phrase this question differently, ask the same group of people if they think gays and lesbians have the right to raise their own children, for example, and the results would almost certainly change drastically in favour of the 'good thing' slice of the pie.

Question number three is an illustration of one of the less obvious but certainly useful weapons in a pollster's arsenal: the forced correspondence. Related to the dichotomy issue, this technique allows pollsters to force a link to be drawn between one thing and another, whether or not that correspondence existed in the mind of the respondent before the question was asked or not. In question three, the pollster forces the respondent to consider homosexuality as a moral issue. Is it necessarily, for most people? For some it is, but anyone who thinks it's an amoral or morally neutral matter of choice, or of biology, has no room to manoeuvre here. It may seem a small point. Surely those who thought it was not a moral issue could simply respond that it's not morally wrong and be done with it. Except this sort of forced correspondence has lasting effects, a lot like the US Induction Centre questionnaire during the Second World War. Roving troupes of pollsters are daily going from door to door, from call list to call list, reinforcing or indeed planting politically expedient ways of seeing ourselves and the world. Individually, none of these polls makes that much difference, but in their multitudes, and in the enormous media use to which they're put, bandied about from the *New York Times* to CNN to *Maclean*'s magazine to ITV to Oprah and back again, they become a major cultural force, spirally making opinion at the same time they're reflecting it.

But, you say, they're the only way we have of knowing anything about what anyone thinks. If things were considerably simpler than they are, if things were as simple as we'd all so much like them to be, then perhaps. If polls were limited to dredging up people's grocery-buying habits (Do you buy potatoes? Yes/No), then perhaps. But they're not. And all the vast majority of polls do is provide us, and politicians and scientists and reporters, with interesting anchors for our cocktail conversation, husting speeches, hypotheses, and stories.

But, you may additionally say, just because polls can be tampered with does not mean they are always tampered with. Surely there are honest and noble pollsters out there doing honest and noble work, genuinely trying to find out a little bit more about the way things are. Yes, there almost certainly are. But it's not only the intent but the very form, the very concept, that does not work and necessarily skews socially complex (ie, human) things in their inevitable misframing.

The problem with polls, and specifically with polls and matters of sex, even extends to the most noble and rarefied of all polling forms, scientific data collection. This is where the science of sex begins, and where it ultimately fails.

After reading a paper he'd published on the subject of the history of selves (more interesting than it sounds), I visited Kurt Danziger, a professor emeritus of psychology at York University in Toronto. After more than forty-five years in the psych biz, he's grown somewhat sceptical of a few of the basic tools of his trade and how they're used. 'A word like data gives the impression of being something rock-bottom fundamental,' Danziger warns.

> But it's the product of an elaborate process of investigation on the part of the investigator and on the part of the person who's responding. If a respondent keeps on saying 'I don't like your questions,' he'll be discarded from that investigation. Either that does happen to you and you don't show up in the data, or you decide, 'OK, if I'm going to be part of it, I'm going to play the game.'... Given that they've got to operate within certain distinct categories, those investigations can never criticize those categories. If you were conducting an investigation, asking people to tell you about their heterosexual experiences, that [heterosexual/ homosexual] distinction is already built into your question. The results you come up with cannot criticize your imposition of those categories. That's your instrument.

Science has been used, it's barely necessary to say, for all sorts of nefarious purposes. Entire species and societies have been destroyed on the basis of what appeared at the time to be wholly reasonable scientific studies. But it is not only evil intent that undermines scientific credibility. In fact, scientists of whatever stripe are almost always working towards the good as they perceive it, whether it be to find an AIDS serum or to make the human gene pool a nicer

131

place to swim by eliminating nasty genes like the ones that cause mongoloidism or those awful character traits associated with Jews. Whatever the specifics of the wrong turns science has made in the past, what's unquestionable is that science can take wrong turns, that strict obedience to the scientific method can result in truly egregious misunderstandings of the world being examined. And that's when the scientist is able and thorough.[72]

But take one of the more celebrated recent cases of gay science, the now retired Simon LeVay's 1991 findings about the hypothalamus glands and certain clusters of cells in them (called third interstitial nuclei of the anterior hypothalamus, or INAH3 cells), first published in *Science* in August of that year and later in popular book form under the title *The Sexual Brain* (1993). LeVay seconded forty-one brains from hospitals in California and New York, most belonging to people who had died of AIDS and all between the ages of eighteen and sixty, and sliced up their hypothalamus glands, that part of the brain that had already been determined to be the activator of the pituitary gland and a major player in the brain-controlled end of sex. It had, a few years earlier, been discovered that in rats, lesions in the hypothalamus impeded heterosexual rat activity while not lessening the general sexual drive to any great extent. It had also been determined that the human hypothalamus was sexually dimorphic, which is to say, certain clusters of cells in the gland were dependably larger in men than in women. Hypothesising that perhaps the cells were dimorphic for sexual orientation rather than sex, LeVay found in his forty-one brains that the clusters of INAH3 cells in the hypothalamus glands of men who had apparently been gay were consistently smaller than those in men who had apparently been heterosexual. The brains of the women, all of whom were (almost groundlessly) presumed to be heterosexual, had similarly smaller INAH clusters. LeVay ultimately decided that the size of the INAH3 clusters was determined by the sexual object choice, and not by sex itself. So, brains that were attracted to women had large INAH3 concentrations, brains that were attracted to men had smaller ones. Much hoopla followed.

Not that there weren't reservations and problems. As LeVay

himself pointed out at the end of his *Science* report, AIDS could have played a role in the varying sizes of INAH3. INAH3 could also be determined by one's sexual behaviour rather than being the cause of it. Or there could be some third factor that triangulates with sexual behaviour and INAH3 clusters, mitigating the cause-and-effect link between the two. Problems he didn't pay much attention to included the presumption of sexual identity in corpses that were doing no talking for themselves. If an AIDS patient had denied any homosexual activity to doctors before his death, his brain was labelled heterosexual. The presumption of heterosexuality among the women, as well as among the men who had died of causes other than AIDS, was based primarily, according to a note, on that misinterpreted Kinsey 10 percent. Chances were, LeVay said, these people were straight.

But what else could be done? you might ask. Since you can never know such things for sure, science's initial steps must be taken on a certain degree of presumption. It'll all come out in the wash later. Which would be all well and good were science conducted the way it seems once to have been, in the relatively splendid isolation of the scientific community, when only enthusiasts, professional or amateur, could be expected to notice various low-level developments and discoveries. But we have the media to factor into our calculations. And it's studies like LeVay's, and Dean Hamer's putative discovery of the gay gene (more on him shortly), that highlight the dangers posed by this peculiarly modern intersection of science and the media.

Like most initial forays into areas of study, LeVay's hypothalamus findings are tentative. One study, forty-one brains – an indication of a possible direction, but little more, as LeVay would probably be the first to acknowledge. But when the science touches on an area that's as media-friendly as gayness has been since the nineties, there is no more splendid scientific isolation. The study appears in *Science*, some science reporter at the *Washington Post* or the *Frankfurter Allgemeine* gets hold of it, writes a story with something catchy in the headline like 'Gay Brain Discovered' and before you know it *Oprah*'s got some scientists and activists talking very briefly, and not at all contextually, about the biological roots of homosexuality. And since several hundred thousand people have read those newspapers' necessarily potted version of things, and since several million have seen *Oprah*'s even more cursory interpretation of events, and since very few would be moved to look up the original *Science* article, or even read the putatively popular book that's always sure to follow, their understanding of the issue boils down to the very simplest one possible: gay brains are different from straight brains, therefore brains make people gay. And because the walls surrounding the scientific community are porous, popular understanding of even scientific issues filters through to future scientists doing research in similar areas, a good illustration of which is LeVay's own popularly inspired misuse of the Kinsey numbers.

We have a longstanding tendency to be able to see right through certain sexual facts. We can stare straight at them and not see them. Take Kinsey's *Report*, a thoroughly scientific document that has become the Ur-text of modern sexuality, even though almost no one, at least these days, has actually read it through. That famous percentage, a part of almost everyone's sexual vocabulary by this time, is taken as a scientific proof, the incontrovertible result of Kinsey's twelve thousand interviews. It's also been turned into a magazine (*10 Per Cent*), several books (with titles like *Two Teenagers in Twenty*), and any number of T-shirts and confident conversations ('How many people are in your class? Thirty? That means there are three fags in your class. No, it's true, it's a scientific fact.') The statistic made flesh, forming as it has the basis for what is now widely considered a race of people that cross national boundaries and account for 10 percent of the world's population. The world is 52 percent women, 48 percent men, and 10 percent gay. As we've seen, Kinsey said nothing of the sort. But he remains the ultimate source of this utterly pervasive view of the matter. Numbers can be useful. But they're double-edged.

Something similar happened more recently, something that threatens to join the ranks of that hackneyed percentage, when Dean Hamer first published his findings about the relationship of genes to sexuality in *Science* and, a little later, in a popular book called *The Science of Desire*. In both report and book, Hamer made it clear that he did not figure he'd found a gay gene. He'd found a conspicuous concurrence of a specific genetic marker among self-declared homosexuals. The findings were statistically significant, but the relationship of the genetic marker to the behaviour was as yet undetermined. None of which stopped the newspapers from using the euphonic 'gay gene' in their headlines, nor other interested parties from citing this fantastic discovery as further proof of the firmly rooted, unchangeable nature of homosexuality.

Euphony, especially the alliterative kind, is a funny thing. It makes certain things stick in your head. As it was meant to. It's how storytellers in pre-literate times are said to have been able to recite stories the length of the *Iliad* and *Beowulf* from memory. Advertisers know it (I know, for instance, that choosy mothers choose Jif, and that, if I ever chose to drive a car, I might want to put a tiger in my tank), and so do tabloid headline writers. And unfortunately, the power of alliteration carries clear over into the realm of ideas. Like 'gay gene' (well, hard and soft g – I guess that's only partial alliteration). Or, better yet, 'nature or nurture'. It's catchy. It sticks in the head. And in this instance, on top of the alliteration, in a world where ever increasing complexity is prompting us towards ever simpler ways of sorting it all out, phrasing the fundamental questions about why we are the way we are in this binary way – Which one is it, A or B? – is an obvious way of going about things. Terms like nature and nurture, used to play off each other, are extraordinarily resilient. But they unfortunately also describe, as so many binaries do, a false dichotomy. It frames the question as if it were possible for something as complex as human behaviour – in our case, as complex as human sexual behaviour – to be attributable to either biology or environment. It assumes these two things are not inextricably linked, not thoroughly complicit. Which they are. It assumes that one can work in isolation from the other in the construction of a human behavioural trait. Which it can't.

But then, what do I know? I dropped biology after grade ten, when it became clear that even Mr Gardiner's wandering glass eye would be unable to frighten me into remembering the difference between myosis and mitosis.

But Dean Hamer – now, you'll believe him. He's head of a big lab at the National Institutes of Health in Washington, D.C. that's working on this Human Genome Project, mapping out all the millions of genes in the human DNA and trying to figure out which does what. Back in the early part of this decade, after he got fed up with so many of his friends dying from Kaposi's sarcoma, he decided to look into a possible genetic predisposition for gay men to get this anomalous and now predominantly AIDS-related cancer. He didn't find any, but in the course of studying the gay-man DNA he'd collected, he noticed a greater than average coincidence of a certain genetic marker along a certain part of the long arm of the X chromosome. After a little more casting about, he came up with some results that showed that the marker, Xq28, seemed to play some role in the sexual orientation of somewhere between 5 and 30 percent of gay men. He published a paper with this findings, which proved to be so media-friendly that he wrote a book about the whole thing, in which he said several times that as far as he knew there was no such thing as a gay gene, and that, even if there was, he hadn't found one. He also, quite early on in that book, helpfully pointed out that the whole nature versus nurture thing probably caused more problems than it solved. 'Most scientists now agree that the very wording of this question represents a false dichotomy,' he and co-author Peter Copeland wrote, 'and that both biology and the environment play some role in virtually all human behaviours.'

There it is, from deep inside the nature camp, straight from the horse's mouth. And for that, as well as a generally thoughtful book and all sorts of excellent little scientific titbits, I thank Dr Hamer.

However, his way of looking at the world does present some problems, problems that feed into our completely understandable desire for absolute, data-based answers to whatever questions we come up with about ourselves. Take a look, for example, at the way he sees human sexuality in his argument against a largely straw-mannish school of thought, called social constructionism, which he sees as antithetical to his own school of thought, which he doesn't name – presumably because he sees it as the One True School – but which we'll call Scientism (since Scientology is already taken):

> The trendiest of behaviorist schools is called social constructionism. It postulates that there is no such thing as heterosexuality or homosexuality, only definitions of sexuality that are imposed by culture. Proponents of this theory are fond of pointing out, at every opportunity, that prior to 1892 [sic] the word 'homosexuality' did not even exist in English. Therefore, they argue, homosexuality (without the quotes) is merely a cultural label; it has no universal meaning, much less any biological component.
>
> This kind of thinking in other areas would have left us in the dark, literally. There wasn't a unified theory of 'electricity' until James Clerk Maxwell came up with one in 1864, and electricity has been well understood and harnessed only during the past one hundred years. So, taking social constructionism to the extreme, electricity did not 'exist' until quite recently and even now has no 'real' meaning. Try that theory on someone who's been struck by lightning.

Well, yes, all well and good, I'm sure. But electricity and sexuality? Come on. This is an excellent illustration of why science has made such a balls-up of sex since it thrust its rubber-gloved hands into it a century and a third ago. Electricity is a physical phenomenon, sexuality a human one, and to compare the two is like comparing apples and economics. And in addition to their incompatibility as analogies, all Hamer shows here is that things can exist without being named, not that things once named have necessarily always existed.

We are, each one of us, extreme examples of the Heisenberg Uncertainty Principle. The fact that we are involved with ourselves changes everything, and it changes it all the time. We're slippery and fluid, and though we may, from time to very limited time, be able to pin ourselves down (and that only when we decide to put a conscious halt to all that sloshing about to make things a little more comprehensible), we can certainly never get anything more than the most approximate handle on anyone else. We can come up with theories if we study and observe and disquisit long enough. But what can brigades of men and women with electron microscopes and reams of carefully calibrated questionnaires tell us about something as amorphous as sexuality? Very little of much use to us. They can tell us that brothers of gay men have a 22 percent chance of being gay, that brothers of straight men have a 4 percent chance of being gay. And they can tell us that there is a general consistency coefficient of 92 percent in men polled on their sexual attractions and self-identifications, indicating a high degree of internal consistency between the various facets of sexual orientation.

But take a look at that consistency coefficient, for example. It was arrived at through conducting a series of interviews with pairs of brothers, some of whom identified themselves as straight, some as gay. Hamer & co. wanted to find out, among other things, about the relationship of self-identification and what they considered actual sexual orientation. After interviewing the pairs, they assigned them Kinsey numbers, from 0.0 for absolutely heterosexual to 6.0 for absolutely homosexual. They then set out to determine the sexualities of extended family members – aunts, uncles, parents. Sometimes they were able to interview the family members themselves, sometimes they relied on their initial subjects for evidence. They labelled people 'definitely heterosexual', 'definitely gay', 'possibly gay' and definitely or possibly bisexual. The researchers were fairly careful – just like the media are, or like most of us are – about labelling people gay, taking only direct statements from the subjects themselves, or credible first-person reports ('I know my brother is gay, because we talk about it all the time, we go out to gay bars together, and once we even dated the same guy'). But in order to label someone 'definitely heterosexual', they took statements like 'I sure hope she's heterosexual; she's got five kids' and, in direct interviews, a statement from an elderly woman that she had been married faithfully to the same man all her adult life, as sufficient proof.[73] Using this standard of proof, Hamer could also have proved that a pre-scandal Oscar Wilde was 'definitely heterosexual' ('I sure hope he's heterosexual, he's got two kids'). And do you think if he, a stranger, had sat down with Eleanor Roosevelt and asked about her married life she would have said anything other than that she'd been faithfully married to the same man all her adult life?

There are problems here on at least two levels, self-definition and admission. Because sexuality is an issue so layered with guilt and incrimination, and because it is so complex, people's definitions of themselves can vary greatly from standard definitions. I remember a scene from Jeremy Podeswa's film *Eclipse* in which a hustler eases a married john's worries about having sex with him and being unfaithful to his wife. It's not unfaithful to see a dentist at the same time as you're seeing your doctor, he says. Different things entirely, and fidelity is not the issue. So the two have sex, and the john could go on about his life, if he took the hustler's line of reasoning to heart, and tell any researcher who might ask him that he had been faithfully married to his wife his entire adult life. Then there's Russell T. Davies' friend, the one he based his Bob from *Bob & Rose* on (about which, more later), who insists he's a gay man in love with and married to a woman, and father to her children. Where exactly would he fit in? And many of us are probably familiar with people like a certain character in a novel called *Reel Time* by Julia Willis, a woman who insisted on being seen as a woman-loving woman despite the fact that she has a boyfriend and has never had any sexual or romantic relations with a woman.[74] The point is that asking someone about sexual identity, or even about sexual activity, is not as clear-cut as asking them about what school they went to or what their blood type is, and not at all the sort of thing to base scientific studies and charts and graphs and statistics on. 'All too often,' Kurt Danziger points out, 'a lot of what is most valuable about the raw interview material is just abstracted away and all you're left with are these sets of numbers.'

One of the bases of science is the idea of the final solution. Every bit as ominous as that phrase sounds, the notion is that everything is quantifiable, that if you study something long enough, you can figure it out. Newton. Gravity. Got it. Next.

True, new scientists do come along who seem compelled to question accepted truths. But it took three hundred years from Newton's musings on gravity before someone came along and toppled them. And even now, about eighty years later, the average person's understanding of the universe is still essentially Newtonian, not Einsteinian (or Hawkingian, despite his sales figures). Ideas are adopted by the public based not necessarily on their proximity to truth, but on their comprehensibility and familiarity. Which is why questionable science backing up anti-Semitism could convince a nation, and most of a planet, that Jews really should just be got rid of. Science promises to make things comprehensible, and whether the most conscientious of scientists work along these lines or not (and a great many of them do not), policies and practices based on science are read through the lens of popular comprehension. One-dimensional scientific solutions are applied to various personal and social problems. In the 1970s it was discovered that African-Americans are much more prone to sickle-cell anaemia than any other group. Result: African-Americans are barred en masse from entrance into the US Air Force Academy because it was figured they're more likely to suffer in high-altitude, low-oxygen situations. In 1980, the *Diagnostic and Statistical Manual of Mental Disorders* decides that hyperactivity, a condition treated in schools during the preceding decades through educational and counselling techniques, is Attention Deficit Disorder, a treatable condition rather than a modifiable behaviour. Result: students are prescribed a pharmacological cognate of speed called Ritalin to pacify them, just as young women two decades before came to rely, through the diagnoses of an enthusiastic and concerned scientific community, on Valium.

The problem here is that there are practical justifications and benefits to all these things. Not one of them seems at all dastardly. The Air Force Academy is just looking out for the best interests of African-Americans – it doesn't want them to get hurt. And classes that were once disrupted by kids jumping out of their seats every five minutes are now calm and much more educative places.

There is just one very big but really not that difficult question.

What is the ultimate goal of society? Is it to be efficient? Or is it to foster happiness and fulfilment among the broadest possible base of its constituents? Despite what trickle-down theorists will tell you, the two are mostly incompatible. The scientific solutions to things mentioned above cater very well to efficiency but do little justice to happiness and fulfilment. Insurance companies have made very convincing arguments, if you are in the efficiency camp, that they should be allowed access to genetic profiles of potential insurees. They are in the risk-assessment business, and they feel it unfair that they might be legislatively prohibited from being able to take all the risks into account. Oughtn't they to know if someone applying for life insurance is likely to develop Huntington's disease and cost the insurer oodles of money? Shouldn't they be allowed to either refuse to insure or raise their rates accordingly? After all, they're just trying to run a business, and they can't be expected to do that with one grabby hand tied behind their corporate back, can they? And what about the judicial system? Wouldn't it be useful, when determining parole possibilities for criminals, to be able to run a brain scan to see how likely they are to recommit? Sure it would. And they're doing that very thing already in California using positron emission tomography, or PET, scans, which track radioactive tracers introduced into the brain to show up brain abnormalities that have been associated with violent behaviour.

We live in an increasingly complicated world. Trite but true. Out of the whorl of it all we jump, predictably and reliably, on simple solutions to complex and probably insoluble problems. And what's wrong with that is as subtle as it is profound. Take another judicial example. Present-day: a baby has disappeared from home. A frantic mother notices a baby she's sure is hers being strolled by another woman in the neighbourhood and claims it as her own. The other woman swears that baby's hers, and the case comes to trial. The judge orders DNA testing, it's determined the baby is almost certainly the first woman's, and various restitutions and criminal proceedings are initiated. Three thousand BCE: same case, brought before a judge who, faced with two women who swear maternity and unable to do any DNA testing, tells the guard to slice the baby in half and divide it between the two women. As the sword is raised, one woman screams and drops her claim to save the baby's life, at which point Solomon figures out whose baby it almost certainly is. In both instances, the case is satisfactorily solved to a near certainty. But the pre-DNA decision, for all its melodrama, has two definite advantages over the simple modern-day solution. First, it was predicated on an understanding of the human condition developed by necessity in the absence of scientific benchmarks, an understanding that takes into consideration not only what is determinable by biotechnology but also the results of the almost infinitely complex interaction between a person's biology and their history and culture, an understanding that is far more pliable than any battery of tests. Second, since both methods allow for a small possibility of error, in the ancient case, even in the event of an error, the baby has gone to the woman who has made it clear she will put the baby's welfare before all other considerations.

Which brings us back around to sex. Is the purpose of investigating human sexuality to make it easier and more efficient or to make participants in it happier and more fulfilled? One need only bring up the fairly recent reinterpretation of stalking and sexual harassment to make the case that submitting human sexuality to hard, fast, and easily codifiable rules fucks it all up. Under current understandings of the terms, and the general mindset that produced and fosters them, Romeo could certainly have been brought up on charges for appearing under yonder window just before morning's break mere hours after meeting Juliet. No matter how Juliet might have felt about Romeo, laws and standards such as we have been busy implementing over the past decade or so teach us, all but the most iconoclastic of us anyway, that a young man, no matter how good looking, who follows you home without your invitation or permission after seeing you once at a party is a stalker, and stalkers are likely to continue to pester you, perhaps to try to abduct you, maybe rape and kill you. Normal men, the sort you would want to get involved with, obey the regular rules of conduct in such matters. They approach you in open, well-lit public places and express their interest, at which point they are met with either encouragement or discouragement. If discouraged, efforts must cease or their actions quickly become actionable. It is healthy to do so, unhealthy to do otherwise.

Now, no matter how few objects of affection would actually pursue the matter to its possible legal resolution, the fact that the rule of law states that romantic pursuit after discouragement or rejection may be defined as sexual harassment or stalking even in the absence of malicious intent is an illustration of the retrogressive effects of overly regimenting human sexual behaviour.

So when we apply polling and charting and genome mapping and brain slicing to building a definition of human sexuality, we must ask ourselves whether we are gaining more than we are losing. True, there are measurable benefits to approaching sexuality this way, just as there are to imposing strict sexual harassment laws. But the fact that what we are sacrificing is less easily quantifiable, the act of sacrifice more in the realm of a sin of omission than commission, does not mean it is any less real and destructive. It makes it, in fact, a self-fulfilling, self-perpetuating cycle of a peculiarly vicious variety.

Pure scientists should probably just give right up on the Big Sexual Picture and limit themselves to bits of it, like figuring out how to give us bigger and better erections, ever increasingly luxuriant breasts, and maybe putting a cap on this whole AIDS thing (and herpes too while they're at it). Simply because a subject is of profound interest does not necessarily make it liable to what in the end is one very specialised, limited, rigid form of inquiry. Along with love, sex is probably best handled by people working on a different plane, or better yet, by individuals on an individual, anecdotal level. Not as satisfying, perhaps, as a scientifically recognisable unified field theory of sexuality, but in the end far more useful, and more honest.

The Western World was finally ready to talk about sex. And though Kinsey and some of those who followed him had given it both the permission of respectable society to do so and the vocabulary to do it with, it would turn his language of nuance and boundarylessness into a patois of percentages, proportions, and identities. It could not really have been otherwise. What Kinsey was asking his readers to do was skip a step or two in the evolution of their sexual thinking. He wanted people to see sex as an amoral activity, within certain very broad boundaries delineated only by mutual respect, that ought to be a far more participatory sport than he saw his peers treating it. Starting with probably prescient notions, and following them up with thousands of personal interviews, Kinsey was asking his readers to tag along as he brought sex out of the hands of religions, past the already smouldering fires of identity, and into broad rational daylight. They weren't ready. So they used what he gave them to help them along paths they'd already set out on. Edward Sagarin, Harry Hay, and Daughters of Bilitis founders Del Martin and Phyllis Lyons used it to help them forge communities. 'Tailgunner Joe' McCarthy and his tailgunning pal Roy Cohn used it as ammunition to ignite a nation's fear of a Homintern ready to sell the nation's nuclear secrets for a blow job (or to keep one secret). And the average person used it to feel a little less tense about whatever it was she or he was already doing.[75] This did not mean that people were all of a sudden finding themselves able to speak frankly and openly about their sex lives. Though certain discussions were easier now than they had been before Kinsey, and though the media was now more likely to address sexual issues directly, most of Kinsey's immediate effects were, one may presume, largely internal. In the days before the media became plurally the most powerful force in the American and European world, things like that took time. In fact it took until the middle and end of the fifties for the Beats to start making popular literature out of the sex that in previous decades was the purview of the specialist (like Henry Miller, for example), and till the sixties for a whole generation of boys and girls who'd grown up in the years since the Reports had been published, those charming boomers who'd never known a world in which sex was simply not discussed, to act accordingly, making love not war in free open spaces when they were in school and, when they started to earn money, in the sex clubs, bathhouses, and discos they founded and funded.

## The End

Shine enough light on anything and it disappears.

The combination of AIDS and the media has had a still unmeasurable effect on the way we see sexual identity in the West. And quite enough's been written about this most recent historical phase of the construction of gay identity. It interests me primarily here for the crystallising effect it had on the gay communities, and the shock it created, forcing large sections of the gay population into survival couples – two-person garrisons against ubiquitous intimations of imminent mortality. It provided gay society with a watershed, similar in symbolic nature, if not in scope or cause, to the Holocaust for Jews and slavery for blacks. It is one of the many disasters of AIDS that it has bestowed upon the aforementioned generation of gay activists and community members a type of often overweening self-righteousness that only truly mass martyrdom can engender.

AIDS has had a dual effect on sex. As it's made male homosexual sex less mysterious and led a general population from sympathy to tolerance to, increasingly, acceptance of this particular form of previously unacceptable sex, it also cast a pall on sex in general. For people growing up during the depths of the crisis – people who reached puberty between, say, 1982 and 1997 – sex and death were linked in a more intimate way than they had been since childbirth had been a regular killer of women. More so, certainly, for boys thinking about having sex with boys, but really for everyone, even if it was only lurking somewhere in the back of the head, pregnancy or herpes or crabs were no longer the worst possible side effects of getting laid.

But what AIDS has really done, on a social, cultural level, is put gay in the brightest spotlight that was ever shone on it. From the mid-eighties, when the media caught on to AIDS as a result of the inevitable celebrity factor and heterosexual crossover, right through to, let's say, November 10, 1996, when the *New York Times Magazine* ran Andrew Sullivan's cover story, 'When Plagues End: Notes on the Twilight of an Epidemic', about the disappearance of the writer's viral load with the cocktail treatment, people all across North

America and Western Europe were treated to regular references to and descriptions of anal sex, swallowing semen, rips in the walls of colons. This they had never seen outside the confines of pornography and medical textbookery.

AIDS compacted the equivalent of several decades of thinking about and understanding of same-sex sexual behaviour into about fifteen years, complementing and extending the effects of the modern gay movements, bringing us closer to the end of the phase in our societal sexual development known as gay.

## The Consumption of Gay Identity

But of course it's not only disease that's been shining bright lights on gay over the past couple of decades. From the time Calvin Klein and Bruce Weber first got together in 1979 and came up with that photo of the Pepperdine University waterpolo player lying in a hammock, shirtless, the top button of his jeans undone, a hand tucked in the waistband, there was a whopping great crack in the popular representation of the sexes and the expression of sexual desire and desirability. Ralph Lauren and, more enthusiastically, Versace followed suit, and together they set the tone in advertising for the decades that followed.

Women had always been used as sex objects to sell products, to both men and women, and though men had also always been used to sell products to men and women, and sometimes as sex objects, they had never so explicitly been so passive, so sexually receptive. Weber's Pepperdine Boy was not a sexy man to dominate you, like the Marlboro Man – he was a sexy man to be dominated. And he was selling stuff to men as well as women. Men were meant to respond to this ad. And they did. Though Calvin Klein had been founded as a company in 1968, it was only with this campaign, and the follow-up by Richard Avedon – the early-teen Brooke Shields bent over *Pretty Baby*-style, telling us that nothing came between her and her Calvins – that he started to get attention and to become a force in fashion and commerce. And when he continued on this exact same tack, continuing that same ad campaign right up to the present day, he not only remained a force in fashion and commerce but became a defining force in the general culture, extending the tools with which companies could sell products and tapping into what was, fairly obviously from CK's sales figures, a pretty universal appreciation of male beauty.[76] By the time Weber found model Tony Hinthaus and launched the first CK underwear campaign in 1984 (remember that overly tanned body, those bright white briefs, that appendectomy scar?), the mould was set. Klein was taking what was becoming a matter of course in Studio 54 – where the busboys were always beautiful, and always to be had, by anyone with the gumption and money to take them – out onto the streets and into the magazines.

Of course, he couldn't have done it alone. In addition to his back-up designers, this new brand of Calvinism was supported by other cultural phenomena, like *American Gigolo*, which came out in 1980, with Richard Gere walking – and falling off – the newly drawn thin line between stud and whore. By 1981, a short-lived sub-subgenre of films, a diluted version of *The Graduate*, was launched with the release of *Private Lessons*, in which a pubescent boy is taken in hand by an older woman and taught to fuck.[77] Though both fit well into Everyboy's dream, both scenarios also portray the male as the passive partner in sex, the one who is controlled rather than controlling. Men had been 'unmanly' before in film, but never in such profusion, and never so explicitly sexually.

So men's sexual roles were changing – that is, society was acknowledging a difference, a fact reflected in the popularity of these films and images. And just as they were, smack dab in the middle of 1981, AIDS happened. Just as people were changing the way they saw and talked about men and sex and women and sex, sex itself changed, at first just for gay men, but pretty soon, through the increasingly popular discussion of the disease as much as through its increasingly non-partisan spread, for everybody. Stick all this in a mortar with the gay activism that emerged from society's initial reaction to AIDS, add in the shock-troop work done by Stonewall, the ERA, Jagger, Bowie, Joplin, and John, pestle it around for the decade it takes to figure out such monumental earth-shiftings, and you get, among other things, the two-headed calf that is the modern gay movement. On the one hand – or shoulder, if we're gong to stick with this two-headed calf image – we have Madonna and Sandra Bernhard and Michael Stipe and the rest of the people more interested in sex than sexual identity. And on the other, you have a new gay activism based on issues of consumption, a positioning of gays not only as a market but as a market to be reckoned with, which activists see as using consumer society to their own ends.

It's this face – or head – that's been getting most of the attention and that's been drawing fire over the past few years for its mainstreaming ways. It's been called the fall of gay culture. Its opponents have been called anti-gay and have included columnists and filmmakers like Bruce LaBruce bemoaning the disappearance of gay-as-taboo or outlaw, and others like Gregg Araki looking forward to the disappearance of identity.[78] It could be seen as an anomalous strengthening of gay identity coming at the same time that its foundations are falling away, the proponents of gay similar to the proponents of ebonics – segregationists who delay rather than encourage general acceptance of larger issues (the immateriality of race in most basic realms, and the fact that sex is a practice, not a state of being). Gay rights are about the preservation of gayness rather than anything more fundamental (like the fostering of more universal human rights, or an evolving understanding of sexuality), and for the past couple of years it's been shoring itself up against increasingly obvious internal opposition, in the face of more and more evidence, including the relatively insignificant obstacles encountered by gay white men in the workplace or the body politic in general, pointing, of course, to the essence of bias and prejudice having less to do with sexuality than it does with race, gender, and class (especially class).

This sort of activism has given us most of the legislative victories won over the past few years legalising various sex acts and evening out various rights and comforts. It's also given us Gay Day at Disneyland and Canada's Wonderland, car companies and home furnishing stores defining and then targeting a gay consumer market, and gay people's – especially men's – evolving notions of themselves as people with money to burn, who have to keep up consumer appearances not only to feel good and look good for their friends but to not let the gay movement down by not responding to ads directed at gays, which are being seen as triumphs of acceptance rather than co-optations.

This face of gay is totally concerned with building a parallel world for gay, running right up alongside the straight one it's been peering into, nose pressed up against the window, ever since it was little. Oddly, though this movement has much in common with what would once have been called assimilationism, it's actually closer to being a separate-but-equal sort of arrangement. It's that calf's other head that's doing the assimilating, gay into straight as well as straight into gay.

# Part Three

## One False Move

I've been hopping around North America over the past year or so writing in friends' homes and in motels and hotels and talking to various likely and unlikely people about sex. My initial impression was that our problem stemmed from an inability to integrate sex into our lives, and our lives into sex; from our tendency to register sex as either sacred or profane, ignoring any roles it might play in between. I thought that if we could only be a little less uptight about it all, treat sex a little more like we treat eating, for example, we might all do a little better.

Expressed like that, it gave Clive Barker the horrors.

I went to visit the novelist-filmmaker-painter at his family compound in the Hollywood Hills to talk sex with him. We'd met about a year previous when he was touring a book. I'd begun by talking to him about his book, but soon, since I'd already started thinking about my own book, talk turned to sex. He was extraordinarily articulate in his not-so-obvious views of things. So when I was able to manage a trip to L.A., I dropped by. Trying to focus on our conversation and not on his panoramic window overlooking the Hills trying to figure out whether you could see Tom and Nicole's place from here and whether that really was Bette Midler I saw sunning herself on a balcony about a kilometre away, I mentioned my hope that we might learn to treat sex a little less liminally – he blanched.

'It would be terrible if the forbidden went from this, it would be terrible if taboo went from this, it would be terrible if we were to be eased into a general state of not so much homogeneity as the idea that everything becomes acceptable. That would be wretched,' he said, envisioning a world in which sex was just another appetite, as socially condoned as a football game; the kind of world that, when I walked in, I thought mightn't be that bad a world to live in. 'That's a nightmare of the future for me. It's a nightmare of cloned hermaphrodites who are gently, passionlessly lusting after one another, and then going home to eat the sort of pre-prepared pap they eat in *2001*, you know, the red stuff then the green stuff then the white stuff. Horrible.'

I could see the film version of Barker's dystopia, a horror the exact opposite of his Pinhead, with all its sharp and pointy edges tearing into you; this hell would have troops of grinning Caspers bouncing after you like that weird threatening fluffy balloon from *The Prisoner*.

What gave Barker visions was the loss of pain, existential perhaps as well as physical, the loss of detail that is for him the very essence of sex. It was a world without taboo, a world utterly lacking in sexual specificity. Sex, for Barker, is about being especially, viscerally attracted to something you see 'in the nick of a scar in somebody's lip'. 'It's not about perfection,' Barker figures. 'The erotic's about the specific – and that's where the ecstatic experience is so powerful.'

I hadn't thought about it in quite that way before. I hadn't thought about the possibility that a greater understanding of sexuality and a greater acceptance of sex would drain it of the stuff that makes it so juicy. So I went away to think a bit more, to figure out how we might escape our current sexual boundaries – boundaries of social propriety, of political correctness, of sexual identity – without encouraging either some sort of Ecstasy-like haze of silly grins and mushy kisses or an 'I'm OK, you're OK' banalisation.

Sex into life, life into sex. As I rode my cab back from the Hills, wondering if that dog we almost hit was anybody famous, and down onto Sunset Boulevard and into the courtyard of my motel (where I'd heard gay porn's first big bottom, Joey Stefano, had died in the shower), I thought that the shift would require a realisation that sex, like ambition, is an appetite that is linked not only to our need to survive but to our need to enjoy life. If sex were to be like eating, we'd have to be foodies, taking pleasure in it not because it's wicked or dirty, but because it is, or at least mostly can be, inherently pleasurable, like well-spiced food, food you've never tried before, or food that's been cooked with obvious love. We'd also have to think about sex, unlike hunger, as an appetite that filters into every aspect of our lives. It would require acknowledging that we tend to favour attractive people of either sex over people we find less attractive, that the attraction we feel towards people who become our friends is simply another version of – and perhaps not that different from – the attraction that draws us to our lovers. It would require thinking along the lines Thomas Moore implied in a *Mother Jones* article I'd read a few months earlier: 'A more substantive weaving of sex into life may be accomplished,' he'd written, 'by softening the barriers between ordinary living and sexuality.'

When I stumbled across that line in an article Moore had written for the magazine as a synopsis of his forthcoming book, *The Soul of Sex* – I thought I might just have found a way in. I'd heard of Moore, about his bestselling *Care of the Soul*, but I'd never read him and had only vague impressions of what sort of a writer and thinker he was. An ex-monk, I recalled, and maybe a psychoanalyst or therapist of some sort. None especially esteemed professions in my opinion, but this excerpt seemed just the sort of thing I'd been looking for. So I called up the publisher and ordered an advance copy of the book so I could take a look at how he expanded on his ideas.

His apparently level-headed talk in *Mother Jones* – about our current obsession with venal sexual activity as attributable to 'the old theological idea that humanity is contrary to divinity', saying that we're 'working up a fever making new laws against touching, and we're more scandalized by a photograph or painting showing a nipple or a penis than by the image of a starving child on a dry, dusty road' – seemed right on track. And pretty exciting coming from an ex-monk, too.

So from L.A. I went to a gracious friend's empty house in Ottawa – with a stopover at home to pick up the Moore pages that had finally arrived – to sit and read and think. The essay in *Mother Jones* led me to believe that *The Soul of Sex* would be about working sex into everyday life in a more rational fashion than we seem to be able to do at the moment. And being by Thomas Moore, I figured it might even have some effect on the way people saw sex. Now that I've read it, I really hope it doesn't.

It didn't take long to figure out what sort of thinker Thomas Moore is – his use of the word 'softening' in that *Mother Jones* passage was crucial. He's exactly the sort you'd expect to leave the spiritual womb of the monastery for the psychic grotto of Jungian psychology. Protected by all-encompassing philosophies his entire life, this man has no edges. If philosophies were shapes, his would be a big bubble. It's just what Barker had been worried about.

What had seemed at first to be a simple recognition of the role of sex in the traditionally un-erotic parts of our lives turned, over the course of Moore's book, into a radical redefinition of the word 'sex'. But more than just redefine sex, what he did in his book was write 'sex' on a balloon and blow it up big, so big that the word became illegible, meaningless, a series of pixels that covers a lot more surface area but no longer signifies much of anything. Kind of like what he'd already done to 'soul'.

Starting off with Carl Jung's 'people think that eros is sex, but not at all, Eros is relatedness', Moore ends up by taking Jung's notion of Eros and applying it to sex, making sex not about sex but about relatedness. Which is just unhelpful pudding to anyone who wants a way to deal with all the sex that's out there and inside them, anyone who does not see the point in sublimating certain forms of attraction, of taking literally only those forms that best fit Moore's world of pleasant shops and clean neighbourhoods unspoiled by 'wild graffiti'.

'Leisure, less exploitation and more honouring of nature,' Moore writes in *The Soul of Sex*, 'some openings of time and space at work, some relief from the purely health and convenience aspects of food, some imaginative building in public and private life, and public gardens, the keeping of old buildings. This is all sex.'

Ironically, for a man so spiritual, so concerned with the soul, with eternity and the infinite, Moore is far too deeply stuck in the world from which he writes, a world in which the commercial use of sex is 'unpleasant'. As if people who agree to be sexually exploited for cash are in any way different from those who agree to be exploited by other, more intrusive sorts of employers who demand their employees sell off half their waking lives for a cheque every two weeks. It's a world in which he can write a book about sex only if he redefines it to include all sorts of things that aren't sex and are therefore neither offensive nor likely to be controversial, in which abandon is a quality to be cultivated, unless it results in anything upsetting. Moore's basic Christianity (spliced with strips of Greek, Hindu, and Buddhist mythology added for colour, or to get him out of the occasional dead end Christianity hands him) disables him sexually. He stares out through double-paned windows at the Aphroditic and Priapic stories he relates – stories in which the true, difficult, and ultimately antisocial nature of pleasure is illustrated – but insists on sublimating rather than investigating ways in which they might be genuinely and radically useful to us, ways he dismissively describes as grovelling in the 'lower regions of sex'.

'In a sense,' he writes in his heart-crunching book (I'd expected so much; so many people were going to read it), 'this book is inspired all the way through by a simple revelation of the goddess [Aphrodite]: if you want to know what sex is, think long and hard about a flower, especially its beauty and its appeal to the senses.'

A flower. I should have guessed from the name of that first chapter, 'The Nymph of Sex', but I was optimistic and figured he just had a funny way of saying things. Which is true in a way, he does have a funny way of saying things. Describing an orgasm, he writes that 'in the moment of passion a person may look at his or her partner and catch a glimpse of Aphrodite herself, no longer disguised as the person who slipped into bed'.

Aphrodite herself? Unfortunately he has a funny way of thinking about things, too. Not funny ha-ha (the man exhibits absolutely no playfulness), and certainly not funny queer (at least not in the more entertaining definition of that word – his three or four references to or allowances for the homo variety of sex seem to have been parachuted in to catch a wave). It's more funny as in funny that a man this bland can sell two million books.

But Moore does offer his readers enough that is different, and enough of a vicarious glimpse of the sexual freedom represented in the myths he draws on, to reel us in before he draws back and warns us against doing anything rash. Enough even to convince us he's helping us out along the road towards a more thorough view of sex, when in fact all he's doing is allowing sexually dysfunctional middle-class married couples to iron out a few of their more basic problems without rocking the boat or causing the neighbours to talk.

Though the book is muddled by poor analysis and contradiction, it's the patina of sexual progress that Moore creates with his diluted vocabulary (great and big words like 'purity', 'sublime', and 'passion', not to mention 'soul' and 'sex', mean close to nothing by the end of the book) that causes me to take it as an example of what can go wrong in the evolution of sex if we don't whisk it decisively and entirely out of the hands of the religions that have been grasping and clutching at it for millennia.

Thankfully, Moore's book, like most books, sank beneath the surface within a couple of months of publication. The real problem is the direction the book points. That it was written by someone who has shown with sales figures that he has some insight into or natural sympathy with the zeitgeist worries me. It's what Barker was worried I was working towards. English-speaking cultures are extremely, distressingly prone to convincing themselves they are progressing sexually, becoming more liberal, less 'Victorian', when all they're doing is sweeping sex under different bits of furniture, allowing themselves to catch only brief glimpses of it as it's scuttled from underneath the settee to over behind the china cabinet. As Noam Chomsky says (or would if he were given to aphorisms), it doesn't take a conspiracy to hide something, just a general disinclination to look it in the face.

Thomas Moore is the unhappy result of trying to use sexual dross to forge with. Of course history does not work in fits and starts and breaks the way synoptic histories often lead us to believe. Of course old sexual knowledge, sexual theory and sexual mores will be worked into a continuing process of human sexual evolution. But like sexual attraction and sexual acts themselves, wit, will, and reason must be employed in the selection of what to take from the past and what to discard.

That continuing process is subject to U-turns, however, as became clear in Canada on 20 May 1999, when the Supreme Court decided 8–1 in favour of support responsibility in the lesbian divorce case known as *M v. H.*

After a ten-year relationship ended in 1992, M pursued the usual legal channels to get H to pay some form of spousal support. Because the Province of Ontario defined spouse as a partner of the opposite sex, M also asked the initial lower court to determine whether this distinction violated the Charter of Rights and Freedoms. Though M and H eventually settled the issue between themselves, various parties felt this was an important enough test case to continue to appeal and pursue anyway. The Supreme Court decided it was a violation, sending the provincial government away to change its Family Law Act within six months or have it declared invalid.

The decision sent the House of Commons off to resolve that it still defined spouse as a member of the opposite sex, a version of the American Defence of Marriage Act in the form of a resolution rather than a piece of legislation, which passed 216–55 a few days later.

Despite this bit of parliamentary poo, *M v. H* was declared a major victory by gay groups far and wide. And in a limited way, it was; there had been a discrepancy between the rights accorded to same-sex and opposite-sex couples – the decision set the ironing-out process in motion.

But the skirmishes over gay marriage, in Ontario, Denmark, Hawaii, Vermont and elsewhere, remind me of nothing so much as one of those awful and endless World War One battles over some little numbered hill on the French countryside. Backing and forthing, damages on both sides, and it matters not a bit who eventually wins or loses because the war is elsewhere. This struggle to be admitted to a moribund social institution the mainstream has been in the process of sloughing off for decades smacks of limited vision and a sort or puerile insecurity. It's like stomping and screaming and demanding a game that's already over be played again because you were left out the first time. It's obviously better to simply get in on the organisation of the next one. And that next one, when it comes to domestic partnership, is so clearly in the shoot and ready to ride, all this gay marriage fooling and stomping seems myopic to the point of blindness.

Consider these merely talking points. I do not expect, in these few pages, to make a comprehensive argument against a rite of passage that men and women have considered sacred for so long. Aside from being a sign of love and commitment, part of the fundamentality of marriage through the centuries has been its major ability to mark time. We're born, we may or may not get circumcised and/or have first communion and/or our first period, then we get married, reproduce, and die. Marriage is the way some of us know we've reached adulthood. It gives others at least the illusion of security after being tossed about during a few tempestuous years of mating and dating.

Marriage has had a lot to offer. It's nuclear and it provided a degree of trans-generational stability in times when little else could be counted on. It's provided assurance of paternity to men, and sets of vicarious rights to otherwise discardable woman. It's allowed even the poorest man at least one valuable asset, and the poorest woman some means of respectable support. It's also given religion a means of reining in sex, and a way of nosing in to and exerting influence on people's most intimate relations with each other.

Another major reason for the traditional centrality of marriage to the social fabric has been its role as a common denominator. Everyone got married. Marriage was even used as the metaphor for the celibate Christian religions, where women became brides of Christ and the men were wed to a Church often referred to with a feminine pronoun. But then, without any special pleading, without any activists marching to decry this or that inequity or injustice, marriage began to erode. It's another case of us looking out for ourselves, or beginning to shed practices and institutions at the cultural moment when they began to hinder us more than they helped us.

You could blame Elizabeth Taylor. I do. But there were also other forces at work. Women now have rights of their very own, unattached to the men they associate with, and we have, in North America and Europe, all kinds of support systems for children – mass education, for instance – as well as for the poor. Marriage can be nice, but it is certainly no longer necessary, and just as certainly no longer central. The shift has already been made. It is only through wilful self-deception that anyone entering a long-term relationship, married or otherwise, would genuinely believe the chances are better than even, given both partners are fairly young and in good health, that it will last until one partner dies. One hopes, surely, but no longer expects.

And with this reasonable expectation of impermanence, long-term monogamous relationships ought now to take their rightful place in the social order, allowing other relationships – non-monogamous, non-sexual, and non-romantic – a little elbow room in the rights and privileges department in the form of transferable benefits-and-responsibility packages given to everyone upon reaching the age of maturity, conferable upon anyone. Not only would this allow people in relationships with their aunts, domestically partnered brothers and sisters, single children taking care of an aged parent, and other people whose primary relationships are with people other than the ones they're having sex with, some very useful benefits and legal assurances, it would also expand our notions of the possibilities of domestic partnerships. In the years between the time gays started to think of themselves as a people and now, when spousal equivalency has become in some parts of the world a reality, people have come up with the first mass rethinking of the ways in which couples could live together the Western world has seen in ages. Out-of-town rules (a return to those Arabic only-fuck-the-camel-boy-on-the-road rules), open relationships, domestic non-sexual anchors amid fully acknowledged seas of sexual partners – all these may not work for everyone. But one thing the gay communities have shown themselves – and the rest of the world when it cares to look – is that these sorts of things do work for many. It's these sorts of eminently reasonable, workable arrangements that tend to get demoted to the realm of the irresponsible when marriage comes along and homogenises things.

For gay to leave all this behind, all this gathered breadth, for the restrictions and disappointments of marriage is, as the pharmacologists say, contraindicated. Far better to win rights and privileges for newly expanded notions of partnership and human relationships. Not as easy to argue for, surely, but eminently possible, and the pay-off makes way more sense. Without disenfranchising anyone – there's no need for marriage to disappear, after all – it would improve the lot of more than just the staid gays who so desperately want to marry each other.

## Porn

At the time AIDS threw its great viral spanner into the works of modern Western sexuality (and clobbered African sex into something that's more likely to produce death than life), prompting Europeans and North Americans in their ever more enthusiastic pursuits of gay stabilisers like marriage, another force was slowly and much less painfully transforming our relationship to sex, allowing a degree of sexual introspection and experimentation previously unavailable to all but the most sybaritic thrill-seekers. It was in the early eighties that the VCR started to become inexpensive enough to be standard issue in Western households. And, as with the two previous advances in visual technology, photography and film, one of the first and most consistently popular uses to which it was put was the advancement of pornography.

Though photographic porn has long had an enormous influence on the sexual development of boys, and more lately girls, movies, a more immersing experience, had been available only in semi-public places like adult cinemas and peep shows, which tend to attract only truly devoted – or desperate, or socially adventurous – fans of the form. But with the introduction of VCRs into everyone's living rooms, the viscerality of moving porn was available to anyone who could get up the nerve to rent or buy any of the exploding variety of movies, whether over the counter or, even more easily, by mail-order.

As is the way of such things, in both market and production early video porn was pretty standard stuff, more straight than gay, more blow jobs than fisting, more young people than old. But as people became more and more accustomed to enjoy-at-home porn, a universally accessible freedom was realised, and people started demanding, and producing, an ever wider variety of stuff. As anyone who cares to step into one of our larger cities' larger porn shops will discover, there's almost every possible variation available.[79] But more interesting than the gay/straight/bi/animal/oldie/black-on-white/Asian-schoolgirl/facial pornplex that's out there is the use to which people are putting it. If anyone is curious about any form of sexuality, they have this Encyclopaedia Pornucopia at their disposal as a first-level educational tool. No one need ever again wonder what boys and boys do together, or girls and girls, or boys and girls, for that matter. You can not only learn with porn but get turned on by it at the same time, in a wonderful union of education and stimulation that is exactly what the University of Indiana people back in the thirties had hired that entomologist marriage instructor to avoid, and also just what modern-day educators seek to avoid by enforcing sex-ed curricula that discuss biology, anatomy, disease, and even love and responsibility but perversely leave out the pleasure.[80] With video, boys and girls can get off watching boys and boys having sex. Girls and girls can watch boys and girls. Et cetera. Which they do. And as they do, they easily and agendalessly learn that sex is sex, hot is hot, and that the world can be one big turn-on.

It's what Annie Sprinkle has spent the past twenty-five years trying to tell us.[81] And it's something that's been broadened even further with Internet porn. Now here's something that's truly easily accessible – at least to the percentage of the population that has regular access to the Internet. Even more anonymous than trench coats in cinemas or brown-paper packages in the mail, all you've got to do is type the word *sex* or *fuck* or *cock* or *girls* or *teens* into the search engine of your choice and up pop tens of thousands of sites, many of them free, where you can see everything the videos have and a whole lot they don't. And with sex, which is in such a large part defined for us by that which we cannot see, that which is kept discreet, that which mustn't be spoken of in polite company, the mere seeing is of truly enormous value. You may not be turned on by seeing a snake crawling out of a woman's vagina, but seeing it eliminates blind spots, causes you, however briefly, to think, to consider, to wonder a little bit about the nature of arousal, maybe to think about things like exploitation, or cruelty to animals, wonder whether this woman is being exploited, whether that animal is being harmed, whether something as far out of polite discourse and

163

acceptable sexual behaviour as this is truly beyond the pale, or just unusual.

For all the talk we have about sex, for all the books and talk shows and magazines and billboards and song lyrics, we generally cover a pretty slim bit of ground. We think and talk a lot about doing it, about having done it, about hoping to do it, and about feeling bad about how you did it but very little at all about the role it plays in our lives and in society (except to say that it's somehow leading to or indicative of decay and declines and falls), about what attraction is and what our relationship to it is, about why we like what we like and how we express that like. Even the freak-parade genre of talk show brings out the difference only to slot it in to pigeonholes. So this sort of access to the weird, far from being potentially harmful to our children or to the rest of us, is a positive good.

But even more radically, the Internet allows for the most involved form of sexual role-playing we've ever had. Through chat rooms and online sex sites, we can on the Net be whoever we want to be. Stories are flourishing of young men pretending to be older women meeting middle-aged women pretending to be young men over the Net, getting off, falling in love, meeting and initiating face-to-face relationships. The Internet is able to strip away everything but that which the users are in control of, and in enabling us to be attracted to, and to attract, utter creations gives us an early and easy peek at the possibilities of interpersonal relationships based on will and attractions created by rational and reasoning people who can not only take the good with the bad but make the bad into good.

I'd started hearing about all this odd sexual behaviour a few years ago, with rules unlike I'd heard of in any other sexual arena, and finally got around to logging into a chat room to see what really went on.

Once you get into a chat room, you're given all sorts of different chatting options. You can go into rooms for teens, for twentysomethings, for people from Chicago, for girls looking for girls, for people interested in *South Park* ... the first site I found had something like forty choices. You pick a nickname, which appears onscreen when you type in your chat, and you can fill out a profile form with as much or as little information as you like. I picked an ambiguous sort of name, Albie, which I could say, depending on who asked, stood for either Albert or Alberta. And the way the windows work, you can be involved in private chats with several people at once. So in one window I was a seventeen-year-old girl, precocious and kind of punky, talking to a twenty-year-old red-headed college boy from South Carolina with very soft skin. In another, I was a thirtysomething rouée convincing a fortysomething guy from Philadelphia that sucking a guy's cock to turn a woman on would be kinda cool. Then there was this Egyptian man in Florida who after about thirty minutes said if all Canadian women were like me, he was going to move up.

No one going into a sex chat room knows anything about the people they're typing to. Presumably many people take some advantage of the anonymity to spruce themselves up a bit – a forty-year-old becomes a thirty-year-old, a five-foot-four, 210-pound woman becomes a five-foot-ten, 130-pounder, a twelve-year-old becomes a twenty-year-old, and in every parent's nightmare, a thirty-year-old becomes a fourteen-year-old and gets to talking with other fourteen-year-olds.

Everyone does it, and everyone knows – especially the kids – that everyone else is doing it. And they also know that more than age and weight can be played with. But they don't for the most part care. They're playing. And as long as you're into the same stuff they are, as long as you can come up with the verbal goods, you're hitched, and become very intimate – after a fashion – very quickly.

A little later on, after my red-headed college boy went to bed and my Egyptian disappeared, I ran across a fourteen-year-old boy from Australia who decided he was really interested in me and called me away into a private chat, without any indication of my age, size, or gender. He really wanted to get off and never bothered to ask me if I was a boy or a girl or how old I was. Now, this fourteen-year-old boy could have been a thirty-five-year-old woman for all I know, but whoever it was – we'll call him a he – he was having fun. And so was I.

Now, some may wonder what's so great about a forum for lying and manipulating in pursuit of sexual gratification – aren't bars bad enough? And, further, what's so special or interesting about the habit of trying to impress people – fan out the feathers – to get a little?

True enough, people have always lied, cheated, exaggerated, and manipulated in order to get laid: yes, I'm on the pill; no, I'm not seeing anyone; my other car's a Jag; I'll pull out. But there's a limit to how much you can get away with in the regular, face-to-face course of events. It is only when everything is up for grabs that you realise just how manipulated attractions can be. The Net is not genderless, but it allows us to play with gender. It is not classless or raceless or without prejudice, but it allows all these things to be juggled, switched around, recontextualised. It allows users to dip in and out of any number of things, the only significant limitations being imagination and spontaneous creativity. Of course, most people do not use the chat rooms this way. Most people who do use the chat rooms employ one or two standard fantasy types and communicate in standard pornese. But as with other social accessories, like money or literature, the fact that it's not always used in the best or most imaginative ways does not lessen the importance of the possibilities it holds, nor dampen the force of this new variable that expands the number of ways we think about ourselves and interact with each other.

Over the course of about two years, I ended up chatting with scores of people in various sexual contexts, meeting dozens of them. All in the name of research, of course. And in all those dozens, I had not one bad experience. Some people were a little heavier than they'd said or implied, others a little older, or younger. But the very way we made our connections, the only way other than pen-paldom I know of in which impressions are made verbally to the exclusion of everything else (except when, as is increasingly prevalent as more people get scanners and Webcams, people start demanding pix), made it not only possible but obvious not to get that worked up about such things. I found myself, in many instances, so fully attracted to someone by the time I got around to meeting them, that no potbelly or mouth full of bad teeth could fully dispel it. I met and had sex with people who were decades older, more than a decade younger, one guy who was probably retarded after a fashion, someone else who was in a wheelchair, and an extremely sweet, maybe vaguely neo-Nazi rave boy with a cough-syrup addiction. The one thing most of them had in common was that I would never have thought of having anything to do with them had I encountered them in any other context. I was not, when I started using phonelines and Net chat, an especially catholic sleeper-around. By the time I stopped (having, as it happens, met the person I now love and live with on one of the franker sex sites), I definitely was. They were all attractive in so many ways I'd never even bothered to consider. In so many ways so few of us ever bother to consider. The Net, at least up to the point at which it becomes completely corporatised, has the very real power to be the great identity crusher.[82]

## Nineteen-Ninety-Four

Heterosexuals are more and more like homosexuals, except for the sex of their sexual partners. Political scientist of sex Dennis Altman calls the growing legitimacy of recreational heterosexuality the 'homosexualisation of America'. Heterosexual ways of life, he suggests, no longer differ essentially from gay and lesbian life modes. The homogenisation of heterosexual and homosexual heralds a paradoxical emerging trend: the declining significance of 'sexual orientation'.

– Jonathan Ned Katz

Though the Net's big and mysterious and chock-full of potential to change the way we see and interact with the world, it's television that is, without a doubt, the primary cultural force at work today. And it's getting pretty gay.

We've come a long way from Mr Wilberforce Clayborne Humphries or Jack Tripper. The relevance of *Ellen*, lash back as we might, is enormous and, I figure, not undoable. As the *New York Blade* reported, by October 1998, there was not one prime-time slot on US network television that was not at least partially occupied by gay.

By and large, these new TV gays are not allowed to have mates. The creators of *Will & Grace*, the big show that's been filling the *Ellen* hole since 1998, have said that though Grace'll have all sorts of boyfriends, they don't want the show to be about being gay (or something), and so Will'll have none, or at least, none onscreen. As of the beginning of 2002, they'd pretty much kept to their pledge. Will still seems to be trying to get over some long-term boyfriend he had before the show started. So it's true: all those other shows really aren't about lawyers and policepeople and doctors – they're about heterosexuality. I knew it.

But that's not really the biggest problem. The biggest problem is that gay TV will slip into the prescriptive role straight TV has always had, and gays will be stuck in a time-capsule cultural existence I've calculated as being sealed up somewhere around 1994. *Ellen* was pure 1994. As soon as she came out on the show, homilies about what gays were and were not started popping up all over the scripts. Nineteen-ninety-four was the year of Stonewall 25, when a million or so people marched through the shops of New York City's Christopher Street buying anything with a rainbow on it. You remember the march that year, surely – the one the organising committee banned leather and drag and dykes on bikes from? It was everywhere, and for many media agencies, it was the first big gay thing they'd covered.

That's what TV is grabbing hold of in their constant quest to have their novelty and eat it too – that year, that ethos, that awkward but familiar transitional period. There's a great chance not only that popular opinion of gay will fixate on this 1994 vision but that gay's will, too.

Nineteen-ninety-four is to gay as 1956 is to straight. It was around 1956 that the American view of the family, of straightitude and, not uncoincidentally, anti-communism, really gelled.[83] The war had been good for the economy, bad for people. Everything, for the second time in thirty years, had been up for grabs. The Axis could have won. You never knew who was going to come home, who wasn't, or what the world was going to look like next week. After years of instability, years in which it was entirely possible that everything that had been taken for granted one moment could be erased the next, people and their governments slid easily into a back-to-basics approach to life. It was an ideological imperative. The greatest insecurity the modern world at large had ever known had to be countered by as much security as governments and families could muster. And since the issue of variant forms of sexuality had been brought up by the military during the war, it had to be dealt with the same way most other subtleties and nuances – personal, political, culinary, sartorial, architectural – were dealt with during this twenty-year decade we know as the fifties: identified, simplified, vilified, nullified. It was also about this time that TV started its career as the enormously powerful normative force it is today.

Nineteen-ninety-four was also a time of aftermath decompression. AIDS had plunged first the gay communities, and then most of North America, Europe and most especially Africa, into a world of sexual uncertainty during the eighties and early nineties. We found out about it around June, 1981, and within a decade, it was clear an entire generation of European and American gay men was being wiped out. Those skeletal faces became commonplace, and the fear surrounding the equation of sex and death reached a piercing pitch. Would gay disappear entirely? Would it be quarantined? Would anyone ever again be able to have sex and not think that it might be killing them? Would gay ever mean happy again?

But abject fear and loathing can only last so long. We get tired. Our attention wanders. We get antsy. And petulant. It's what makes us so much fun. By 1994, we were seeing some of the positive effects of the massive amounts of attention AIDS had got gay, and things didn't seem quite so bad. It's when gay started appearing on TV in something other than purely comic, villainous or pathetic ways. It's when legislative victories were starting to be won. Gay'd come a long way, baby, and it was time to celebrate and be happy and, most important, it was time to banish all that AIDS-inspired uncertainty. We're here, we're queer, get used to it. By this time, gay was mature enough as a culture to be more or less OK with itself, at least in urban places or when it was left to its own devices. ACT-UP and OutRage! had done their thing, and it was time to start nailing the benefits.

Nineteen-ninety-four was the year gay truly started believing its own hype. The year it became clear gay was not going to accept its successes and continue moving forward, the year it became clear that it preferred to accept its successes and dig in its heels. It was the year gay got scared straight.

We don't need that. And we don't need gay TV. What we need is queer TV. Like *Roseanne*, *Absolutely Fabulous*, *The Drew Carey Show*, *Bob & Rose*, *Friends*.

*Friends* was, at least for a few years, on the other side of something, on the other side, I think, of gender and sexual awareness. Despite its formulaic adoption of lesbian ex-wife/mom, and the completely tired jokes dependent on her, gender and sexual attitudes come from the other side of an awareness that did not popularly exist in 1990. Aside from the parts of the show that actually deal with named same-sex sexuality, the situations, the relationships, the understandings, are all post-*Ellen* (as they were even before *Ellen*) and go some distance towards fulfilling the predictions and postulations of Dennis Altman and Jonathan Katz.

Take the episode with the ballroom dancing. Friend Joey, in order to keep his apartment (or something), has to help his super out. His super's got this date coming up, a big formal affair, and he doesn't know how to dance and he doesn't, for whatever sitcommie reason, have a female partner to practise with before the big day. So he enlists Joey. As the sessions begin, Joey feels weird, and all the typical homo-discomfort sight gags ensue.

But before long, Joey starts to enjoy himself. He feels a little odd about enjoying himself at first, too, before he gives himself over to it. The fact that he's dancing with a man soon becomes for Joey less important than the dancing itself, less important than he assumed it would be. The two end up dancing well together, and when the time rolls around for the date, when the super figures he's practised as much as he needs to, Joey goes into a funk and tries everything to get to dance again. The episode ends with the super relenting and a big sweeping romantic rooftop crane-shot dance number that wouldn't have been out of place in *On a Clear Day*.

You could read the dancing as metaphor for sex if you like. But the thing is, you don't have to. What starts as awkward utilitarianism ends up as genuine pleasure. In previous series, in previous eras, though the same set-up is feasible, the only possible positive end-point for it would be a brushing off of each other after a momentary lapse into comfort, probably with some pledge never to speak of it to anyone. That's a big difference. The pleasure, despite appearances and initial reluctance, that's allowed in what is quite essentially a romantic interaction between the two men is one big quiet step forward for television-kind. That there's no hint of anything tumescently sexual between them is irrelevant.[84]

Joey's a pretty interesting character. He seems to be the most ardent heterosexual on the show. But look a little more closely and it turns out that Joey is simply the show's most sexual character, no prefix necessary. He's nowhere near as heterosexual as Ross, who is in constant search of a mate where Joey is in constant search of sexual pleasure. Where there's pleasure to be had, Joey takes it. When he wakes up after falling asleep and being buried in the sand, a mermaid from the neck down, he looks at his sand breasts, yelps, and then grins and feels himself up. He went out with a transsexual without knowing (or caring) and both he and his father have been going for years to a tailor who has a tendency to take liberties while measuring inseams. He is, to boot, the most unabashed about the emotional attachment to his male friends. I get the impression that if certain sitcom influencing elements of society were not so hung up on sexual identity, Joey would be the first to take the show's already established lead in exploring what happens to friends who become lovers. And what's stopping him on the show is, I figure, the same thing that's stopping men and women all over: the perception, the myth of one's impotence to follow pleasure and relationships across boundaries that have so calcified over the past few generations that it seems that you can't cross them and still stay you.

There's another Joey on TV at the moment who was, at least in that show's first season, before its creator abandoned it, bringing up some questions that bear thinking about. This one's on *Dawson's Creek*, and the show's central question, among many having to do with sex and the average thirty-year-old (dressed up for allurement and market segment purposes in the show as a bunch of fifteen- and sixteen-year-olds), is an old one, about the difference between love and friendship. As we know, the Greeks folded their notion of education and friendship into love and sex with fairly good temporary results. And some of the more admirable and profound marriages through history – Havelock and Edith Lees Ellis, Leonard and Virginia Woolf, Iris Murdoch and John Bayley come immediately to mind – have been at least as much friendships as love matches. But the question of the difference between the two relational states, of where the boundary is, how thick or impenetrable, or, sometimes, whether there even really is one, has never been answered to my satisfaction. So I was pleased to see this show devote such a huge part of its screen time to considering it.

A quick rundown: Dawson and Joey are lifelong friends, next-door neighbours who've been sleeping over and talking about everything forever. The pilot episode deals with the first roadblock in the no-holds-barred friendship – talking about masturbation. To test the newly perceived limits of the relationship, Joey asks Dawson when and how often he does it. Dawson doesn't feel comfortable talking about it. It's an especially well handled *Fox and the Hound* moment: the two realise that this is the first crack in the inevitable breach that forms between all adults. But they do Disney one better and just as that crack is about to be solidified and widened by that first refusal to relate on sexual issues as they've always done on every other issue, Dawson leans out his window and yells to Joey across his creek that he usually does it during *Good Morning America* watching Katie Couric. Roll credits, love-friendship question postponed. Until Dawson falls in love with Jen, the new girl in town, and Joey falls in love with Dawson.

And as Dawson experiences love for what he figures to be the first time, he quickly distinguishes it from what he feels for Joey, which, he tells his other best friend, Pacey, is friendship. The difference? Love is about romance. The problem of defining one problematic term using another is overlooked, but a sanguine Pacey urges Dawson, once again in a boat on the creek, to think a little more about it and the question is once again left mostly up in the air, to be dipped into from time to time over the next few seasons.

What exactly is the difference among different sorts of attractions? There's the sort that kicks in when we walk by a cologne billboard, but there's also the kind that develops over time that is nonetheless physical for being largely attributable to elements other than instant rubberneck arousal. And then of course there's the attraction that's involved when we pick our friends. Are these attractions, as is commonly assumed, entirely different things? They seem to operate in the same way – there are those we'd really like to be friends with and those we want nothing to do with, those we make an extra special effort to maintain as friends and those we don't really spend much time on at all. Is it possible that there's a continuum of personal attraction rather than a bunch of different sorts? And if so, is it possible that there's less of a difference between friends and lovers than we think? Is it possible that Dawson's dichotomy is a false one, that he shouldn't feel the need to set up such solid divisions between his relationship with Jen and his relationship with Joey?[85] Though he's more automatically romantically turned on by Jen, should he entirely rule out the (admittedly lesser) sexual element of his much fuller relationship with Joey? Are friendships perhaps even inherently sexual?

In a slightly less obvious way than the first *Star Trek* used to handle social issues – perhaps even unconsciously – *Dawson's Creek* is providing us with one of the key weigh stations on the road to the disappearance of sexual identity. By looking into that perceived gap between friendship and love and exploring the possibility that the best friends make the best lovers, as the show began to do in its second season when Dawson dumps Jen in favour of Joey, it also goes some way towards implying that there is no necessary boundary between the two, that there is no magic ineffable separating one from the other, that this particular *je ne sais quoi* is more of a *pas de quoi*, that in fact good relationships are good relationships, and all we're doing by abnegating responsibility of will in the realm of sexual attraction – saying 'sorry, he/she just doesn't do it for me' – is roadblocking what could be some of the most fulfilling, complex, and, if we like, lasting relationships of our lives.

And though Joey's a girl on this show, the ramifications of the investigation, no matter what conclusion they eventually come to on *Dawson's Creek*, are more universal than American television is currently allowing itself to admit.[86]

It is significant that both these shows, *Friends* and *Dawson's Creek*, do in fact have gay subplots, and that these subplots are the least sexually adventurous, the least original bits in these two otherwise well written shows. On *Friends*, it's Ross's lesbian ex-wife, the source of the most inane dyke jokes and some of the show's corniest, safest storylines (though she's not been brought up that often in the last few seasons). On *Dawson's Creek*, it's Jack, Joey's ex-boyfriend who's now gay and has gone from being an erotically charged character to an utterly flat one. Things may change, but the basic fact seems to be that where mainstream sexuality is getting ever broader and diverse, gay is getting crystallised, left behind. Heterosexuality is quietly dying, though not so's many people'd notice. But gay, though moribund as well, as befits the Siamese twin of a dying brother, is pretending that everything's just peachy, thanks, please pass the olives. It's become sacrosanct, with handle-with-care stickers affixed by gay watchdog agencies warning not to bend, spindle, or molest.

Something different did happen in the UK in the weeks leading up to 23 February 1999, when Channel 4 broadcast the first episode of Russell T. Davies' *Queer as Folk*. The show itself, good though it was, fell squarely into the category of gay, as opposed to queer, TV. The characters were handled with less care, and so came across as far more human and interesting (and sexy) than their predecessors, but they did still play pretty much to type. The barriers delineating what was sexually possible and what was not were still in place, wavering only slightly when it came to age (the sex scenes between 29-year-old Stuart and 15-year-old Nathan became the meat of what made the series sensational). It was, when it came right down to it, little more than an especially well-written gay soap opera. It was still 1994, in other words; it was just better at it than anything that had come before.

What makes it noteworthy for us here is its marketing and reception. It was among the biggest TV events of that year, with billboards up everywhere around London. It was news, and it was on everyone's lips. It was not, as its American remake would be two years later, a gay person's event. This was TV for everyone.

And as it turned out, it was just the opening act for something better.

*Bob & Rose* was also written by Davies and broadcast in the UK on the populist channel ITV. As Davies explained in a piece he wrote for the *Observer* in September, 2001, the series is based on a friend of his named Thomas. Thomas, Davies wrote, well known on the Manchester gay scene, 'was, and is, the happiest out, loud and proud gay man you could meet'.

But then he fell in love with a woman.

'Of course, Manchester ignited with rumour,' Davies wrote.

Especially among those of us whom tabloids love to call 'the gays'... Faced with something which didn't fit our view of the world, we started inventing... in no time at all, savage smiles were telling me that Thomas was having a nervous breakdown; that he was only doing this to have kids... I was even told that recently he fell out of a 12-foot Christmas tree and landed on top of his secret male Russian lover.

Thomas said: 'Sometimes she goes to bed before me, and I sit downstairs, and I panic. I'm scared. I'm gay, I'm completely 100 per cent gay, and I wonder what the hell I'm doing to her. And I dread going upstairs. Every night. And then I go up, and I get into bed. And we talk. We talk, and she makes me laugh, and the next thing you know, we're doing it. Because I love her...'

Since the mad explosion that was *Queer As Folk*, I've had 20 dozen opportunities to stand at a microphone and demand equality – but there I was, as prejudiced as the next bastard, completely unprepared to allow this couple to fall in love. I was acting out of fear, the same fear I'd condemned in every homophobic thug.

But...prejudice lingers on in that amorphous beast, the Gay Community. Every night out on Canal Street, I'm asked: 'Why have you written that story?' Stuck in ghetto thinking, maybe through no fault of their own, these critics have got an agenda of the things I should be writing, and Bob's simple challenge doesn't fit the game plan. And in fairness, there is one, tangible fear: stupid people will assume that the series is saying all a gay man needs is the right woman. But the key word there is 'stupid'.

## The Word

Before the word, everyone in the Western tradition, and most of the others as well, got married. It has been for millennia one of the foundations of almost every society, and rightly so. Survival through propagation is a social and political as well as a biological imperative. But propagation and sexuality, in the human species, are quite simply and quite completely separate things. They're related, to be sure, but not interdependent. Reproduction can occur without sexual desire, and sexual pleasure can be had without the possibility of reproduction. And as the quest for pleasure, and through pleasure satisfaction and contentment, and through satisfaction and contentment happiness, became over the millennia the ultimate human pursuit – the reason, in fact, for our being – the pleasure derivable from sex became a prominent and going concern for men and, more quietly (since the men have always had the megaphones) but no less concretely, for women.

As old and ancient letters and paintings and pottery and poems tell us, women and men have been taking their sexual pleasure where they find it, from both the opposite and the same sex for as long as there have been letters and paintings and pottery and poems.[87] They were married all the while, of course, and often having children. And, for almost as long, they'd had some religion or other, whether in adherence to Baal or Athena or Shiva or Yahweh or the angel Moroni, telling them where and how to have sex, and with whom, and when and, more important, when not, and whom not, how not, and where not. Sex is one of the strongest impulses we humans have. And along with the drive to survive and the will to power, any authority or social organisation that lasts anything more than about a decade must incorporate into itself rules and restrictions reining these impulses in, for it's a sure bet that given their head, any of those impulses holds far more sway with any individual than any authority or organisation that claims her as a member. And so, in all these successful religions, as in all successful states, we find laws and edicts telling us what we may do to survive and what we may not, over whom we have dominion and whom not, and whom we may have sex with and whom we may not.

We have had our rules, and we have, for the most part, obeyed them – one might say to the exact extent to which they truly benefited us. That is, we did go forth and multiply, and we did raise our children in various forms of families, and those children did also multiply, and so on. This was to our benefit. What we most conspicuously did not do, however, was limit to any great extent the ways in which we pleased ourselves sexually. We masturbated, though most every religion and society (even the Dalai Lama, for Buddha's sake) said it was bad. We had oral and anal sex, though we'd been told not to. And we had various sorts of sexual relations with members of our same sex (we've also had a persistent habit, especially the more rural among us, of having sex with animals, but we'll leave that to another book, shall we?). Priests did it with their acolytes, priestesses with theirs. And not only did the master of the house do it with his stable boy, his stable boy did it with the groom. And the maid with the seamstress. These sexual relationships weren't, with some notable and thoroughly anomalous exceptions, formalised or even officially or personally recognised by many or any; this is, to its everlasting credit, what the gay rights movements of the last century and a third have achieved for us. But the relationships did happen. And pleasure was had, and bonds, of whatever description and whatever duration, were formed.

If you're interested in evidence, an excellent Chinese piece called *The Embroidered Couch* was published in English for the first time in 2001. The plot is pretty standard porn. Easterngate, a well-placed youngish man married to a pretty younger woman, Jin, keeps a fuck-buddy on the side, the younger-still Dali. Dali's young, widowed mother, Ma, hasn't got laid in years; as a result, she is drawn in, through a little lesbo-diddling on Jin's part, to a delightfully rompy relationship with Easterngate, who likes the idea of fucking his fuck-buddy's mother in a kind of partial turnabout for his fuck-buddy's marathon-fucking Jin, whom he'd had a crush on for a long time.

Like most current porn, the dialogue's charmingly bad.

Dali hurriedly bowed twice. 'Elder Brother,' he said, 'you are so kind-hearted! I'm willing to let you ride anal whenever you want to. Even if you pound my asshole into the shape of a barrel, I'd not say a word.'

Or, put another way a few pages later:

'Oh darling, I didn't know you are so in love with me!' Jin exclaimed. 'I'll let you do it with me any way you want and I'll not complain a single word even if you pound me to a nad-shattering unconsciousness.'

But the most extraordinary thing about *The Embroidered Couch* is that none of its gender-hopping is portrayed as being anomalous. The various couplings evolve naturally out of the well-constructed characters and their relationships to each other. No one is classified as a nympho; there are no extenuating circumstances, like prison or the military or absent boyfriends, no miraculous aphrodisiac is lowered onto the stage like a *penis ex machina* to let the players, and therefore the readers, off the hook for a devotion to sex greater and broader than is otherwise allowed.

Dali, when he's not dicking around with Easterngate or Jin, is described as being off with a couple of other male fuck-buddies.

Dali, it seems, just likes it. And, also unlike other catamites, Dali's also a big ol' het stud, too.

In its basic assumptions about sex, this book has a lot more in common with, say, Gore Vidal, Jane Rule, Michel Foucault, Tony Burgess, D. Travers Scott and Dale Peck – people who write with an understanding of human sexuality that does not assume that there is such a thing as innate or immutable sexual identity. The book's utterly different approach to gender (as well as age, for that matter – Dali's about thirteen when he and Easterngate hook up), and the ease and reasonableness with which it's handled, offer some support, some historical context and foundation, for what I'm suggesting are turning into some very current ways of thinking about sex.

Writing like that was never very popular for long, no matter how prevalent the practice. But soon, even the practice began to wane. At some point, we changed, as a Western culture, from what Ferdinand Tönnig called a *Gemeinschaft*, which translates as 'community', to a *Gesellschaft*, by which he means a 'society'.

The pre-urban *Gemeinschaft* was a culture based on close, dense inter-relationships centred in small communities like towns and villages. And, as happens when relationships are close and personal, not too formalised. Things tended to be made up as they went along with certain microcosmic templates. The difference between this type of culture and the society the information age is taking us out of now, is vast, but what it meant sexually was that everyone got married (that's the macrocosm) but everyone had all sorts of unscripted sex (microcosmically). Because people had no notion of such a thing as a zoophiliac, for example, they didn't stop themselves from doing things with the pigs that would, in later generations, label them and get them a spot on some talk show specialising in entertaining outrages. As long as the power structures were without, and we were alone with ourselves within, this happy dichotomy between the macro and the micro could exist, they with their rules, we with our negotiated adherence to them.

But then something cataclysmic happened: the Modern Era. Governments and religions and whole philosophies crumbled in a very short time, and people like Nietzsche and Freud came along and conferred upon us, each one of us, all the power we had for millennia invested in those exterior structures. All of a sudden – and it was all of a sudden in the human span of history – that old dichotomy was not nearly so easy to maintain. It was, in fact, nearly impossible. All of a sudden, we were not responsible to something outside of us to which we could lie, however whitely. We were responsible, ultimately and only, to ourselves. And lying to ourselves, as Freud made abundantly clear, was something we could never really get away with.

And so we had to come to terms. Walls had to come down, and we had to make some decisions. For along with all this newfound autonomy came something with shoulders broad enough to support it – identity. And this identity had its components, which as of 1868, in addition to various things like citizenship, gender, class, and race, began to include sexual orientation.

Now, the notion of identity, of an individual's notion of herself, can seem like an exceedingly abstract concept. But the fact of the matter is that, perhaps more than any other single exceedingly abstract concept, it has made our increasingly homogenised society what it is today.

It is arguable that the first real step towards our modern Western notion of identity was taken by the Roman Catholic Church in 1215, when the practice of confession was brought out of the monasteries and into general practice and made an annual and universal requirement. Though there had of course been a concept of personal culpability before this time, what the actual ritual of confession required was something quite new to people of the Christian Era. Though there would not be an English word for it until the late seventeenth century, what was being required of these people was introspection. Previously the exclusive purview of philosophers and theologians, the Church now conferred this responsibility on us all.

Introspection, as it turns out, is a funny thing. In the process of introspection – of sifting through the memory, the soul, the self, to find the nasty bits you want expunged – there is a tendency to create something that didn't exist before. Without introspection, we are a collage of our various thoughts and actions, chronologically discrete, not necessarily coherent, and probably contradictory. We are, prior to introspection, defined by things outside us rather than in — by who our parents and grandparents were, by who their parents and grandparents were, by whom we serve and whom we marry, the children we bear and sire, the place we live, the god we worship, the trade we practise. All pretty easily identifiable signposts, easy to compare with others', easy, in fact, not to think about at all.

But the post-introspective us was something quite different, and almost incomprehensibly more complex. Once we started mucking about inside, we came up with all sorts of other, far more amorphous identifying features. It happened slowly, as so many things seem to have back then. And, truth be told, it happened without anybody much noticing, and certainly with very little record. In fact, we can only tell it happened from evidence provided several centuries later, after the Reformation shifted the emphasis even further from its pre-1215 state of ignorant bliss, past concentration on individual acts and sins, to a picture of the individual's life as a whole. Self-examination became a far more regular, in some traditions even a daily, requirement. And this led, perhaps inevitably given that we are, *homo narrans*, a story-loving, story-making people, to diary-keeping.

From this point on, our lives became stories, and we were the collaborative tellers. People started feeling it necessary to be able to tell themselves and others coherent stories. This affected both the way we looked back on our own lives — encouraging sometimes subtle, sometimes egregious revision — as well as how we made our day-to-day decisions. 'Am I the sort of person,' we began to ask ourselves, 'who goes to bear-baitings?' And increasingly often, it was the answer to questions like this that determined what we did, how we saw ourselves and, as a result, how others saw us.

It's sort of a Heisenberg Identity Principle: one cannot investigate oneself without recreating, or at the very least altering, that self in the process.

It's the sort of thinking that led to Maoist identity reconstruction, the idea that one could change something called an individual into something called a citizen, an intellectual into a worker, and so on.

It also leads to notions like 'real women' and 'real men'. As the last emperor of China, Pu Yi, wrote – or had written for him – in the final paragraph of his autobiography, '"Man" was the very first word I learnt to read in my reader, the *Three Character Classic*, but I had never understood its meaning before. Only today, with the Communist Party and the policy of remoulding criminals, have I learnt the significance of this magnificent word and become a real man.'

Become a real man.

The phrase, when I came across it for the second or third time in the course of thinking about this book, reminded me of a 1992 book called *Becoming a Man*. It's by Paul Monette, a not-so-well-known American poet who, once he realised he was HIV-positive and began to concentrate on the personal repercussions of that, became the memoirist for an age. In *Becoming a Man*, the book – subtitled 'Half a Life Story' – that won an American National Book Award and, with its predecessor, *Borrowed Time: An AIDS Memoir*, established its author's new reputation and status, Monette wrote: 'Every memoir now is a kind of manifesto as we piece together the tale of the tribe.' Taking himself and his readers through what were at the time of his writing becoming familiar stations of a less and less tortuous cross, Monette found his story amidst the 'genocidal' homophobia that was, as he saw it, 'the national sport of straight men'. Just as Pu Yi found the real meaning of the word 'man' through the Communist Party, so Monette describes his initial adoption and, as he later saw it, misunderstanding of the word, until he realised what he was. 'Let them [the straight men] be the male-bonded unit...,' he wrote, 'swapping ball scores, crowing over the Celtics as they sit down to a killer game of cards. Me, I can't tell the plays from the players even with a program.' After his lifelong search for the meaning of 'man', he finally decides, 'on the brink of summer's end', that 'no one would ever tell me again that men like me couldn't love.'[88] Men like me. He had learned the significance of that magnificent word and become a man.

Although he says his story is particular and that he speaks for no one but himself, he says that he's 'come to learn that all our stories add up to the same imprisonment. The self-delusion of uniqueness'. Whatever his intention, what Monette wrote became for the gay community very like what Pu Yi's story became for Chinese communism. Despite the many particularities in Monette's life – he was involved in sexual relationships with women till quite late in life, for example – he assimilated himself into a vision of gay, as Pu Yi did to a vision of communism despite what he saw at the end of his book as a long history of resisting and deceiving (himself, the party – they had become one by the end). And it was not only assimilation, it was assimilation for a purpose, for a political purpose, for the greater good of 'the tribe', as it was for Pu Yi and the greater good of the party. In both cases, the falling in is of both emotional and social importance. For the last emperor, it made it possible to continue living in a very literal sense; for Monette, it offered hope and greater cause in the face of imminent death, and allowed him to tap into a power, a well of emotion and imagery that fed him an extraordinarily productive period, from the publication of *Becoming a Man* through the publication of *Last Watch of the Night*, till his death in 1995.

I am aware that this is not the first time that homosexuality and communism have been yoked by seeming violence together. And I do not mean, in doing so, to cast aspersions in either direction, only to draw attention to useful similarities.

As I sit here writing this, I'm listening to my roommate Randy on the phone, having the conversation that gay men have, over and over again, apparently for their entire lives, never tiring. I've had it myself, I figure, at least thirty times. They talk with people they are just getting to know of their gay beginnings, of their becoming gay, discovering gay, relating each other's stories one to another, finding significance in similarities, significance in difference. Randy is talking about coming to the big city, about discovering the gay community, and about fitting himself into it. He is, he's decided – or discovered – an ageing (that is, in his mid-twenties) muscle club kid who doesn't do casual sex. This telling and retelling of stories, honing bits, figuring out past experiences in the context of others' stories, is a lot like those prison writings and rewritings Pu Yi and others did in search of their new selves.

The process is helped by outside forces – by the various gay industries that have sprung up around the (mostly mythological presumption of a) supersufficiency of disposable gay income. But the most obvious bolstering comes from a not-for-profit organisation. In fact, the tactics it uses exceed the usual definition of bolstering and bleeds right into various premises and methods that would not have been at all out of place in Mao's China. The Gay and Lesbian Alliance Against Defamation, grinningly called GLAAD for short, made its name around the time of the *Basic Instinct* controversy, when people got to thinking that yet another film in which a sexually irregular character is also a killer was doing gay more harm than good. Since then, they have, among other services, been providing weekly e-mail media alerts, informing people on their lists when some media organisation has either done an especially good or, in their opinion, especially bad job of representing gay and lesbian issues. A fine activist service, if that were all it was. But at the end of every one of these items they run little injunctions – balder versions of the items they've just alerted you to. For example, after telling us about a story in the December 21, 1998, issue of *Newsweek* about Wyoming bashing victim Matthew Shepard that GLAAD felt was slanted in the wrong direction, it says, 'Write to *Newsweek* and tell them this coverage was disrespectful and gratuitous.' Every one of their items features a wind-up action notice like this: 'Please thank the *San Jose Mercury News* and the writers of "The Two Dads" (Russ Quaglia and Doug Hall) for their perceptive and responsible column'; 'Please thank the *Toledo Blade* for cutting through the hype and giving a straightforward account of Scott Amedure's murder'; 'Please express to *Reason* magazine your appreciation for this substantive contribution to the important work of debunking the ads' misleading and harmful claims'. The occasional exception, like 'Please watch "Transgender Revolution" and let A&E know what you think', only serves to highlight GLAAD's more general tone, which is pure condescension.

Like me when I read Signorile's book and put on my T-shirt and boots, but more so. GLAAD is the broadest, boldest, most maddening example I know of what can happen when causes overtake people. In a world of uncertainty, confusion, and moral ambiguity, GLAAD is saying with its action alerts that at least one thing is certain: gay identity and the modes of its oppression. So, you may read that *Newsweek* story about Matthew Shepard and figure it tries to answer a few of the questions outstanding at the time about just why it was he went off with his murderers. The story, surely a little odd in parts, doesn't glorify Shepard, but neither does it vilify him. But for that very reason, because it questions the wrong things, suggesting that Shepard may have had some self-destructive personal problems, that he was sad and lonely and that in this case at least it seems to have taken both bad judgment and villainy to end a life, it is disrespectful and gratuitous. In GLAAD's eyes, those who are not part of the solution are part of the problem. One voice, one view, one vision is required to win the war. And just as in a military operation, the actions of the many are dictated by the views of a few. And as in war, victories won this way can only be pyrrhic.

Women have, more than men, lately taken up the question of life-and identity-as-narrative that Pu Yi and Monette left half-baked and begun to wonder about it, many deciding that a narrative is not something we're necessarily in thrall to, something that exists so that we can enfold ourselves in it for protection and reassurance the way Monette did, but something we ourselves create and manipulate over the course of our lives to suit our own ends.

We can see some of this in a fun book by Lindsy Van Gelder and Pamela Robin Brandt called *The Girls Next Door: Into the Heart of Lesbian America*. It's sort of a lesbian cognate to Edmund White's 1980 book, *States of Desire: Travels in Gay America*. The differences between them are interesting. Van Gelder and Brandt's book was published sixteen years after White's and it's tough and probably pointless to try to determine what's attributable to history and what to mere difference, but the following passage from an interview with a woman named Denise whom the authors met at the Michigan Womyn's Music Festival has absolutely no equivalent in White's book. Asked about sexuality and the possibility of its fluidity, this straight woman from Detroit says:

Well, I can't believe you mentioned that! You know, before I came here the first time, I wouldn't in any way have been open to it. I was walking around with blinders on. See, I think it is true I carry, and so do many other women – which is maybe why they won't leave their bad relationships with men – the idea that gay people are all born that way; that's who they're attracted to and it couldn't be any other way. For the longest time, to justify my acceptance of gayness, I've just said, 'Well, they don't have a choice. Why can't people accept that? I can't change that I'm not black.'

After almost a week at Michigan, Denise admits,

I'm still not sure the whys of gayness all compute for me. Tell you the truth, you're kind of an experiment, because this is stuff I haven't said to anyone yet; I've just started thinking about it myself, and I suspect it's gonna take a lot longer than this festival to sort it out completely. But after being here, I can see how easy it would be to be with a woman. I certainly can! Even just the intensity of watching one woman touch another woman . . . It's overwhelming, just something else.

First off, as far as I can recall, White didn't talk to any straight men. Second, the notion of the frangibility of sexual identity never came up, nor could one imagine it coming up, except in teleological terms, in which the misguided or intimidated straight youth realises his true self and sheds his faux identity for a real one.

But listen to Denise. The intensity of watching one woman touch another woman. Instead of the standard non-neurotic male response to seeing two men holding hands or in some way lovingly touching each other, which is to say, 'That's great for them', Denise sees how easily it could be her, how, despite previous notions about the boundaries of sexual identity, she sees possibilities of commonality when confronted with it in a context in which she has time and is allowed to think about it.

Susan G. Cole, a self-confessed old-time Toronto lesbian who came out in the early seventies and has just turned 50, figures that 'in the last twenty-five years, any woman who's really smart has thought about sleeping with another woman at some point'.

It's this sort of reaction to the issue of same-sex sexuality that I find in a lot of women – far more women than men – and while it's absent in most older men, it's very similar to what I'm seeing in younger men like Todd Klinck, those Webcam boys, or those most definitely not closeted straight men I mentioned having snogged or slept with.

The same goes for the gay communities. It's an issue lesbians have been dealing with for a number of years now – women who refuse, despite going through periods of intense and militant lesbianism, to block themselves off entirely from the possibility of opposite-sex attractions and relationships. One of the higher profile instances even made it to *20/20* early in 1998. JoAnn Loulan was a prominent lesbian activist in the seventies and eighties who, a few years ago, met and fell in love with a man. The first time we hear her voice on the *20/20* episode, it says, 'My name's JoAnn Loulan, and I'm a lesbian' – a statement and an identity she stands by for the whole show, badly but I think usefully confusing people in the process, including Barbara Walters. 'Oh, Lynn,' Walters says to the segment reporter Lynn Sherr after the piece is over and we're back in the studio, 'I am confused.'

'It's very confusing isn't it?' Sherr herself says in the piece, talking to a medical expert. 'If 'lesbian' doesn't mean a woman who is attracted to other women or who is sexually involved with other women, what does it mean?'[89]

'By her making such a statement,' says one interviewee earlier in the show, a lesbian-on-the-street named Alexa Rodriguez, '[Loulan] is going to create even more confusion for individuals out in society that may or may not have a clear understanding about what it is to be a gay or lesbian.'

You can see how these people are thinking. Sexual identity's confusing enough to many, but to call a woman in love with and living with a man a lesbian? Confusion worse confounded. You can understand Barbara, speaking as she always does, kindly, understandingly for the good people out in her viewing audience who have only just come to terms with the whole gay thing, and are now being asked to shift their sexual goal posts once again. Oh, Lynn.

And they're right. But to use a distinction, simple but fundamental, I heard drawn a couple of years ago by Michael Ignatieff, understanding things and getting things done are two quite different affairs, and the former ought never to be sacrificed to the latter. And confusion? Well, what's wrong with confusing people? Keeps them on their toes. But more than that, if you're defining confusion to mean questioning a couple of basic tenets, as these ABC TV people are, confusion's likely the very stuff of life.

And on this particular issue, mightn't this new confusion be seen as an analogue to the confusion we went through in the sixties and seventies when we were first encountering new forms of sexuality, like free love, same-sex sexuality, open and happy interracial sexuality? Mightn't we be just about ripe for a little more sexual confusion now that those other sorts of sexuality, while not universally approved of, are, I think it is safe to say, universally understood, universally lived with?

But confusion is, at its best, a transitional sort of thing, a catalyst to take us from one place to the next. And in my estimation, Loulan and people like her, people who stand by their identities while seriously challenging (some would say compromising) them, are just that. In between. In between what? Well, I'd say in between Susan Cole and, say, Pat Califia. It's not, as you can see, entirely a generational thing. All three of these women are approximately the same age, but I'd say the zeitgeist, the future, is with Pat. Cole, the entertainment editor at Toronto's *NOW* magazine and a former local rock star, places an awful lot of political and personal emphasis on community ('I don't know who her community is now,' she says of Loulan) and conscientious, responsible use of identity. 'I understand why some people are saying "Now, I'm not a lesbian, now I feel I'm getting what I need I'm expressing myself, having my most creative time in a heterosexual relationship," ' Cole says, 'but there'll be a point where you have to be living as a lesbian to call yourself a lesbian, there's a point where she's no longer living as a lesbian, living with a woman, physically, in a way that is a fundamental challenge to the way sexual things are organised ... Women-identified? great word; lesbian-friendly? a great word; lesbian-positive? fantastic words to use, but lesbian? I don't think so.'

Loulan still feels that identity is inherent and of great importance. 'I clearly am bisexually active,' she told *20/20.* 'But I think sexual orientation has to do with much more than that. If this relationship ended, it's not like I'd say, "Well, whatever comes along next." I'd go right back to my lesbian community and hang out with the women, and I'm sure I would be with a woman next.' But at the same time she says that 'sex is an activity, it's not an identity', moving away from the having-your-cake-and-eating-it-too problems with lesbian identity combined with heterosexual privilege, making a fundamental crack in the connection between sexual behaviour and identity.

Califia's twisted the crack into a break, and in a way that no male as popularly read or ingested as she has – yet.[90] She's written oodles, including a bunch of pornography aimed at gay men,[91] but to take one essay of many, 'Identity Sedition and Pornography', included in *PoMoSexuals*, gives a fair picture of her ideas about, as she puts it, 'colouring outside the lines'. She says that 'gay male and lesbian culture is obsessed with purity of identity as the only basis for figuring out who you can trust or dance with. This creates a lavender breed of segregationism'. She talks about going to an S/M club called the Catacombs where she describes what usually goes on there as dyke sex, despite the fact that everyone doing it was male. 'Everyone at the Catacombs was usually much too stoned to make use of his dick. Sex involved hands and buttholes and mouths.' In her opinion, just as bisexuals blur the separation of gay and straight, and the transgendered between male and female, the practice of S/M sex challenges 'the whole idea that sexual orientation ought to be based on gender in the first place, since many of us care more about the fetishistic aspects of our partners' apparel or the equipment they are prepared to wield than we do about the contents of their laps'.

Califia's writing, and much of the writing that appears in books like *PoMoSexuals*, *Boys Like Her*,[92] as well as the underpinnings of such books as *Switch Hitters: Lesbians Write Gay Male Erotica and Gay Men Write Lesbian Erotica*, is confusing. There's talk of women being fags, boys being dykes – it's all very messy. And though some would interpret this as nothing more than cutesy manipulation of nomenclature, I'd say it's cusp-talk – it's trying to get across notions popular frames of reference do not yet allow for. It's trying to come to linguistic terms with the implications of what these writers have experienced as a deflation not only of sexual difference but of the sort of gender difference Kate Bornstein talks about. It's a language and conceptual crisis that's prevented me from taking gender into as much account in this book as Bornstein convinced me we ought to – it just gets too abstruse; ridiculous, as often as not.

Which is one big reason people are not paying more attention to it. And when the talk turns to S/M, well, it's easy enough for most of us to distance ourselves from that – sure, maybe those S/M people don't bother as much about gender as they do about leather and tit clamps, but then, they're not normal, are they. And those other people writing their stories of fucking boys like girls, girls like boys, girls as if they were boys, boys as if they were girls – it's just beyond most people's ken. Most people, as a friend of mine pointed out recently, are chiefly monogamous – they don't get to play around that much. All this play and talk of play presumes multiple partners, she told me. So do I, I replied. I assume, apparently unlike my friend, who's about twenty years older than I am, that most people I meet have had or certainly will have multiple partners, that long-term relationships will be measured in years, perhaps, but not in lifetimes, and that in the context of those long-term relationships, there will be other interim, probably quite brief, sexual relationships. It has, as far as I can tell, been ever thus for men – maybe the generational difference has something to do with the fact that women are now doing it more, or at least are now being seen to be doing it more. Whatever. It's still probably incontestable that the norm, at least among the older and more conservative and less confident younger people, is some form of lifetime monogamy. But that rather dull fact does not, as it happens, have too much of an impact on our discussion. What we're talking about here is possibilities, contexts, ways of understanding ourselves and others, ways of looking at the ways we look at ourselves. And it's about freedom, too. That subtle, rarely enacted aspect of freedom that lets you know that even though you may have done things the same way every day for the last thousand days, there is no reason in the world that you can't do them entirely differently today. Or tomorrow. Or the next day. It's the sort of freedom that comes from getting ever closer to an understanding of yourself and your interactions with the things and people around you, before you, after you.

Which brings us back to Van Gelder and Brandt's book. Here's Jorie, another of their interviewees:

> In terms of attraction, I think I'm not entirely a lesbian. I met a young guy – twenty-three – recently who made me think, 'If more young guys are like this they're doing something okay.' He was not just New Age sensitive; he was genuinely interested in women, and different. I realised I could be attracted to a guy like that. I think if I'd met more lesbian role models when I was younger, I would have been a lesbian first, and then bisexual, instead of straight and then with women. I'm more lesbian, because I've found I have more profound relationships with women, and I'd rather be in that community. But I'm still attracted to men – almost against my will.

What prevented Jorie from being interested in men before was not their manhood but their disposition, their world view, their relationship to sex and their take on gender relations. The two have been perceived to be the same, manhood leading to certain sorts of dispositions and world views. But if it ever was that way, it certainly isn't any more – or at least, not so reliably. Jorie is more lesbian, she figures, because she has more profound relationships with women. The profundity of the relationship is the determining feature for her – not the gender that engenders it. There's this twenty-three-year-old who seemed capable of offering her that profundity, which made his being a man of secondary importance.

And then there's the issue of surprise. 'Almost against my will' is how Jorie surprisedly describes her sometime attraction to men. She's being surprised, I'd say, by her own consciousnesses, which has developed along different lines from those people under whose rules and definitions we've been living and fucking. Jorie assumes fellow-feeling with the gay communities of which she's become a part, but when her own varying reactions, built from personal histories lived entirely post-Stonewall, come up and smacks her at a party, she's surprised by feelings or thoughts she would not expect from a paid-up member of the club.

It's a surprise that won't remain surprising much longer. As more and more mostly younger people feel the surprise, and every once in a while decide to think a little bit about it rather than tuck it behind a mental or emotional couch to avoid embarrassment or difficulty, and maybe even write about it once in a while, as Todd Klinck has done,[93] as D. Travers Scott has done,[94] as Pat Califia made a career and a reputation doing, it, too, will become a part of people's notion of what is allowable, precedented sexual, emotional experience. It will become an option where no option seemed to exist before, and the de facto essential nature of sexual identity will continue to crumble.

Because when Loulan says that sex is an activity, not an identity, she's simply using different words to explain the same basic notion – that life is a narrative, a story we tell ourselves.

It's a concept that another former lesbian activist, Jan Clausen, came up against for the first time about a decade ago. It inspired her to write an essay in *OUT/LOOK* magazine in 1990 that made her a lot of enemies in the lesbian community. In that essay she talked about leaving her long-time female lover for a man and described what she figured that meant about who she was.

In 1999, she decided to extend that argument and make it more explicit in a full-scale memoir, called *Apples and Oranges*, in which she talks about the 'vertiginous absence of plausible narrative structure' she felt once she stepped outside the boundaries of sexual identity and her initial 'sense of unease at my inability to furnish a credible (never mind seamless) account of my past'.

Having fallen in love with this man after spending her entire adulthood as a very central part of the New York-Brooklyn lesbian community, she writes, 'I had to ask myself some difficult questions, not only about my current choice, but about how I'd been telling the story of my life. My habit of stowing my early pre-lesbian years in the sub-basement of my autobiography began to seem suspicious.'

## Ex-Gays

In the middle of 1998, a media storm ended up adding to people's general perception that gays are getting far too much media attention. Baseball player Reggie White told people god didn't like homosexuals or some such thing, and on 13 July, the *New York Times* ran an ad, under the title 'Toward Hope and Healing for Homosexuals', featuring a picture of Anne Paulk, which described how her own lesbianism had been the result of having been molested by a boy as a child, and losing touch with her femininity. Her heart became cold, she wrote in this ad copy, and as she pursued her lesbian lifestyle, she continued to feel something was missing. She felt a god-shaped hole in her heart. Until she found an ex-gay ministry:

> Thousands of ex-gays like these have walked away from their homosexual identities. While the paths each took into homosexuality may vary, their stories of hope and healing through the transforming love of Jesus Christ are the same. Ex-gay ministries throughout the US work daily with homosexuals seeking change, and many provide outreach programs to their families and loved ones.

Paulk used no reasoning in the ad copy, which runs to several hundred words, so I'll refrain from arguing the points. But there are a fair number of assumptions, premises, and techniques at work, and the opposition the ad set up between gay and god is one that touches a lot of hearts in the wacky old United States. And the opposition is so egregious, so blankly stated, and so kindly sounding, it polarised the debate once again. Gay caused by early-childhood molestation; a conflation of gayness and gender-identity; and under all of that, the notion that some sexuality is learned or inflicted, while other bits are inherent.

On one side of this newly reopened wound, people wondered openly if the *New York Times* could be charged with publishing hate literature. Would they have run a similar ad advocating the conversion of the Jews? On the other, a collective sigh of relief that all the politically correct crap was finally out of the way and, right there in the *New York Times* (and a good number of other newspapers around the US), the real deal was finally being stated in plain terms. This ad explicitly stated the underpinnings of much Christian teaching on the subject. Hate the sin, love the sinner was the message I got from Cardinal Ratzinger when I was in college. And though much protestant rhetoric – and Christian action – tends to dispense with the latter half of that equation, it pretty much sums up the Christian – and to a large extent the continuing American establishment's – take on things. Sounds not that bad to a conscientious believer. Except, of course, that we all have sex drives that will out (even if some of us go through a good deal of effort to imply they don't and won't), and so if someone's going to have to stop the sin of same-sex sexual activity, they're going to have to either take up a pretty comprehensive regimen of masturbation (which, despite official teachings, most churches are considerably less sticky on than sexuality involving other mammals) or start having some opposite-sex sex. Which, in most systems of sexual belief, adds up to some sort of conversion.

So, at precisely the time when the gay movements had come so far along that even their boundaries were beginning to break down, along come the ex-gays to make everyone circle their wagons again. (And by October, the gruesome reporting of the killing of Matthew Shepard, and the continent-wide protests and vigils that stemmed from it, furthered the effect.) As Andrew

Sullivan argued in his cover story for the *New York Times Magazine* on October 11, 1998, this ad campaign was the eruption to the surface of years of subterranean American political conservatism percolating itself back into puritanism, a conservatism, Sullivan argued, that had 'lost sight of the principles of privacy and restraint, modesty and constitutionalism, which used to be its hallmarks'.

It seems very much like a sign of the twilight of the gods of conservatism to me, but whatever the ultimate source, or effect, of this renewed anti-sexualism (and Sullivan argues well for his take on the case), the fact is that it goes to the root of the way a lot of us, some thoughtfully, most thoughtlessly, believe. Its attraction, and its effectiveness, is based in the same corner of the human soul that responds to the black-and-white triumphalism of Jimmy Somerville, the gay pop diva and Michelangelo Signorile's musical equivalent who provided the soundtrack to the late eighties' and early nineties' read-my-lips gay activism and whose apotheosis was his performance at the 1991 gay March on Washington at the height of both gay and AIDS activism, where he sang to the gathered hundreds of thousands, 'Here we are and standing our ground/And we won't be moved by what they say/So we'll shout (Shout!)/As loud as we can/And we'll shout (Shout!)/Till they hear our demands/Money is what we need, not complacency/Read my lips and they will tell you/Enough is enough is enough is enough/Finding cures is not the only solution/And it's not a case of sinners' absolution/So we'll fight (Fight!)/For love and with pride/And we'll fight (Fight!)/Standing together for the/Right to live and die with dignity.'

The indisputably gay contextualisation of his original love songs and of his remakes of seventies disco classics like 'Don't Leave Me This Way' has a lot in common with the biblical positioning system American Republicans use to deliver their own brand of uniquely twentieth-century socio-moral conservatism. The flag that decorates the back of Somerville's greatest-hits CD, emblazoned with his initials and a pink triangle, is the precise cognate of the American flag that dangles behind as President Bush tells his people who the enemy is. Neither seeks to make a case; both appeal to prejudicial sympathies. Both depend on inarticulate symbols to evoke largely unexamined systems of thought and belief. You can't argue against the flag – it's a symbol of the good – just as you can't argue against liberation.[95] So, just as Jimmy won hearts and minds predisposed to his cause, made them well up with anger and pride and tears that needed a focus, so too did the Christian Coalition, the Family Research Council, and the other sponsors of the national ad campaign appeal to those whose predispositions led them to believe that America is foundering as a result of moral decay (Lewinsky was also unfolding at the time), and that the epitome of moral decay is the growing systemic tolerance for the pain, the cold, the loneliness, and most of all the instability that is homosexuality.

Such extremes of inarticulacy are great for winning hearts and minds but not for changing them, and certainly not for prying into tight-lipped certainties and trying to discern what else might be in there.

Like with the ex-gay issue. It seems to me that they've got something there, these pro-ex-gay people, though not necessarily what they think they've got. I appeared on a talk show, named for its bubbliciously serious-acting host, Arlene Bynon, about this very issue. They were looking for a gay couple with kids to counter the two ex-gays they had on, both members of Exodus, a Christian organisation devoted to helping believers make the change. They couldn't pin one down, so they got me.

The two ex-gays spoke to Arlene in exceedingly measured tones about their situations, about the moments they respectively realised they were gay, about the pain that ensued, about the reasons they figured they might have been gay (the woman mentioned something about having been sexually assaulted when she was fourteen, just as Anne Paulk did, and about feeling more like a real woman now that she'd dropped the whole lesbian thing, just as Anne Paulk did), and the godly course they took out of it. The man was married with children, and the woman was enthusiastically, she said, dating men. Then came the satellited-in fellow with obscured face and electronically altered chipmunk voice (real early-sixties time-capsule stuff) to talk about electro-shock therapy and how it didn't work for him. Then came a psychiatrist, Dr. Allan Peterkin, who regularly dealt with gays who were having trouble with being gay. He said the problem usually wasn't with being gay but was with more generic issues of dissatisfaction, low self-esteem, etc., and that trying to attack the sexuality was a misguided attempt at a magic-button solution to much more complicated problems.

As I was sitting in the green room watching them all on the closed-circuit, it struck me that there was one big possibility that none of them was even entertaining, that in fact none of the debate on the issue since I'd started paying attention to it has even hinted at. Based on my own little experiments, it seems to me that attractions are something we can, if we choose, be actively engaged in. That they are not ethereal forces, inexorable miasmas that well up, over which we have no control. What they are, these attractions, are the paths we use to social happiness. When we fall in, amicably, professionally, sexually, romantically, with someone we're attracted to, the relationship that ensues is more likely to produce greater happiness than similar relationships where there is no attraction. If you recognise this, and allow for the possibility that attractions are manipulable, that they are in your control and not necessarily vice versa, you'll be able to see yourself at point A, happiness at point B, and, using the attraction-as-path analogy, see your way clear to cutting across the field rather than needing to stick to the roads set down for you in your reflex reactions.

Sounds a little cold, I know. But it's not. At least it needn't be. Remember *The Dead Poets Society*? Robin Williams as the Mr-Jean-Brodie teacher-hero John Keating whooshes into the stuffy old boys school to teach them all to really love literature. He opens the text that's been assigned to help them with this and finds a graph of literary perfection some New Critics developed to assess achievement. Outraged by the soullessness of the approach, he hurls the book away to the cheers of the newly rebellious boys who ominously start calling him Captain, and he spends the rest of the movie speaking from his chest and encouraging the boys to get up on their desks and shout a lot of Whitman. Suicide ensues.

Williams's character appeals to that innate sense many of us have that, as it seemed to be for the Romantics and the Beats, the creation and appreciation of literature and the arts in general should spring from previously untapped wellsprings of soulful joy, and that once these subterranean lake districts are tapped, either by the writer writing or the reader reading, one can't help but be overwhelmed by the gushing loveliness. Wordsworth said something about spontaneous outpourings of unpremeditated verse; the Beats had their cut-ups.

Edward O. Wilson defines consilience as 'literally a "jumping together" of knowledge as a result of the linking of facts and fact-based theory across disciplines to create a common groundwork of explanation.' In his 1998 book, *Consilience*, and two *Atlantic Monthly* cover stories based on the same notion, he suggests that the extent to which we have jumped away in the arts from anything that even remotely resembles the sciences may not, in the end, be in our best interest. And as I'm sure someone must have said quite pithily at some point, probably rhyming 'art' with 'heart', people tend to treat the arts in much the same way they do matters of the heart and loins. It's surely chief among the many reasons people dislike critics so much: they're applying their minds where they should be using their hearts. The same goes for difficult art that requires some effort to understand or appreciate – it's not really art, people figure, not like a landscape, not like *Swan Lake*.

But as some critics, and many others who have decided the arts are something worth spending time and effort on, have long known, art is best when it takes us from where we were and plops us down somewhere quite different. It's the basis of the 'transporting' metaphor, which is also applied to love and sex. But the problem with the metaphor, in both instances, is its passivity. One is transported by great art or grand love. But in matters of both, to truly take advantage of all they have to offer and all you can bring to them, activity is essential. With art, or any cultural or social event, this activity involves engaging the material, not waiting to be pleased by it but taking pleasure or understanding from it, or at the very least seizing it as an opportunity for thought.

It's much the same in the movable realm of attraction. Though I am primarily attracted to boys, I find that I am also attracted to girls who look like boys. Follow me. I'm sitting on the back patio of a place I go sometimes in the summers – great big iced coffees and excellent cheap burritos – and I'm losing chunks of my friend's side of the conversation looking over his shoulder to a table set farther back on a little dais. There are five of them sitting there, four women and a man. Great cheekbones on the guy, good chin, the sort of skater-surfer hairdo that always does me in. My friend says something about television, something about pornography, and then something about Terry Southern. But I'm obsessing for a moment, falling in love as I do about half a dozen times a day, with this great skater-surfer dude, when I realise, just as my friend's coming to some point about it all being downhill for Southern after *Easy Rider*, that the skater-surfer dude's a chick. This has happened before, of course; I usually snicker a little and that's about it. But since I've got time and sunshine and a friend with an apparently self-sustaining conversation, I decide to run with this a little.

What does this say about the essential nature of attraction? Does it mean that attraction can be fooled? Or does it mean that we are fooled by attraction? Does it not make some sort of comment on the perhaps fundamentally fetishistic nature of sexual attraction? Does it not mean that I have developed certain fetishes – hairstyle, facial features – that are most often, but not exclusively, found in men? By making a leap, unconscious, from that to an assumption that I am essentially attracted to men, have I not made a mistake, or at least a simplification? And are not fetishes malleable? Can we not choose to indulge them or not? Can we not add fetishes to our repertoire and subtract others?

What is the difference between general attraction and fetishism? Can we learn anything about ourselves, our own attractions, and perhaps how better to deal with them from taking a look at people who cum at the sight of a stiletto heel wrapped in clingfilm?

I think we can.

But we may have to use Freud to say how. Or at least start off with him. In his *Three Essays on the Theory of Sexuality*, he observed that fetishism shows us that 'the sexual instinct and the sexual object are merely soldered together'. Now, I'd much prefer to stay away from Freud, as he seems to have far too great an influence on the way we continue to view sex. But on this point, I agree with him. It seems intuitively correct to me that sexual instinct and sexual object are, in fact, shoved together through a process of what psychologists call overdetermination, which as far as I can tell means the process by which we come into most of our views, qualities, and even physical characteristics – the assimilative process of folding multiple and ultimately untraceable causes into single but complex effects. Freud was a big fan of the much simpler, more elegant, and far more literarily satisfying single cause theory. See your father's penis, develop penis envy. Have trouble on the potty, become exceedingly well organised. And it's this simplicity, as well as his leaning his theories into universal mythological and literary traditions, that have lodged many of his notions in our brains, rather than anything much to do with common observations.

But the reason I agree with him on this point is that I find myself attracted to girls who look like the boys I'm attracted to. Now at first that might seem to be nothing more than getting fooled, a kind of sexual *trompe-l'oeil*. Except that unlike a *trompe-l'oeil*, which could lead you into a cleverly painted wall you thought was a corridor, in the realm of sex, attraction is the thing. If you're attracted to something, you're attracted to it. The effects of being attracted to something you thought was something else are wholly negotiable – unlike the wall. In this respect, attraction cannot, like your spatial relationships, be fooled. It is only our established and socially supported notions of ourselves, of our identities, and of the set of acceptable attractions included in those identities – once we realise it's a girl and not a boy or a boy and not a girl – that kick in and shut us down.

But what would happen if you didn't let that kick connect? What happens if you, like me this day on the back terrace of this charming little burriteria, continue to look, continue to get turned on? Well, you could go up to the object of your attraction and start a conversation, express an interest in her in that coy way you have that works so well with all the boys, and if she's as interested in you, maybe go home and have sex with her, maybe even start up some sort of relationship. But that might mean you're not gay, or at least not as gay as you thought you were. So it's far more likely, of course, that you'll do no such thing, that you'll file it away as one of those funny little missteps, maybe mention it to a few friends by way of cocktail chat, and that's that.

But that's identity getting in the way, isn't it? An identity founded in attraction getting in the way of following through on an attraction that runs contrary not to the foundation of the identity but to the ancillary accretions developed from suppositions made as a result of those initial attractions, suppositions that this apparently anomalous attraction could very well prove to be mistaken.

Let me unpack that a bit.

You, for whatever overdetermined reasons, developed a basic set of attractions some time either before or during puberty. And as these attractions firmed up over time, solidified through various processes of positive and negative reinforcement and whatever else solidifies attractions, you noticed they tended to clump more around either boys or girls. Now, depending on your own gender, you either found your set of attractions the topic of all sorts of schoolyard and media conversations and representations and had them further crystallised and extended by that, or (if you grew up in the eighties or earlier) you found an odd sort of silence, far fewer representations and conversations, deduced difference, perhaps uniqueness, from this relative absence, and developed and extended these attractions along those lines, perhaps denying the attractions, perhaps following them along lines of increasing difference (into those most obviously unlike your perception of yourself – cheerleaders, say – or into your perception of some extension of yourself – queens, perhaps). Whatever the case, as sexual identity crystallises, you develop attributes that are essentially ancillary to the original attractions, attributes of the real-men-don't-eat-quiche variety. Depending on your class, your nationality, and the nature of your education, these attributes might include either an interest or a distinct lack of interest in ballet, in sports, attention to personal grooming, certain groups of sensual pleasures, dominance or passivity in the initiation of sexual contacts, the physical form of one sex over another. But the most fundamental of these is the gender dichotomy: straight people don't get involved sexually or romantically with members of the same sex, and gays don't get involved with members of the opposite sex. And it doesn't take long before the construction becomes an essence, before you are genuinely not attracted to anyone outside your declared or perceived gender group. And though there are oodles of people out there ready to tell stories of an utter lack of interest in members of the opposite or the same sex from the delivery room onwards, I'll simply have to disagree with them; disagree with them on the basis of personal experience and introspection – which, since polls and statistics are utterly unreliable, is, I am certain of it, the only way into such issues.

I was once myself convinced that I was utterly unattracted to members of the opposite sex, and further, that I never had been. I remembered my prepubescent relationships with Stacey and Corinne and Kimberly and Susan as being essentially sisterly, or at least lacking the urgency of my equally early relationships with Scott and Michael and Richard and Brent. It was only when I decided that this part of me was worth investigation that I realised, consciously attempting to remove the retrospective filter of a gay identity, that the relationships were pretty much the same; it was only then that I remembered I played prepubescent sex games with Brenda (which I found just as naughtily alluring as learning about erections – in theory – from Kenny), that I had a just-presexual crush on Monica, and that I never played sex games with boys, nor even thought of it. And though I can hear explanations like I must have felt safer playing sex games with girls, in whom I wasn't really interested, than I did with boys, who I thought might be too incriminating, I've heard the opposite reasoning put to work far too often to explain same-sex sex games to put much faith in either scenario. And when, in grade six and seven, I first started feeling those more visceral rumblings sitting beside certain people and not others, even though that dreamy set of Calgarian twins named Christian and Richard were the first to set things in motion, the buxom-before-her-time Jennifer ran a close second. Before I sat down to write this, I had completely forgotten about Jennifer, and about Brenda and Monica.

But enough about me. Let's talk about you.

I think it would be fairly uncontroversial to suggest that your own attractions have changed over time. Perhaps you were once attracted to girls in kilts? Or skaters? Maybe Kurt Cobain or Helena Bonham Carter once did it for you. And now, though you may either retain vestigial attractions for these or have developed a distinct dislike for them, you are perhaps attracted to the lawyer type, or the matronly sort, or maybe you've just moved from Kurt or Helena over to, say, Ewan McGregor or Gwyneth Paltrow. It seems to me that throughout our lives we are continually adding and subtracting attractions as a result of our experiences, of our changes in circumstance, of our aging. Very rarely, I think, do those initial pubescent attractions – to Mister Rogers or Wonder Woman – stick around in anything other than nostalgic or ironic form. All sorts of barriers are crossed in the development of our attractions – when once we were attracted to teenagers we become attracted to adults, when once we were attracted to people because of how they looked we become attracted to them because of how they think. Not everyone undergoes drastic shifts, but we all suffer alterations in the nature of our attractions. ('What did I ever see in her?' is a pretty common sort of thing to ask yourself.) True, sometimes these shifts may be seen as a honing, from Wonder Woman to S/M, from Mister Rogers to daddy types, but the change remains the same. And most people, I'd guess, see this and take it as self-evident that since we don't do this with the sex of those we're attracted to, it's in a different category from, say, superhero outfits. Very few people, they'd say, go from being attracted to women to being attracted to men.

But since attraction is overdetermined, and since not only aging and financial advancement but also societal pressures and cultural norms all play a role in its development, and since fluidity in the choice of the sex of the sexual object has not been permissible, it has not been an option.

But things have changed, and continue to change. Unrestricted sexual choice, which was once common but unspoken, became less common and more spoken about, then even less common and even more loudly talked about, and is now more universally shouted about than ever and becoming more common once again. In the few years since it has become acceptable to create reasonable portrayals of same-sex attraction in the American and northern European mass media, those who are young enough, independent enough, or sexually introspective enough have started – just started, mind you – to accrete a little less seamlessly. As it becomes obvious through public representation that there are no particular types of people who are either straight or gay, that there are very straight-seeming people who have sex with members of the same sex and very gay-seeming people who have sex with members of the opposite sex,[96] and all sorts of stuff in between and beyond, the connection between act and essence is becoming weaker in people's minds. Echoing my own de-revision (or re-envisioning) of the development of my attractions, Edmund White, one of the most prominent creators of English-language gay literature of the eighties and nineties, said in a review of Marjorie Garber's book on sexuality that reading it had made him realise that he had 'denied the authenticity of my earlier heterosexual feelings in the light of my later homosexual identity'. The same cultural markers that led Garber to write her book and me to write mine are allowing people younger than the fifty-something White to avoid some levels of those original denials and revisions-on-the-run. It's by no means a universal, or even remarkably common, thing for teens and young adults to completely ignore sexual identity and follow less walled-off paths of attraction and relationships. Not yet. But the common teen habit of sexual experimentation, on this far side of gay rights and cultural sexual discourse, has come to mean different things. Experiences that were once singular, or at least confined within age boundaries, are becoming less so.

According to Todd Klinck – who is young enough, socially and financially independent enough, and sexually introspective and active enough to be fully affected by these changes in sexual development – one of the possible new grounds for attraction may in fact be a common sexuality uninhibited by gender.

'I hear guys say that they enjoyed their relationships with girls but there was something "missing", but I don't know if the something "missing" was the fact that the girl didn't have a cock. I think maybe the something "missing" for me was the fact that these girls weren't in on my jerk-off fantasies about boys.'

What Todd is suggesting is that it's an open, actively, enthusiastically pro-sex sexuality that attracts him, people who see sex and sexuality as he does, rather than possessors of certain gender-defined characteristics. Which is not that different from more common notions of sexual compatibility – people who like penetrative sex, for example, tend to find something missing in sexual relations with those who don't. Except that Todd's devalued it (or de-reified it, in kulturspeak), shuffling it down from its traditional top spot to somewhere around second or third. Though Todd usually finds himself going for men, he has had girlfriends and has felt definite sexual pulls to women, and later decided it was the overt and queer sexual sensibility that did it for him. If he could picture her strapping on a dildo, or getting into some of those jerk-off fantasies, along with all the more usual sexual stuff, he would be able to get into her fantasies and she would become a potential sexual partner.

'It wasn't that I wasn't interested in women, didn't find women beautiful, didn't get aroused by the kiss or embrace of a woman,' the gay writer Frank Browning writes of gay in *Queer Geography*. 'My neuro-physiological responses functioned just fine with the opposite sex, though perhaps a little less quickly. The great fear was that should the woman at hand catch my errant glance at a man, should she divine my lust for a male breast, I would be undone. I would be revealed as a fraud. I would be other than a man. Somehow the exclusionary categories of gay and straight that I had constructed in my mind prevented me – and I believe a vast number of my generation – from enjoying multiple desires in multiple ways.'

This realisation came to Browning and Todd – much the same way as it did to Van Gelder and Brandt's Jorie – not out of the blue but as a result of thinking through the implications of a couple of anomalous twists and tugs and images that popped into their heads – the sort many of us would ignore, or perhaps not even recognise, passing them by like those piles of rocks that become cairns only when we know what we're looking for.

It may be too late for Edmund White or Frank Browning, both men in their fifties, to really bother doing anything about what they now see as their misunderstanding of sex and attraction. For me, twenty years younger, though I still find it easier to fall into relationships of various kinds with men, there have been women since the men, in between them, and I fully expect there to be more. But for people ten years younger than me, I suspect as they travel around, there are even fewer initial barriers. And for those twenty years younger than me, just now on the verge of puberty, just now, as you read this, in grade five or six sitting down next to some classmate and feeling that first little tummy jumping and heart fluttering, there shall, I suspect, be fewer still.

Browning sums up his observations in the form of an interview with a Neapolitan named Marcello D.:

'Homosexuality and heterosexuality don't exist. There doesn't exist an identity common to everyone. This homosexual model of life isn't a liberation. It is a limit to the personal experience of each of us. I'm not homosexual twenty-four hours out of twenty-four... The risk today is living the ideology of life rather than the experience of life.'

To mistake the model for the experience... is sure not the particular burden of the gay movement, Italian or American. It is, Marcello D. would say, the particular burden we all face in contemporary consumer society, where we accumulate concepts and slogans about experience instead of living inside of experience, where we spend thousands of dollars and hours sculpting ourselves into models of erotic attraction in place of touching each other in direct erotic engagement, where under the slogan of 'coming out' we confuse primal tensions of intergenerational autonomy with phantasms of sexual identity.

Living the ideology of life rather than the experience of life, accumulating concepts and slogans about experience instead of living inside of experience. It's precisely this living inside of experience that younger people, especially younger women, seem more able to do now that we've been talking about and assimilating the whole gay thing for so long. In February 1999, Stephanie Nolen wrote a piece in the *Globe and Mail* about going to Kingston in search of a sexual frangibility she felt herself and was experiencing anecdotally everywhere. She describes going to Kingston's only gay bar and seeing 'grinning young women in midriff-baring tops and platform shoes . . . in this once-foreign land because they just might want to sleep with some girls. They have come visiting, because the land's not so far away any more, and the order can be crossed without any trouble at all.' She quotes a Queen's University student as saying, 'It's like eating Indian food without joining an anti-racism group.'

What Nolen sees, what I see, and what all sorts of elements of culture have been showing us for a few years now is a space opening up to get through the politics and into the pleasure. As Nolen writes, 'This is about young women experimenting with sex the way their parents' generation did with drugs. It's about young women sleeping with other women without feeling any need to take on questions of sexual identity, and without worrying about the L-word – not because they reject it but because they're not interested in any label at all. This is not about feminist response to patriarchal society; it's about girls on a Saturday night.'

Which brings us back to ex-gays and my theory that attractions are learnable. Where ex-gays and their advocates go wrong is that they also believe attractions are erasable. You can expand your sexual horizon, but I'm not so sure you can contract it. Decades of therapy, shock and otherwise, have come as close as anything can to proving that reversals are not on. However, centuries of instances of personal sexual expansion – from the marriage of men and women who were predisposed towards same-sex attractions, to the situational sexualities of the military, of prisons, convents and boarding schools – imply that additions to one's sexual repertoire are possible, and always have been.

Problematic? Sure, gay men and women have been forced into marriage for ages, for millennia, and sure, they had kids, which I guess means they had sex, but it was all under duress, extreme social and sometimes even more extreme judicial and clerical imperative. Fuck or be outcast, fuck or die. Hardly an expansion, you could say, of one's sexual horizons; more like Muslims and Jews being forced to convert by the Inquisitions.

True enough, if you're also willing to believe that Oscar Wilde was, except for certain technicalities, purely gay. It's a form of circular reasoning; it doesn't allow for the possibility that categories of sexual orientation are not innate or natural or prone to evolution. It's a closed system, a way of thinking that allows you to ignore evidence, overlook the obvious, and see a man having regular sex with a woman, fathering children, and call him gay. He may not be straight, this man who also has sex with men, or at least thinks sexual thoughts about them from time to time – but he's certainly not gay. Which is exactly how I'd describe ex-gays. No longer gay, perhaps, as they date and marry and concentrate their sexual energies on the pudenda of the opposite sex – but definitely not straight. You can paint an orange red and shoot it full of apple juice, but that doesn't make it an apple. Like the tree of the knowledge of good and evil or Pandora's box, there is no going back, only forwards. Primary attractions may, and mostly do, change, either as the cause or the effect of changes in sexual or social behaviour, yet the rest remains, perhaps in secondary or tertiary positions, but always there to be called upon. We are, in more than just an epidemiological sense, a collection of everyone we've ever slept with, or even thought of sleeping with.

## Queerness

*Queer* is a word useful to bigots and activists and no one in between. It's extreme – like *nigger* or *cunt*. But like *nigger* and *cunt*, it points to an enormously important and only partially discovered country. Reclaiming of terms of derision is all well and good, and provides temporary empowerment and comfort for those traditionally derided. But sandwiching the reclamation and the derision for blacks is the fact of basic differences that will never be eliminated because the colour of one's skin is so raucously visible, and people never ignore difference. With *cunt*, it's about the sexuality of women, about pleasure, about overcoming baby-making and becoming as potentially sexually voracious as men have always feared women might be. It shocks and serves its purpose – but only briefly.

*Queer*'s even bigger. *Queer* is, in its logical extension, all consuming. Despite the use of the term by organisations like Queer Nation that emphasised radical difference and marginality, the basic precepts of *queer* are that sex is just another word for fun, that sex can be had by all without reference to gender or religion or morality of any sort, that sex is, qua sex, morally neutral. It means that sex with dildos is no more perverse than eating with chopsticks.

But *queer* is more or less synonymous with marginality and, the way many use it, with identity. It stakes its existence on exclusivity. So let's dispense with the sloppy signifier and go directly to the signified. As Garber hints, sex can be taught when the reward is fun, though this flies in the face of how most people tend to see sex. *Queer by Choice* is the title of a little, popularised academic book by sociology professor Vera Whisman, in which she interviews, analyses and hypothesises on the subject of choice as it relates to sexuality. One of her many interviewees tells her: 'I don't see how a person can pick and choose. I mean, it's like a person likes spinach or doesn't like it. I don't think a person chooses not to like it. You just eat it or not eat it.'

Now, I, for one, hated cooked spinach when I was little. The smell was too strong and it was too limp and soggy. I also hated mushrooms, tomatoes, garlic, and any number of strong-tasting things, like black liquorice and hot peppers. I quite liked bologna and processed cheese slices, and loved celery with Cheez Whiz. As I got older, and started getting tired of picking things off pizzas and pushing bits of meals to the side of my plate, I began nibbling the things I didn't like. I was remembering what my mother told me about olives – what it seems every mother tells her children about olives: you keep eating them, and soon you begin to enjoy them.

An acquired taste. The implication is that certain pleasures are learned, worked for. They are nonetheless pleasurable for being the product of effort. In fact, a few of these things, olives included, have overtaken my older gustatory pleasures and become more exquisite for being the instruments that educated my palate. But when my mother first told me about this special relationship olives had to the palate, I figured her tack on it was typical parental nonsense, like the whole bed-making thing (why on earth? you're just going to mess it up again in a few hours). Why pop these vile things in your mouth when eating's all about things that taste good?

A little later, in an introductory course on philosophy, I came across Aristotle's thoughts on happiness in the *Nichomachean Ethics*. He goes about discerning and defining happiness at some length, distinguishing among its different types – sensual, commercial, political, and contemplative in ascending order of precedence. It's only through using those faculties that distinguish us from animals, he wrote, that truly valuable forms of happiness may be achieved. The happiness of a philosopher is therefore, by definition, of a higher quality than the happiness of a pig. There are pleasures you're handed, and there are pleasures you achieve, and like the money or reputation or love you've earned yourself, the latter are always more lasting, more exquisite.

Though it works well enough for practising Jews and Muslims, the food–sex analogy is not perfect. Few social conventions prohibit most of us from eating any sort of food we might want to try. And food is not, for most of us, an emotionally pregnant commodity. But neither are the payoffs for culinary expansionism as profound. As another of Whisman's interviewees told her, 'A lot of people are so lonely, they're unhappy; they say "I need someone to love me", but they never think about their own sex. They look for the perfect man or the perfect woman, when that "person" could be sitting right next to them. But because of whatever stereotypes or biases they have, they don't look. They think that that perfect person is going to be in the opposite sex. That's not the case sometimes.' How many times have you experienced best friends complaining about their matelessness? Every once in a while, you hear of two friends getting together after years of not even considering each other, or of one not considering the other, like Cybill Shepherd and Ryan O'Neal in *Chances Are*. But those are generally opposite-sex relationships.

*Chasing Amy*, a 1997 film by Kevin Smith, is an exception to this. Two geeky, though of course kind of attractive, comic book artists, pals since childhood, meet a cool, beautiful comic book artist named Alyssa with whom Holden, played by Ben Affleck, falls instantly in love. The fact that she's a lesbian makes only a little difference to him as he leads himself through some typical straight-guy rationalisations about her just not having found the right guy yet. In what could have been a stereotypically homophobic turn of filmic events, Holden's constant hounding actually works, and the two end up in bed together. And in love. But listen to what Alyssa tells Holden in bed when he asks why she turned for him:

> I came to this on my own terms. You know, I didn't just heed what I was taught – men and women should be together, it's the natural way, that kind of thing. I'm not with you because of what family, society, life tried to instil in me from day one. The way the world is, how seldom it is that you meet that one person who just gets you. It's so rare. My parents didn't really have it. There were no examples set for me in the world of male-female relationships. And to cut oneself off from finding that person, to immediately halve your options by eliminating the possibility of finding that person within your own gender, that just seemed stupid to me. So I didn't. But then you came along. You, the one least likely. I mean, you were a guy. And while I was falling for you, I put a ceiling on that, because you were a guy, until I remembered why I opened the door to women in the first place – to not limit the likelihood of finding that one person who'd complement me so completely. So here we are. I was thorough when I looked for you, and I feel justified lying in your arms, 'cause I got here on my own terms, and I have no question that there was someplace I didn't look. And for me that makes all the difference.

In addition to that excellent and even pretty radical speech, what really transports the meat of this movie from the ordinary to the extraordinary is that not only does Alyssa change, Holden does too, and in pretty much the same way. Over the course of the developing romance, Holden's lifelong buddy, Banky, gets more and more sour, digging up dirt on Alyssa and generally just trying to bust things up and get back to where they were before she came along. After considerable meditation on the issue, Holden calls them all together and suggests the only way to keep these two very important relationships going is for them all to have sex together. He kisses Banky long and full on the lips and tells him that their friendship obviously has more to do with love and sex than either of them's been willing to admit, and that this expansion of their relationship into bed is a natural progression. Banky agrees, hesitantly, taken off guard, and though Alyssa doesn't go for it for other reasons and things fall apart, the sexual distance all three characters cover over the course of the film, in thought and deed, is significant, novel, and very much to the point of our discussion.

This kind of thinking bespeaks a practicality that most consider anathema to sex. Sex is supposed to serve no practical purpose (other, of course, than reproduction). To seek out sex for practical purposes is like creating art for a purpose. Dance critic Arlene Croce made a big stink a few years back when she refused to review Bill T. Jones's *Still/Here* in *The New Yorker* because it dealt with HIV in too direct a fashion. She called the piece 'undiscussable'. Mavis Gallant has the same view of art. 'The purpose of art,' she told me once, 'is to enhance your life, to make your life richer, to give life itself a meaning. I think that art is an aim in itself, I think that writing is an aim in itself without it being useful like painting a house.' Substitute *sex* for *art* and *writing* and I think you've pretty much got the general view of it. There's an aura about art (and sex) that serves as an armour, despite so much evidence that great art has been created for purposes any number of times. My grade-eleven English teacher, Grenfel Featherstone, told the class once that Byron's 'She walks in beauty, like the night' was written to get a woman he'd met at a party into bed. And it seems Shakespeare's sonnets may have also had very practical purposes, as so much painting and music has through so many ages.[97] But in a world in which complexity (or at least the degree of white noise) frightens us into slotting everything into safe and immediately recognisable categories, art that's meant to win someone's favour, or get you money, or a job, is considered not-art. As with sex. Sex erupts, sex happens, sex is a visitation; when we are aroused, we are aroused, and when we're not, we're not. *Will, reason, effort, purpose* – these are words not to be spoken in the same breath as sex. Why is that?

I can offer one possibility. Most people still consider sex ideally sacred, even if they do not always treat it that way. And when it is not sacred, it's profane. There's that black-and-white dichotomy again, those binary 0 and 1 slots we try to fit everything into. Good sex is sacred, bad sex is profane (and even when bad sex is good sex, like something delicious with a mistress or a stranger, it's still second-class sex, maybe more fun, but still not right, and certainly nothing to make a habit of and remain socially acceptable). Penis-in-vagina intercourse is the pinnacle of the sexual hierarchy, below which everything is considered foreplay or fooling around. And just like with the Sex Act itself, sacred sex, sex between a man and a woman who love each other very much, sits at the top of the heap, and everything else is slightly less valuable.

But sex is innately so much more, and so much more diverse. Just as sex can be great without orgasm, without an erection, without penetration, so sex that seems contrived, or perverse, or performed for reasons other than love or even lust, can be of enormous value. Sex for adventure, sex for fun, sex to create a lover of a friend, even sex to get a promotion at work – why on earth not? It's only because sex is seen as sacred, with the body as temple, that people tramping in for reasons other than to kneel at the altar are seen as intruders and heretics. As Garber's pointed out, 'We have resistance and reticence, sometimes even recoil and repugnance, at the idea that sexual versatility could include the widest range of consensual partners and pleasures. Sex isn't supposed to be an invention, or a sport, or a labour-saving device.'

## Monkeys on Each Other's Backs

Ever heard of bonobos? They used to be called pygmy chimpanzees.
They've been around for a while. Eight million years ago humans,
gorillas, and chimps shared a common ancestor. In the next million
years, gorillas split from the common human-chimp ancestor; two
million years after that, humans and chimpanzees split into distinct
species. Much later, about one and a half million years ago, bonobos
and common chimpanzees separated into two species. This makes
chimps of both varieties closer relatives to humans than the more
human-looking gorillas. But they've not been discussed much, these
bonobos, in *National Geographic* specials or other forms of popular
infotainment for three reasons. First, their existence was postulated
only in the 1920s, when some bonobo skeletons were discovered
along the Zaire River, and it was not until primatologist Takayoshi
Kano actually saw some live ones in the seventies that true study
could begin. Second, probably because of their late appearance on
the primatological scene, they never got their own media-attracting
Leakey-monkey-lady the way gorillas, regular chimps, and orang-
utans did. Third, it soon became quite evident that their behaviour
would be a little difficult to discuss. They rather like sex, it seems,
and have no compunctions about doing it with anyone at any time.
I just saw a recent documentary on them, and they're downright
lascivious. And a little arousing too, truth be told.

Unlike most other animals, and quite a bit like people, bonobos
have sex without regard to periods of fertility. As Meredith Small
describes it in an article on nerve.com, males regularly grab each
other's penises in their hands and mouths, and females engage in
what the behaviourists have called a genital-genital, or G-G, rub.
'Two females place their pelvises together,' Small says, 'either face-
to-face or rear-to-rear, and rub each other rapidly with yelps of
delight.' There is generally an enormous amount of sex had, mostly
for fun, with some other uses thrown in – like smoothing over spats
or jockeying for position in the clan hierarchy. And anatomy is never
a barrier.[98]

We use animal sex to understand our own sexuality in various
ways. We watch rabbits and describe our more enthusiastically sexual

friends as fucking like bunnies. We can fuck doggie-style or, if we read up a little, in the butterfly position. Stallions or bulls are used as male sexual ideals, queen bees or black widows (if we're feeling nasty) as female types. We learn from animals some of the fundamentals of attraction, can observe them without all the baggage that observing ourselves comes with, and figure out what we presume to be biological and evolutionary imperatives behind sex. But until very recently, we've been doubtful about animals experiencing any pleasure in sex. They're driven to it by instinct, the need to survive as a species, greedy genes, whatever. It's only people, divorced long ago from many of our more natural instincts, who require pleasure as an instinct stand-in. In fact, in many animals, it seems sex is pretty far indeed from a pleasurable experience. Females often have to be cajoled, and then there's those cat-penis spikes that sound downright cruel. So, for those increasing numbers of us who like to describe us as human animals and emphasise the similarities to the rest of the mammalian kingdom rather than the differences we've been trying to cultivate for the last couple of eons, these animal lessons tend to corroborate the standard sex-pleasure discontinuity, the serious utilitarianism that religion and other forms of government have imposed on sex for so long.

So bonobos' sex-play and their very obvious erotic pleasures provide a pleasant change. And, in their extreme genetic and evolutionary proximity to we humans, they're an indication that maybe the closer animals get to us, the more complex, nuanced, and idiosyncratic sex becomes; that maybe, in sex matters at least, people do – or at least could – work better than other mammals.

Much of bonobian sexual behaviour points us, if we care to follow, in the direction of our own suppressed sexuality, elements of our sexual selves that we have moved away from as a result of the various not-so-very-nice anti-sexual elements that have evolved in most human societies. Take the fact that older female bonobos are often seen to be caressing the genitals of infants. In a very little but very good book, *Toward the New Degeneracy*, Bruce Benderson describes the still common but wholly undiscussed practice among various sections of what he describes as the culture of poverty –

mostly Latino in his experience – of mothers stroking their infant and young sons' penises into erections to build their male sexual pride. Older male bonobos have a tendency to stroke younger male penises as well, reminiscent of a sort of sexual comradeship and mentoring that has more or less ceased to exist among humans. As Small describes it, bonobos 'use sex not just for reproduction, as we expect nonhuman animals to do, but for a variety of nonsexual purposes. They bestow "sexual favours" (as we humans say) for appeasement, to gain food, to show affection and connection or to reduce stress. In captivity, when food is delivered by the keepers, the excitement usually triggers a round of sexual behaviour that calms the group down. Sex functions as a social balm.'

We could also see bonobo sexual behaviour as addressing larger sexual issues. As Small says:

> Bonobos call into question assumptions about the evolution of human sexual behavior. Researchers have previously thought early bipeds lived in male dominated groups where aggression and violence were the rule, and where female sexuality was useful primarily as a tool to manipulate males. In the traditional scenario, the genital swellings that signalled fertility in pre-human females were lost over evolutionary time because it enabled them to look less sexual and make peace among the males. At the same time, this theory presumed, ancestral females became continuously sexually receptive, willing to mate during non-fertile periods, in an effort to keep one male close to home.
>
> But bonobos suggest another possibility. Bonobo males and females live peaceful, egalitarian lives, and they use sex as an integral part of their calmer social order. Perhaps our common ancestor was more like bonobos in this regard than common chimps. Perhaps ancestral human females 'lost' their swellings and became continuously willing to have sex not to manipulate males into monogamy, but to facilitate a more promiscuous lifestyle. Bonobos suggest that our idealisation of private, monogamous sexual behavior might be a relatively recent

deviation from our evolutionary heritage. Indeed, our ancient ancestors, like bonobos, may have used heterosexual and homosexual sex on a daily basis to make alliances, trade goods and favours, establish friendships and keep the peace.[99]

If we truly are the proprietors of our bodies, with rights freehold absolute as various political and medical debates of the moment seem to be indicating, then why not, as long as we are in charge of what we're doing with our bodies, do a whole lot more with sex than was ever dreamed of (or at least allowed) in religious philosophy?

Queerness, then, could be seen as the programmatic desanctification (as opposed to desecration) of sex. But let's stop calling it queerness, shall we? As long as we call it queerness, it sounds like something other, stranger people do. Let's try calling it sexuality, something we all do.

## The Stories We Tell Ourselves

Sit in any café or marketplace in any part of the world and if you eavesdrop, you'll notice that the vast majority of conversation consists of telling stories of events just passed, of turning experience into narrative, of fitting experiences into various recognisable and accepted forms. Only a minute portion of conversation consists of idea-making, of busting forms rather than catering to them. For some of us, there's the stupid-boss story, the idiot-co-worker character, the insufferable or, with luck, charmingly thoughtful spouse, and, on a broader if not deeper level, the incompetent head of government, the sex and financial lives of celebrities, and the ever popular comparative tales of meteorological wonder. Each has a fairly restricted number of narrative forms, ways not only of making the story interesting or recognisable and therefore enjoyable to those across from you, but ways for you to understand what's happened to you in the course of your day, your week, your month, or even your year. Why did the boss tell you to check all those numbers a third time? Because she's Stupid Boss. How is it that you're simply unable to bear the heat today? Well, because it's The Hottest July We've Had In Years, isn't it? In this way casual conversations – that is, conversations not meant to achieve any specific end other than a state of general amicability and a cursory organisation of the events of your life – are formed, and formed into broadly influential templates for lives and perspectives. It's mostly a shorthand – the boss may have asked you to check those numbers again because of some recent troubling activity in German bond trading, or because she's worried that her husband not being able to get it up for the past three weeks has something to do with her elongating cleavage and she has to work out her stress through her employees. But leaving yourself open to consideration of so many possible reasons for your boss's mistreatment of you simply takes more time than it's worth. It may be better on some ethereal level of general human charity or something, but it won't help you get your own house in order.

It's a relatively small jump from this sort of quotidian story-making to the writing of fiction. There are relationships between truth and fiction that it has been the job of legions of academics to define or deconstruct, and we'll stay away from that. But what the average person who is not especially interested in allusiveness, intertextuality, subversion, form, or linguistic experimentation wants out of a story is as important as it is obvious. Check out the *USA Today* or *Bookseller* bestseller lists, which are, at the time of writing, the only two English-language lists based reliably on actual sales figures, and you'll see the same names popping up again and again, names of writers who have latched on to archetypes and basic storylines that people recognise and like. The characters are easily definable as types or simple combinations of types (the ambitious young lawyer, the conscientious young doctor), and in none of the perennial bestsellers will you ever find anything that challenges the average cultural notions of the way things are or the way it is popularly perceived that they should be. That is the realm of literary or alternative fiction. Authors of these sorts of books may show up on a bestseller list from time to time, but never for long, and rarely more than once. The doctor-lawyer brand of popular fiction is by some people's definitions bad fiction. But by virtue of its very popularity, it has not only cultural significance but cultural worth. It tells us something about ourselves and, depending on where you stand on such matters, it either reflects or creates a common vocabulary and way of thinking about ourselves and our place in the world. And one thing that both popular fiction and enduring mythology tell us absolutely for certain is that people like, have always liked, and will almost undoubtedly continue to like, stock characters and stock footage. You can read as much nuance as you like in ancient favourites like Odysseus or Lancelot, but they are, in their originals, pure stock – the wily jokester hero, or the noble hero-lover. They don't bust out of type, and you can bet that though they form the basis of our notions of these particular types, they were not, when they were created, anything more than manipulations of archetypes that existed for centuries or millennia before either Homer or Malory.[100]

If you take a brisk look through the evolution of literary fiction, you see characters growing less and less archetypical and more and more human, until we reach the twentieth century and come across characters like D.H. Lawrence's Rupert Birkin, to take one example of hundreds, a character possessed of at least as much conflict and contradiction as assonance. And since about the time of Lawrence, fiction and its characters have been judged by how complex and contradictory – in short, by how real – they are.

James Baldwin wrote in 1949:

It is quite impossible to write a worth-while novel about a Jew or a Gentile or a Homosexual, for people refuse, unhappily, to function in so neat and one-dimensional a fashion. If the novelist considers that they are no more complex than their labels, he must, of necessity, produce a catalogue, in which we will find, neatly listed, all those attributes with which the label is associated... A novel insistently demands the presence and passion of human beings, who cannot ever be labelled. Once the novelist has created a human being, he has shattered the label, and in transcending the subject matter, is able, for the first time, to tell us something about it... Without this passion, we may all smother to death, locked in those airless, labelled cells, which isolate us from each other and separate us from ourselves.

Human beings. It's what the reading few (as opposed to the reading many) have come to expect from their authors in the place of the stand-in (the stand-in for evil corporate bigness, the stand-in for corrupt politics, the stand-in for the horrors of misogyny). But it is not the few that influence the many in grand matters of social movements and structures. And since it is the many who prefer characters simple and labellable, the many who, as we've seen, are in the habit of building narratives out of our lives and then slipping our lives into their structures, it is by those rules that we are all made into characters, by those rules that we are made recognisable, slottable characters in what must be, because we have ever so much else to be worrying about, a very simple play produced on a pretty sparsely propertied world stage.

And so I think it is because we like villains and heroes, lovers and beloveds, tricksters, father-figures, mother-figures, and sages, and not because of any strictures of the 'ruling classes,' that we have heterosexuals and homosexuals and, sometimes, bisexuals.[101] And we've always slotted 'the other – whether it's the Stupid Boss or the Dumb Blonde or the African-American or Aborigine or White Man – wee pigeon holes so it's easier to enslave them or kill them, dispossess or dismiss them. It's a basic human tendency that when applied to gender is often known as sexism, to race as racism, but which, in fairness, is far more universal and far less inherently nefarious. It's the simple separation of other from self, and a resignation both to the extrapolation of broad difference based on particular perceivable difference and to a feeling of awkwardness around that which is unlike oneself.

It's something that's not likely to change much. But the problem when we come to the issue of sexual difference is that these labels are not only given, they're taken, too. It is not generally the case that a group like, say, African-Americans, accepts the simplistic labels given to them by, in this case, Caucasian-Americans. Various radio and Hollywood infelicities aside, African-Americans have generally defined themselves in opposition to, and mostly in very marked transcendence of, the labels they were provided with. Contrast this to what has happened with gay. Over the course of a couple of centuries, as we have seen, the idea was bruited and slowly developed with varying degrees of sympathy and antipathy that, first, there was such a thing as a homosexual and, second, that there were certain external and internal characteristics inherent to this sort of person. It was only in the very late stages of development, really only since the fifties, that those who were so labelled had much overt input into the subject. It was at about that moment, too, that the heterosexual, much slower in forming, came into being (originally as a negatively defined state, 'that which is not homosexual') to complement the homosexual.[102] And so we had, from about this time, a labelling situation like no other: a simple dichotomy that was meant to account for the entire world's population, a dichotomy broader even than the American versus Communist one formulated in the same era, which at least allowed for anomalies like Canada and Sweden.

Once sexual categories were firmly ensconced, once everyone began to think of themselves as part of one team or the other, a new type of character was created. And given people's desire for simplicity in such matters, what was once complex because it was unstructured now began to become quite seriously simple. In what Baldwin described in that same essay as the American male struggle to remain innocent and deny sexual complexity (a Lancelotian struggle that appears to be considerably less central to female senses of self), we managed to level all the curves and dips and hills that lend surface area to our sexual topographies into a smooth, round, wholly visible, wholly explicable and justifiable Teletubbian sexual self.

Just as the way we tell ourselves stories and the way we tell them to others influences the way we see ourselves, so too does the way we have stories told to us.

Almost every autobiographical story, almost every *Bildungsroman* that focuses on the life of a gay boy, and many that concern

221

themselves with gay girls, pay a lot of attention to the breaking of gender stereotypes. Little Chris liked to set the table in kindergarten, didn't much like wrestling with the other boys. Eleanor was always up a tree, knees always scuffed, dresses always torn, doing all the wrestling Chris never did, with a distinct predilection towards Daddy's flannel workshirts. Mum's worried. Dad's worried or violent. Oh, and look – Chris and Eleanor grow up to be gay.

There are an enormous number of problems with this line of narrative, and though not much evidentiary weight can be placed on these anecdotal stories, they are so universal that they acquire practical strength. With the possible exception of AIDS and a few especially effective political movements, books like *The Well of Loneliness*, *City of Night*, *The Front Runner*, *Dancer from the Dance*, *Rubyfruit Jungle*, *A Boy's Own Story* and *Tales of the City* have been the most instrumental factors in the creation of our sense of gay.

These stories become the stories by which gay men and women know each other, through which they communicate, and into which they fold their own perceptions of themselves and their pasts. Never mind that the typical growing-up-gay-male story is almost point by point the same as a certain sort of growing-up-Jewish-male story (take a quick glance through some of Woody Allen's autobiographical boy characters). Fine for comedy – bad for identity. Since Jewish identity rests on vastly more than gender dysphoric childhood experiences and non-Brady sexual activity, growing up a klutz and preferring books to schoolyard fights add up to some entertaining anecdote fodder, little more.

But these stories bear considerably more weight with the rush on gay identity construction – which resembles nothing so much as the construction rush on those prefab neighbourhoods thrown up all across North America immediately after World War Two to accommodate far more people and far more prosperity than had ever been expected. In fact, other than actual sexual behaviour and tales of oppression (which find their first expression in childhood schoolyard-bully and gang-up stories), there is little other primary material than these stories we tell ourselves upon which gay identity is built (community groups and pride marches all being secondary accretions). And the problem is it's the same sort of backwards thinking, the same anachronistic looking at the past that hobbles so much of gay studies.

Let's take a look at a couple of the other common points in these proto-gay life stories used to indicate early detectability. Sport is a big one, maybe the biggest for boys, after gender behaviour (of which it is a subset). Our proto-gay boy, Little Chris, never went out for football or rugby or baseball. And though this does mean that Little Chris belongs to the large number of future gay men who did not play sports growing up, it obscures a lot of pertinent details. Like the fact that, for example, there are any number of reasons boys, whatever their later sexual habits, might not want to engage in sports. Perfectionism and weak self-image for starters (which I think we can all agree are not exclusively gay traits). And then there are the general iconoclasts rebelling against the conformity that's most obviously exemplified by school sports, who are as likely to be ruffians as aesthetes. And don't forget the merely uncoordinated, who in most school systems are covertly or openly discouraged by faculty and peers from joining in any reindeer games. This formulaic life story also shifts attention away from the enormous number of future fags who were, in fact, football players, track stars, basketball heroes, and wrestling champs (pointed out most recently in a truly awful collection called *Jocks* by Dan Woog). Never mind burden of proof, this line of implication falters even anecdotally.

Third in the roster, for the more candid of our raconteurs, are the early same-sex sexual experiences. Playing secret agent, rescue, tum-tums, or just plain cornholing are set pieces in most gay men's (and fewer lesbians') childhood stories. And leaving those charming Boy Scout sex games aside for the moment, these experiences usually involve two people, generally between the ages of ten and fourteen. One, the storyteller, is blown away by the experience, figuring he's finally able to put a finger on what's made him feel so different for so many months or years. The other party is usually drawn as being less emotionally implicated in the scene, just getting his rocks off, or simply being a normal red-blooded boy who's using our sweet young narrator as a trial run for girls. In most cases, his indifference is expressed by his walking away from the sexual part of the relationship – far too cavalierly, in the eyes of our narrator – or by constantly talking about girls, a disinclination to kiss, or saying this will have to stop when they get to junior high.

Our hero generally juices up this first poignant tale by rolling unrequited love into a more overarching rebirth, making the whole into one quite handy and powerful trope. Just as stories of mysterious parentage (Oedipus, Jesus, Pip) or fatal flaws (Achilles, Apostle Peter, Hamlet) help draw us in both narratively and sympathetically to the great bulk of the world's literature by crystallising fundamental fears and personal misgivings into unlikely narrative gems, compelling in their simplicity but hardly representative of actual human experience, so the story of young gay sex makes for an excellent, and often titillating, narrative device to propel the story or ground the character.

But since these stories are used daily to help identity-starved people understand themselves and each other in practical ways, being used, in fact, to construct political movements and legislative changes, the problem of solipsism must be addressed.

Let's go back to our primal scene for a moment. Let's say our Little Chris, age twelve, and his best buddy for six months, Young Brent, have just finished up in Little Chris's basement. Little Chris came (his third time ever), and Young Brent didn't, but since neither's been introduced to the politics of pleasing, they're both pretty satisfied with the whole thing. Little Chris, lying perpendicular to Young Brent on the sectional and wiping himself off on the underside of the sleeping bag (making a mental note to clean it before he gives it back to Dad), is avoiding looking at Young Brent. And being an introspective sort, Little Chris starts thinking about what's just happened. He realises that penises are private parts and that he just made his a little more public. He also realises that he's just discovered a sensual pleasure that totally beats eating the whole chocolate section out of a box of Neapolitan ice cream. And, just like when he's finished that last spoonful, he realises his pleasure has probably got the best of him, that he's likely just done something pretty wrong. If Little

Chris was born in, say, 1985, he's probably made the connection between what he's just done and being gay, too. But for the sake of this story, since things have been getting a little more complicated in the past decade or two, let's say Chris was born in 1965.

He's noticed he's feeling an awful lot closer to Young Brent now than he did before they had sex, something like he'd feel for a brother, he imagines, if he had a brother. He's also noticed, as he snatches a quick glance in his direction, that Young Brent has turned his head away and has gone to sleep. So as he stares up at the ceiling Chris sets about convincing himself that he's alone in the world and totally different, obviously, from Brent, not to mention everyone else. He's maybe even a bad person. And having hit puberty, it doesn't take much to convince himself of any of this.

Following through on his introspection over the next few years, long after he and Brent have parted company over the Kevin Incident (how could Brent want to be that guy's friend – he's a total snob), this sense of difference only increases. Unfortunately, only rarely does a heightened introspective nature coincide with a similarly honed extrospective one. And what the combination of high introspection and low extrospection is most likely to produce in someone – Little Chris, for instance – is a highly developed sense of difference, sometimes extending into feelings of isolation. So although Chris would have been well aware of the depth and complexity of his feelings surrounding his sexual experiences with Brent, all he's got to go on for Brent's end of things is the latter's relatively calm and pleased exterior, and the fact that he lay there still, eyes closed, apparently immune to all the emotional turmoil Chris is thrashing through.

And so sex is added to the list of introspective Chris's points of difference, along with the fact that he's really short, has limp and completely unmanageable hair, and a distinctly uncool appreciation of Glenn Campbell.

And so the process of identity construction is begun. His height leads him to think of himself as maybe cute, but never good looking or handsome. The Glenn Campbell thing will give him a lifelong anxiety about never being quite with it. The introspective habits will make him think of himself as a bit of an intellectual, and the sex thing, the more he thinks about it, the more he figures it meant more to him than it did to Brent, the more it becomes a permanent point of sexual difference rather than the single (or multiple) event that it was, will come to make him think of himself as, first, sick, then perverted, then perhaps evil, and finally, somewhere along the line, gay.

We are all quite different from one another, though not always so obviously. As we're growing up, we have a tendency to hit on certain points of personal make-up over others. Some we're not allowed to ignore – if we're fat, for example, or really blond, or have a really big nose. And an automatic predilection for sexual arousal by a member of your same sex, which I am not denying exists, whatever the (probably eternally inscrutable) reasons for all manner of predilections might be, is most definitely one more point of difference. But unlike fatness or blondness or big-nosedness, sexual difference has in the decades leading up to this one rarely been spoken of, either among children or to them by their elders. And so it has grown, unmediated, unassimilated, undiscussed, into something that appears to those doing the thinking and the hiding to be something wholly, qualitatively different from fatness and the rest of those other qualities that are brought out into the open and dealt with. It's harboured and secreted, and made to colour everything else about oneself, instead of being a simple quality like the rest of one's constitution.

Did I say a quality? Like fatness? So gay is something innate, then, just like everyone figured, and all this talk about the end of gay is as nonsensical as talking about the end of fat or the end of blond?

No. Sex is more complex than cellulite and hair colour. Sex involves attractions, which are subject to context; motivations, which are subject to priorities; and sexual objects, who can be encouraging or discouraging and in the process be (not necessarily respectively) positively or negatively reinforcing. There are libraries to be written on the variables involved in sex. I've tried to cover a few of them between these covers. But what happens to sexual difference when it's hidden away like it has been since it was identified as something that ought to be is that it hardens, it crystallises into something that those subject to it figure is something even less changeable than fatness and blondness, something more akin to height or shoe size. And we've seen, in Grimm's pre-Disneyfied Cinderella, what happens to people who try to change their shoe size. Exactly the same sort of thing that happens to closeted or ex-gays: they become disfigured. In some way or other they are denying the truth about themselves. And for those who choose to alter their sexuality by asking god to relieve them of their burden, I'd have to agree.

But the most basic thing about sexual attraction, other than its very existence, is that it changes. On the most basic level, when we are young, we are mostly attracted to young people and when we get older, we are mostly attracted to older people.[103]

But perhaps that's too basic – maybe it seems transparent. Okay, how about something more extreme, something not quite so utterly common, that originates in the same place. Let's go back to that Catholic college of mine. Once I'd been there a year or two, I began to notice something that happened to the boys I was living with as they entered third or fourth year. The more outgoing, attractive, playful sorts, the ones who'd always had the broadest choice of sexual partners, started altering their choice in the girls they went out with. A great many of them, I noticed, were breaking up with their blond, hard-drinking, hard-dancing, hard-screwing girlfriends and beginning to ask out quieter, perhaps less traditionally attractive but more apparently emotionally stable, women. They'd go through perhaps one or two of these before graduation. Then I'd hear about the weddings. The phenomenon was by no means universal, but it was regular. There was even a distinction drawn between the two women's residence buildings, which seemed to have subtly different admission practices or applicant bases – it was Loretto to bed, St. Joe's to wed.[104]

Now, things were a good deal more structured in this little Catholic college than they would have been in other environments, even in other colleges on the same campus. Girls and boys lived in separate residences, and because most of them had come from sex-segregated high schools, social interaction was formalised to a much greater degree than usual. Fewer friendships developed between the sexes. It was dates and formals, much like it was a few generations before. And because the relationships were rarefied in this way, strategies could be more easily detected. But the only point I really want to make is that these boys' attractions were changing, probably quite consciously. They had started looking for wives, for mothers for their children. It all seems very *Wild Kingdom* – or Christian Coalition – when commenting on it from a distance, but it points to the fact that attractions are not only alterable but multifaceted. To be utterly reductive for point-making purposes, the party girls played to that reflexive sexual urge, born of those complexly constructed predilections; the calmer, less physically and socially extravagant types, to the notions some of the boys had developed of proper wife material. And these boys made rational if not always correct decisions that affected their sexual attractions, behaviours, and futures. And I don't think it's sufficient to say that these guys were leaving behind the purely sexual for the more practical. What they were doing was incorporating further levels, further faculties, into their none the less active and still driven sexualities.

There are all sorts of instances of attraction changes between these two extremes. From being a tit-man in your youth to an ass-man in your golden years, to having one remarkable individual change the way you think about, say, shy retiring types, to sitting behind someone you've known for months or years and, through the play of sunlight through her hair, or the way he tweaks his earlobe, getting turned on when you hadn't been turned on before. These are all examples, to greater or lesser degrees, of the separation of that reflex, rubbernecking attraction and attraction as a whole. The rubbernecking is only one small and simple part of a greater complex whole, and though we have almost all been subject to that greater complexity in one way or another, that reflex is the only type of sexual attraction we're usually willing to dignify with the name. People, we hold, either turn us on or they don't. Hard cocks and wet pussies don't lie. But neither do they tell the whole story of sexual attraction. Sexual attraction is as slippery and sloppy as the bodily fluids it produces. Fitting it into slots serves only to hem us in and dry us up.

## Categories

Some of this fitting into slots is, of course, simply rational thinking. Noticing that every man you've ever slept with has had long hair tells you something about yourself, even if it's only that you're in a rut (or have higher than average plumber's bills). This sort of categorising is usually better done than left undone; whatever the conclusion, it is more useful than harmful. It's only when our slotting incorrectly implies – as categorising has a distinct tendency to do – that there are more similarities than differences among our slotted items, or that the similarities are more significant or profound or fundamental than the differences, prompting us to draw generalising conclusions, or to impose similarly drawn rules, or expect similar responses or impute similar motivations, that categorising becomes a problem. It's a problem of intellectual shorthand, the sort of thing one must do to get through every day without getting bogged down at every decision, every perception, but which when applied to such complex items as, say, people, does us and our understanding of ourselves and the world around us more harm than good.

Let's call the first sort of categorisation, the sort we ought to be doing, the sort that helps us out and lets us see our world in a truer, more organised and comprehensible fashion, 'organising'. The other sort, the shorthand sort that is all well and good when restricted to things that are peripheral to our lives, or that are not adversely affected by being lumped together, but which can otherwise quietly screw us up, let's call that 'fudging'.

It's when fudging is translated into hard and fast rules, systems of thought and systems of being, that we've got a real problem. Then we have false constructions – things we can convince ourselves exist and can even, to a certain extent, call into existence but that are, nevertheless, confabulations. And even so, if such confabulations were beneficial, there would be little problem, little to contest other than in the form of purely intellectual quibbling.

For the last 130 years at least, the gay confabulation, a fudge for any number of things – from what is now termed 'gender dysphoria' to anecdotal or regular same-sex sexual activity and/or extraordinary same-sex emotional attachment or, for that matter, men who have been florists and women who have been truck drivers – has been useful and eminently beneficial. No matter how much same-sex sex there was before gay consciousness and gay rights, what had been impossible in all but a few cultures isolated in time and place through millennia – open and honest same-sex partnerships that combine sex and the emotions – is now possible. Sexual friendships, which had for ages been restricted to two mutually exclusive realms – marriage or scandal – are finally, in North America and Western Europe, Australia, and South Africa, and increasingly in Eastern Europe and parts of South America, becoming not only possible but practical. Gay consciousness has won us that, significantly and irreversibly in theory if not always in practice. And that is a right we should not stop pressing for, not allow to backslide, until it is not even worth a second thought, whether or not we figure we or our kids might be interested in some sort of same-sex living arrangement sometime in the future. That much simply makes sense.

But what is becoming evident, what has been evident to some for years in fact, is that gay is, after certain fundamental victories are won, inherently more confining than liberating. Once it is recognised that people are at root sexual beings – that it is this innate recognition of the connection among pleasure, emotional attachment, and sex that is one of the chief elements that sets people apart from bunnies and chrysanthemums, and that the millennia before Kertbeny and Hirschfeld, Harry Hay, Del Martin, Larry Kramer, and Ellen DeGeneres were not ignorant of an inherent truth about human nature, or prejudiced against a natural variation of sexuality, as much as they were simply stridently and pragmatically attached to certain useful social contracts that officially recognised same-sex sex and unions would have fundamentally upset – only then will gay come to be seen not as an end in itself but a step, a catalyst towards a crystallisation of a modern ability to live lives as fully and humanly sexual as we are naturally wont to do.

It was more out of concern for age-old systems of property devolvement, inheritance, and workforce production that previous ages were so concerned that men not get together in any socially acknowledged way with other men, or women with women, than out of any dastardly desire to put down a species.

And it took a while – almost a century of percolation between the time Kertbeny came up with the homo- and the heterosexual and the time society, with modern divorce patterns, population and consumption problems, and desertion of religion on all but the most idiosyncratic of levels – for the direct effects of the notion of sexual identity to be felt. Just when society was able to dispense with the chattel theory of family, just at the point at which individual freedom from responsibility for propagation of the tribe and the stability of society became possible, practicable, and comprehensible, at just that point, gay was enacted, and a very short while later, accepted.

So, over the past twenty or thirty years – and in some places, like New York, London, Toronto and Berlin for much of the past century – we have slowly learned by watching that same-sex couples and same-sex sex does not destroy society. We have seen, in fact, to the more or less quiet chagrin of at least two otherwise entirely divergent groups – those who are horrified at the idea of same-sex sex, and those who figure it offers to society some sort of transformative properties – that it has very little effect on society's stability or basic make-up at all, nor would it were there four times as many such unions as there are today, nor a hundred times neither.

But not so very long after we noticed this, once we had started groups and parades and lobbies to ensure everyone else realised it too, we also began to notice that in order to get much further in our pursuit of happiness, gay would have to be superseded. For very shortly after gay started being an acceptable label, it became an exclusive one, as, in reaction, did straight. No more movement allowed back and forth, no matter how surreptitious; no more sexual freedom, something we seem to have traded in return for sexual identity (not, as I see it, that much of a bargain).

Not that this lack of freedom was imposed on us by some executive committee of sexual identity and conduct. Opposition to the claims and practices of people like JoAnn Loulan and Jan Clausen mostly come from within. For in the beginning, between the time the notion of gay was concocted and when gay was let out of the closet and into the streets, the only way to exist for people who adopted this new identity was to congregate, at first in most solemn, deadly, and stagnant secret and later in greater and greater states of freedom, fun, and inebriation. The more these women and men who were beginning to define themselves by what they perceived as their more or less unitary sexual difference hung out together, the more their notion of identity, of undiluted ontology, became fixed. They began constructing personal gay histories for themselves, casting early childhood same-sex friendships as proto-gay ones and early different-sex friends as brotherly or sisterly comrades. Before long the notion was set in stone – as it had to be to fight the fights we needed to fight. But just as there are difficulties, writ large and exciting in scores of action films, inherent in integrating people back into peacetime civility after having trained them for and engaged them in war, so there are now problems with gay identity, an identity necessary for social, political, and personal soldiering, but one incompatible with the pursuit of full personal pleasure and fulfilment in the relative peace that's been won for us.

Just as it has been difficult, these last fifty years, to convince many American and British veterans of the Second World War that the Japanese are not inherently any shiftier or more belligerent than anyone else, so it will be difficult to convince the generations of warrior lesbians and gay men to take off their armour of identity and settle into the sexual freedom and unity they've won for us through brutish and sometimes brutal expression of sexual division.

As painful and controversial and certainly alienating as such a process is, it must happen. And, under the circumstances, it's now or never. For we are very close to instituting these soldierly ways into an entirely new social system that is slowly turning into a bifurcated version of what we had before, one old system for the straights, one burnished but no less old system for the gays. The most fundamental, the most valuable victory won by our warrior class has been the space – political, personal, economic – to do as we please, an inherent and necessary part of which is the ability to step back from the front lines and see ourselves as we actually are in peacetime, as sexual beings whose boundaries are inscribed not by gender or anatomy, and certainly not by anything as contrived as sexual identity, but by pleasure and emotional opportunity.

Which means there is still one more thing required of our martial elders before they fade away into the mists of reverend heroism. They must free succeeding generations from the chains they took up to pull us into the modern age. They must realise that whatever concrete notions of sexual identity they hold dear for themselves, they must, to paraphrase Anita Bryant, think of the children. They must, in their mentoring ways, let them know (though they may not be sure about the whole thing themselves) that there may not in fact be such an immutable thing as sexual identity, that these kids should spend a little time thinking, probing around inside their brains, their hearts, their trousers – discerning, as the Catholics might say – and then just following wherever their little souls and loins lead them, feeling free to enter into relationships, casual, life-long, or anything in between, based on personal and purely anecdotal attraction in all its forms, rather than be guided by scripts written for a different age.

# Notes

1     I will, however, be talking about a number of other people's polling, especially Kinsey's, but mostly to point out either their shortcomings or their misapprehension.

2     *Showbiz Today* got its highest rating of the week running 112 seconds of it, *Saturday Night Live* got its highest rating of the season for the 90-second excerpt it ran, *Nightline* ran it uncensored and got its highest ratings of the year, and *The Howard Stern Show*, which ran it with minor censoring, got its highest rating ever.

3     An idea I got from John Greyson's now banned musical film, *The Making of Monsters*. The film's banned, by the way, because two of the recurring characters, goldfish named Bertolt Brecht and Kurt Weill, are portrayed as lovers. Weill's estate was incensed at having their ancestor portrayed as gay and won a court case to ban the film until their claim on the Weill name runs out. The fish part apparently didn't bother them.

4     The Mattachine Society was an early, secretive homosexual rights organisation, founded in 1951 in Los Angeles, a rough equivalent in many ways to other early groups, like the Homophile Association of London, Ontario. Though its founder, Harry Hay, was a devoted Communist, the organisation soon became thoroughly conservative (and Hay left). See *Hay's Radically Gay: Gay Liberation in the Words of its Founder*, edited by Will Roscoe (Boston: Beacon Press, 1996) for the best account I've found of Mattachine and this era in US gay activist thought.

5     Perhaps an opportune moment to point out that I'm a firm subscriber to the Woody Allen School of Qualitative Sexuality – bad sex is a highly relative term in my books, akin to filthy lucre.

6      And Vidal has gone on saying it, most recently in his memoirs, *Palimpsest*, where he writes: 'Most young men, particularly attractive ones, have sexual relations with their own kind. I suppose this is still news to those who believe in two teams: straight, which is good and unalterable; queer, which is bad and unalterable unless it proves to be only a Preference, which must then, somehow, be reversed, if necessary by force.'

7      In an interview with Richard Goldstein, *Village Voice*, June 26, 1984.

8      *Partners*, directed by the man responsible for, among other things, *Cheers* and *Will & Grace*, was written by Francis Veber, who four years earlier had written the screenplay for *La cage aux folles*.

9      The film also makes a rather heavy point of what the experience is doing to Burns. Looking disturbed in bed with his girlfriend, Burns tells her, 'There's a lot about me you don't know.' When she asks like what, there's just silence and an anguished look. Later, she tells him, 'I don't understand what's happening to you,' to which he responds, pensively troubled once again, 'Neither do I.'

10     Though the argument can be made that Valentin changed less over the course of the story than either Burns or Benson did through theirs, feeling as he did neither lust nor love for Molina, though he did, in the spirit of comradeship and appreciation – and perhaps to ensure his complicity – finally have sex with him.

11     This sort of phenomenon was noticed as early as 1929, by a Dr Gilbert Hamilton in his book, *A Research in Marriage*. As John Loughery points out in *The Other Side of Silence* (Henry Holt, 1998), 'Men didn't become uncomfortable when asked if they were kleptomaniacs or bigamists. They simply said that they were not and gave the question no further thought. That was never the case with homosexuality, Hamilton observed, and there was apt to be a compelling reason for that level of uneasiness. Hamilton's speculation was just the sort that the psychiatric establishment had less use for as twenties openness gave way to thirties conservatism: "The majority of American males probably fear their own homosexual impulses," he wrote, "more than they fear all other tabooed components of the human reactive equipment taken together."'

12     How many times have we heard that the biggest homophobes are the biggest closet cases?

13     Listen to 'Nikki,' from 1999, for an example, and compare it to, say, Trent Reznor and the Nine Inch Nails' 'Closer' on *The Downward Spiral* (which features the line, 'I want to fuck you like an animal').

14     Well, almost. There was some very early controversy, and later, a caricature of him did appear in the Dire Straits video for 'Money for

Nothing' during the line 'that little faggot he's a millionaire'.

15   He brackets 'i love u in me' with a 'she says', but in the song's lyrics, as in all pop songs, it's the refrain and/or the title that gets repeated, that gets remembered. It's a man singing I love you in me. Over and over again.

16   And different too from the standard movieland sexualisation of men, which tends to pitch the men as objects of admiration and passive desire. Prince is constantly implicating himself in the sexual acts he describes in his music and videos, where Robert Redford and Kevin Costner and Harrison Ford and Brad Pitt tend to be sexual implications rather than sexual facts, their stereotypical boundaries more or less always in place (with the possible exception of Pitt-as-dildo in *Thelma & Louise*).

17   The grammatical ambiguity of this construction merely serves to increase the mix: doing girls like they're boys could mean the doers are like boys or the girls being done are like boys.

18   It came out later on that he probably had when he was younger, but that's neither here nor there.

19   Since then, things have taken off in several different directions in music. In 1998, 24-year-old Rufus Wainwright became the first successful pop singer to be quietly but unabashedly out from the beginning of his career while not playing on gay to create a niche. That same year, the English band Placebo, which consists, the band says, of a straight drummer, a bisexual lead singer, and a gay bassist, reported to *The Advocate* that a radio station had done a survey and found that 60 percent of listeners thought singer Brian Moloko was a woman. 'When they find out he's a guy and he's bi,' bassist Stefan Olsdal said, 'it's quite a different thing. They have to ask themselves questions, and that disturbs a lot of people.'

20   Their clientele, I have been assured by Amanda, who once worked as a prostitute and is now Webmistress of shemalepalace.com, is made up primarily of more or less happily married or otherwise heterosexually coupled men who are looking for either something they can't get from their female partners or things they'd be too shy or ashamed to ask for (usually involving the butt and/or the she-male's cock).

21   It's entirely possible, in fact, that one of the primary attractions of tits for men is that they are play things, like footballs, hockey sticks, and their own cocks. Which would mean that she-males, on this level, are simply sex partners with twice the toys.

22   Then what would we say about these men's wives and female lovers? Forced into it by circumstance and social imperative? There's a problem

23   For a while towards the beginning of the century in Amsterdam, for example, it was known that an inn called The Serpent was the place to be. It's also about this time that vocabularies started sprouting up. In Rotterdam, a man you might find at one of those pubs would be known, as least to patrons, as a *vlaggeman* (literally, flagman), whereas in The Hague, he'd be called a *nichtje* (the diminutive term for a female cousin).

with this sort of default shifting from straight to gay. In addition to the problems inherent in this 'one drop of black blood' line of thinking, the status quo is not, essentially, changed. We are still placing labels above observable fact for efficiency's sake.

24   Similar things based on similar grounds have also recently been argued in the case of Abraham Lincoln.

25   It bears a striking resemblance, for instance, to the 1996 biography *Henry James: Young Master*, by Sheldon Novick, which seeks to establish a young-adult relationship between James – thought by many to have had same-sex sexual relations, but only much later in life – and a twenty-two-year-old Oliver Wendell Holmes.

26   The first version of the Code, which remains the basis for French as well as Quebec law, was drafted by legal scholar and arch-chancellor Jean Jacques Regis de Cambacérès (1753–1824), who was known for his same-sex sexual interests.

27   His founding notions also included the possibility of identifying members of the third sex by their hips: *Urnings* (male homosexuals) had wider hips than other men, and *Urndinden* (female homosexuals) had narrower hips than other women.

28   Among the high-school boys, 6 percent replied that they had at least some continued sexual interest in other boys; the factory workers came out at 4.3 percent.

29   From Neil Miller, *Out of the Past* (Vintage, 1995). Hearts must have been made of stronger stuff back then.

30   Paul Fussell, *The Great War and Modern Memory* (Oxford, 1975).

31   According to another account of the affair by Michael Kettle (*Salome's Last Veil*, 1977), Christian Scientists went so far as to call the purity activist 'Christ the King' and sent a woman to him to conceive his child; he obliged, and she did.

32   For the sake of precision, it should be noted that though *Le livre blanc* is generally attributed to Cocteau, and though he approved its inclusion in a general bibliography of his work, he never formally took credit for writing it.

33   From notes in *The Intersexes: A History of Similisexualism as a Problem in Social Life*, by American music critic Edward Stevenson writing under

the name Xavier Mayne, privately printed in Italy in 1908.

34    Exceptions include Bruce Nugent's piece in the single issue of *Fire* called 'Smoke, Lilies and Jade' (1926), Claude McKay's *Home to Harlem* (1927), and Wallace Thurman's *The Blacker the Berry* (1929) and *Infants of the Spring* (1932).

35    In his under-read *Toward the New Degeneracy: An Essay* (New York: Edgewise, 1997).

36    At about the same time Greta Garbo was doing the same sorts of things, in movies like *Queen Christina* (1933) and her cabaret acts and various personal appearances and spottings, though the brightness of her particular spotlight made her behave somewhat less blatantly.

37    Harlem and other developed Northern urban black communities had, starting in about the twenties, come up with the idea of buffet flats. Originally set up to rent rooms to black travellers with no place else to go in a highly segregated climate, they evolved their money-making enterprises to include entertainments, which, given their wholly private, marginal nature, quickly evolved into live sex shows. Ruby Smith described in an interview with Chris Albertson in 1971 going to one of these buffet flats (this one in Detroit) with her mother, Bessie: 'They had a faggot there that was so great that people used to come there just to watch him make love to another man. He was that great. He'd give a tongue bath and everything. By the time he got to the front of that guy he was shaking like a leaf. People used to pay good money to go in here and see him do his act.' According to the (perhaps inflated) estimates of New York's 32nd precinct at the time, as reported in *Variety*, there was an average of two buffet flats for every apartment building.

38    The draw, though temporary as marginal safe spaces usually are, was large. An article in *Variety* in 1929 observed that Harlem's 'night life now surpasses that of Broadway itself'.

39    Martin Sherman's 1979 play, *Bent*, still widely in print, is a good way into this aspect of this particular part of the holocaust that's still almost entirely overlooked, even in places like the Holocaust Museum in Washington DC.

40    Signorile, *Queer in America* (Random House, 1993).

41    An artistic and domestic partnership which, as described by New York's Museum of Modern Art, 'created work marked by elusive meaning and poignant wit in a range of mediums, addressing both popular culture and mass-media'. It marked the radical emergence of ultra-gay into the international art scene.

42    People were, and Perry's group evolved into the international

Metropolitan Community Church.

43    *The Advocate*'s early years were of extraordinary importance. If there had not been a widely distributed magazine, put together by people with a certain degree of mainstream media experience and connections, devoting itself to covering just such events and issues, it is unlikely the consolidation of the gay rights movements in these years would have occurred as quickly or as efficiently.

44    I take this timeline from Loughery's *The Other Side of Silence*.

45    And a little under two years after the British House of Commons passed a more restrictive but still enormously significant act of decriminalisation called the Sexual Offences Bill, the result of 1957's Wolfenden Report, with a vote of 99 to 14.

46    From Dennis Altman's essay 'The Death of the Homosexual?' in his collection, *Homosexual: Oppression and Liberation*.

47    *Tales of the Lavender Menace: A Memoir of Liberation*, New York: Basic Books, 1999, pp 141–42.

48    C. E. Montague, *Disenchantments*, 1922.

49    Kaiser, *The Gay Metropolis*.

50    *Newsweek*, 8 November 1943.

51    The Lonergan case was fictionalised in a 1997 book, *The Good Life* (Alyson Books), by gay pulp writer Gordon Merrick, who lived in New York at the time and knew Lonergan.

52    There are two reasons, as our chronology progresses, that I am paying more and more attention to the United States. First and most obviously because there has been more extensive, now verging on comprehensive, scholarship and other forms of primary and secondary research done on twentieth-century American gayness than there has been on any other nationality. But second, and more to the point, we are experiencing at the moment full on American cultural hegemony. What goes in the States tends more and more to go everywhere in the Western world, and beyond. And though there are exceptions in various cultural realms (the US view of literature does not, thankfully, seem to have penetrated the French psyche yet) with regard to what was until recently called the queer nation, New York and San Francisco and the two Hollywoods (the old eponymous film one and the new muscly West one) have very much set the rules and the parameters.

53    The navy actually said that it wouldn't accept people 'whose sexual behaviour is such that it would endanger or disturb the morale of the military unit' – an indication, perhaps, that it was at this very moment in American history that the notion of the homosexual as a type was

coalescing out of the larger realm of the general sexual deviant.

54   Harry Stack Sullivan, it should perhaps be noted, was a forty-eight-year-old bachelor living with a male companion at the time.

55   The author of this new paragraph, Lawrence Kubie, in addition to being a member of the National Research Council psychiatric committee, was Tennessee Williams's psychiatrist.

56   In conversation with the author, March 13, 1998.

57   Allan Bérubé, *Coming Out Under Fire* (The Free Press/Macmillan, 1993).

58   It cost a family $35 a month to fund a conscientious objector in the work camps set up for them in the United States during the war.

59   As recorded in a 1948 navy memo entitled 'Proposed Talk to be Utilised in the Indoctrination of Recruits'.

60   There had of course been years and years of oppression of men and women who engaged in same-sex sex, but always as individuals, or as groups of individuals, more of a serial oppression than a class oppression.

61   One of these four was Edward Sagarin, who was, in six years' time, to publish an enormously influential book called *The Homosexual in America: A Subjective Approach*, under the name Donald Webster Cory. There were other quasi organisations, like the one Gean Harwood and his boyfriend, Bruhs Mero, put together in New York in the thirties. And though these meet-and-greet sorts of things were important, and though there were probably quite a few of them, they were inward rather than outward looking, and so are of less importance to us here.

62   Named after a bachelor brotherhood of masked Renaissance Frenchmen, the Mattachine Society was conceived by husband and father and ex-boyfriend of someday-to-be-Grandpa Walton actor Will Geer, Harry Hay, in Los Angeles in 1948 and founded by him and several others in 1950 as a fairly radical, Marxist-inspired organisation for radical sexual social change. It took off, being one of the only gay games in town, but was soon overrun by people with more conservative notions about how to get gay things done. Hay left, and it went on to earn its reputation as an organisation more interested in transforming its members into facsimiles of the mainstream than transforming the mainstream in ways they knew from personal experience would be both possible and propitious.

63   Will Roscoe, ed., *Radically Gay: Gay Liberation in the Words of Its Founder, Harry Hay* (Beacon Press, 1996).

64   The relatively homo-positive Crittenden Report, though submitted in 1957, remained secret for years.

65   In Roscoe, p. 54.

66    Whether he had sex with any of the men he also interviewed is not entirely clear, but we do, as of 1997, have testimony, albeit anonymous, from a contemporary friend of Kinsey that he did have sex with men on these trips.

67    James H. Jones, *Alfred Kinsey: A Public/Private Life*.

68    Within two years of its publication, there were about five hundred magazine and journal articles on the *Report* and its author. Helping in the quick assimilation process, beginning with the G.I. Bill – though it was to be a worldwide trend – was a massively expanded educated and culturally engaged population.

69    Rock Hudson and Sara Davidson, *Rock Hudson: His Story*.

70    Trilling, *Partisan Review*, April 1948.

71    While the *Hite Report* remains in print and continues, presumably, to sell, it is simply too much of an update on Kinsey, rather than a true departure, to do anything more than corroborate and extend the influence of the original Kinsey fervour.

72    And it's important, by the by, to take into consideration the effect of context and intention on method and conclusion. There were reasons for Kertbeny and Hirschfeld making some of the observations they made and drawing some of their conclusions, with us still. This is not to say they're invalid. But it does, ipso facto, mean they should be questioned.

There were, as far as I can tell, three main instigators leading these early sex researchers to look into homosexuality. The first, which we needn't examine too closely, was the general curiosity that pushes all things forward. The second was a search for self-knowledge and, if possible, self-justification. Both these men felt sexual attractions to other men, and at the same time as wanting to know why, they wanted very much to figure out, since these attractions didn't look like they were going to go away, some way to make it all okay. The third factor was the law. At the time these men were working, there were still laws on the books in some European countries that called for execution of men convicted of same-sex sexual activity. And even though these laws were rarely invoked at any time in European history, their lesser cousins, laws calling for banishment, flogging, public humiliation, were used fairly regularly. So, if these sex researchers wanted to make a better life for themselves and others, there was one pretty much sure-fire way of going about it. Western legal theory is based on the precept that though someone can be punished for what they do, they cannot be punished, per se, for what they are. So if these researchers could prove what people did was a direct and natural result of who they were – if, that is, there was a sort of person who did these sorts of things simply because they were born that way – laws, which were then based on the notion that same-sex sexual activity was merely capricious and lewd and on a slightly more disgusting plane, but essentially the same sort of crime, as masturbation and opposite-sex adultery – would have to be changed. Pretty compelling reasons to find what they found, frankly. And when coupled with an analysis of how they found what they found, the mental steps they took from observation to conclusion, well, it calls the whole thing into pretty serious question.

73  And listen to him on describing how he makes some of the assumptions he bases his research on. Here he is describing how he decided one of his interviewees was heterosexual: 'Martin still lived with his mother, which immediately made me suspect he was indeed gay. At least until I saw him. He was big and beefy, crew cut and florid faced, with a potbelly that stretched a t-shirt out over a big leather belt holding up a pair of dusty jeans.'

74  One historical counterpart for Willis's character is mentioned by Caroline Ware in her 1935 book on Greenwich Village. Writing about a certain speakeasy in 1930, Ware notes, 'One girl who came nightly... was the joke of the place because she was trying so hard to be a Lesbian, but when she got drunk she forgot and let the men dance with her.'

75  Though it's not a part of the book that's much discussed, Kinsey's last chapter, immediately following 'Homosexual Outlet', was 'Animal Contacts', which, in its findings that 17.2 percent of farm-dwelling males had had sex with animals by the age of twenty-four (and as much as 29.4 percent of those with a post-secondary education) must have set a lot of rural minds at ease. And just FYI – 'Because of their convenient size,' Kinsey noted, 'animals like calves...burros and sheep are most often involved.'

76  Starting with Brooke, he took advantage of especially frank sexual depictions of women, as well, but that was nothing new.

77  Other members of this charming and underrated genre include *Homework* (1982, with Joan Collins) and *My Tutor* (1982).

78  See, for example, his movies *The Doom Generation* (1995) and *Nowhere* (1997), in which several lead characters' refusal to peg sexual repertoire to sexual identity is one of the chief narrative elements.

79  On a recent trip to New York, I even found a video in one of Times Square's few surviving sex shops devoted entirely to women who had once been obese but had quickly lost weight and now had an extraordinary excess of skin.

80    I say this realising the enormous problems many people have with porn
      on just these grounds – that porn is in fact not reflective of actual sex,
      and that it therefore leads to objectification and abusive sexuality. I
      believe the vast majority of viewers of porn are able to view it with the
      same nuance with which children are able to watch cartoons, being
      entertained by it, even learning things from it, but at no time actually
      thinking that they are as indestructible, or as free from social convention,
      as the characters they're watching.

81    You could do worse than to take a flip through her latest book, *Post-Porn
      Modernist*.

82    Another sexually interesting Net phenomenon is the Webcam jerk-off
      show. Some girls and women put them on, and they can be fairly certain
      that their audiences will be almost entirely male. But plop 'Webcam' into
      your search engine and you'll find an enormous number of boys and
      men putting on weekly or even nightly shows. Some of them – an
      increasing number, I imagine – are part of the porn industry in some
      way or other. But a large number of them are still obviously
      independent. The men are almost always professedly gay, but the boys,
      more often than not, just seem to be doing it for fun. Some say they're
      doing it for the ladies, but even they have to know a whole lot of men
      are logging on. The fact that they're doing it at all means they really don't
      care who's watching, boy, girl, or classmate. And as anyone who's spent
      much time around any sort of strip bar knows, comfortably performing
      sexually for indiscriminate crowds has a great tendency to dissolve some
      of the more regular sexual categories and inhibitions. Webcams allow
      people who wouldn't ever want to go out and dance or strip to get many
      of the same personal sexual benefits in the privacy of their own
      bedrooms.

83    The British history of this period is far more complex than America's,
      given the backing and forthing between Labour and Tory governments,
      and the much slower economic recovery. Though politically less
      conservatively reactionary during the fifties, it was also during this
      period, as a direct result of the warmer Anglo-American relations after
      the war, that American notions of things like family and morality began
      seriously to seep into the UK, with the effect in the UK being ultimately
      similar to what was happening in the States.

84    As Rick Bébout, a Web chronicler of the struggles over sexual identity
      over the past three decades says on www.rbebout.com, there was, in the
      early seventies, 'a politics of polymorphous perversity, a childlike – Freud
      had said "infantile" – ability to find erotic pleasure not limited to the

genitals, nor to partners of only one sex or the other, nor even to "sex" itself'.

85    That's the implication of the latter seasons of *Friends*, when the entire show shifted into a pairing off of former friends into lovers. It started early with Ross and Rachel, though the ground was laid in backstory that there had been a high school crush, which meant there were feelings of love before there'd been a friendship (though the fact that the relationship only happened after they had been friends for quite a while is significant). But then Monica and Chandler got together. And by 2002, Joey and Rachel were an item. The fact that the friendships that turn into love relationships are all heterosexual, though obviously significant, is of less fundamental importance than the narrative investigation of the relationship between friendship and love and sex. Lucy and Ricky were not friends first. Shirley wasn't friends with Carmine first. Neither were Ben and Ria or Roseanne and Dan. Hawkeye and Hot Lips and Sam and Diane were enemies before they were lovers.

86    There is every possibility that this sort of subterranean telegraphing is the modern-day equivalent of all that intentional gay subtext screenwriters, producers, directors and actors stuck into all those thirties and forties movies we saw so brilliantly, movingly uncovered in *The Celluloid Closet*. There are things that, for whatever reason, must not be shown in this or that era, but that creators think important or fundamental or fun enough to indicate again and again, often in very obvious terms, for those who are willing to see what they're looking at.

87    There are loads of examples, for which I refer you to any one of the many books published over the last decade dedicated to unearthing such things. I've stuck a few of the better ones in my bibliography.

88    Paul Monette, *Becoming a Man: Half a Life Story*.

89    The doctor's answer, FYI, was: 'The problem is that we're trying to apply words to a reality that doesn't stay still. And it doesn't work because that's not the way reality is. That's not the way people experience their sexuality.'

90    It looks like D. Travers Scott, Mark Simpson and Michael Lowenthal may be moving in that direction, though. And that Califia's moving in the wrong one. In the last year, I've heard she went and had a sex change. She's now a man. Which just ruins everything. It may throw everything she did in the past into a new light, or it may mean she got too confused at some point, or tired, and gave in and gave up. Whatever the case, my discussion of Pat here is about Pat the radical woman she was, not the

relatively boring transsexual she is.

91  She also used to have a sex advice column for gay males that ran in *The Advocate* and elsewhere.

92  *Boys Like Her: Transfictions,* Taste This (Press Gang, 1998).

93  In one book so far, a very short novel called *Tacones* (Anvil Press, 1997).

94  In his first novel, *Execution, Texas: 1987.*

95  Though William Kristol, editor of the flagship conservative magazine *The Weekly Standard*, tried to in the February 1997 issue, in which he spoke of the abortion issue as the 'crossroads' where 'judicial liberation (from the Constitution), sexual liberation (from traditional mores) and women's liberation (from natural distinctions) come together'.

96  See, for instance, 'Trials of a Gay-seeming Straight Male' by Leif Ueland on nerve.com, posted 12 June 1998, in which Ueland writes: 'Maybe what my people need is a new definition, a nice user-friendly label. Something that says, "not gay, but not straight in the way to which you're accustomed, and maybe not even willing to rule out the possibility of being gay in the future".'

97  Barbara Kingsolver may be bringing us back in that direction with *The Poisonwood Bible*, her successful and wholly political 1998 novel about American diddling in the Congo.

98  'Prime Mates: The Useful Promiscuity of Bonobo Apes', Meredith Small, *Nerve* magazine online, posted 9 September 1997.

99  For more on bonobos, take a look at Frans de Waal's book *Bonobos: The Forgotten Ape* (University of California Press, 1997). You may also be interested in Bruce Bagemihl's *Biological Exuberance: Animal Homosexuality and Natural Diversity.*

100  Carl Jung and acolyte Joseph Campbell were obsessively faithful proponents of this view of literature and life. See, for example, Campbell's now standard *Hero of a Thousand Faces*, which, not insignificantly, gave rise to last century's second most popular new mythology, *Star Wars*.

101  It's a theory propounded by many who oppose the sexual di- or trichotomy that the reason it exists is to make us governable. As the government- and class-minded Gore Vidal said in 1985, 'In order for a ruling class to rule, there must be arbitrary prohibitions. Of all prohibitions, sexual taboo is the most useful because sex involves everyone . . . we have allowed our governors to divide the population into two teams. One team is good, godly, straight; the other is evil, sick, vicious' ('Someone to Laugh at the Squares With', *New York Review of Books*, 13 June, 1985).

102   Given Webster's tradition of prescription over description, it fits that it was in 1934 that the word heterosexual came to mean sexually normal. Prior to this, it had been defined as 'Med.: morbid sexual passion for one of the opposite sex', leaving a temporary absence of description for the sexual nature of those who were not morbidly sexual.

103   There are obvious exceptions, which do not disprove the standard.

104   I don't intend to imply that the women lacked agency in all of this. But I'm afraid all I've got to go on for this little anecdote is my own experience. I've no idea how the women treated or thought of the phenomenon I was witnessing from my side of the fence.

# Bibliography

## Sources

Adam, Barry D. *The Rise of a Gay and Lesbian Movement*. Boston: Twayne/G. K. Hall, 1987.

Ashmore, Richard D. and Lee Jussim, eds. *Self and Identity: Fundamental Issues*. Rutgers Series of Self and Social Identity, Volume 1. New York: Oxford University Press, 1997.

Auden, W. H. *Forewords and Afterwords*, selected by Edward Mendelsohn. New York: Vintage/Random House, 1989.

Baldwin, James. *Collected Essays*. New York: Library of America/Penguin, 1998.

Baldwin, James. *Giovanni's Room*. New York: Laurel/Dell, 1956, 1988.

Benderson, Bruce. *Toward the New Degeneracy: An Essay*. New York: Edgewise, 1997.

Bérubé, Allan. *Coming Out Under Fire: The History of Gay Men and Women in World War Two*. New York: The Free Press/Macmillan, 1990.

Bornstein, Kate. *My Gender Workbook*. New York: Routledge, 1998.

Boswell, John. *Same-Sex Unions in Premodern Europe*. New York: Villard, 1994.

Browning, Frank. *A Queer Geography: Journeys Toward a Sexual Self*. New York: Crown, 1996.

Chauncey, George. *Gay New York: Gender, Urban Culture, and the Making of the Gay Male World, 1890–1940*. New York: Basic Books/HarperCollins, 1994.

Clausen, Jan. *Apples and Oranges: My Journey to Sexual Identity*. Boston: Houghton Mifflin, 1999.

David, Hugh. *On Queer Street: A Social History of British Homosexuality 1895–1995*. London: HarperCollins, 1997.

D'Emilio, John. *Sexual Politics, Sexual Communities: The Making of a Homosexual Minority in the United States, 1940–1970*. Chicago: University of Chicago Press, 1983.

Ellman, Richard. *Oscar Wilde*. London: Penguin, 1987.

Faderman, Lillian. *Odd Girls and Twilight Lovers: A History of Lesbian Life in Twentieth-Century America*. New York: Penguin, 1992.

Fone, Byrne R. S. *The Columbia Anthology of Gay Literature: Readings from Western Antiquity to the Present Day*. New York: Columbia University Press, 1998.

Fussell, Paul. *The Great War and Modern Memory*. London: Oxford University Press, 1975.

Garber, Marjorie. *Vice Versa: Bisexuality and the Eroticism of Everyday Life*. New York: Touchstone/Simon & Schuster, 1996.

Gebhard, Paul H. and Alan B. Johnson. *The Kinsey Data: Marginal Tabulations of the 1938–1963 Interviews Conducted by the Institute for Sex Research*. Philadelphia: W.B. Saunders, 1979.

Gerard, Kent, and Gert Hekma, eds. T*he Pursuit of Sodomy: Male Homosexuality in Renaissance and Enlightenment Europe*. New York: Harrington Park Press, 1989.

Goldberg, Jonathan, ed. *Queering the Renaissance*. Durham, North Carolina: Duke University Press, 1994.

Greenberg, David F. *The Construction of Homosexuality*. Chicago: University of Chicago Press, 1988.

Haeberle, Erwin J. and Rolf Gindorf, eds. *Bisexualities: The Ideologies and Practice of Sexual Contact with both Men and Women*. New York: Continuum, 1998.

Hamer, Dean, and Peter Copeland. *Living with Our Genes: Why They Matter More Than You Think*. New York: Doubleday, 1998.

Hamer, Dean, and Peter Copeland. *The Science of Desire: The Search for the Gay Gene*. New York: Touchstone/Simon & Schuster, 1994.

Hamer, Emily. *Britannia's Glory: A History of Twentieth-Century Lesbians*. London: Cassell, 1996.

Harris, Daniel. *The Rise and Fall of Gay Culture*. New York: Hyperion, 1997.

Hart, Jack, ed. *My First Time: Gay Men Describe Their First Same-Sex Experience*. Los Angeles: Alyson Publications, 1995.

Harwood, Gene. *The Oldest Gay Couple in America: A 70-Year Journey Through Same Sex America*. New York: Birch Lane/Carol Publishing, 1997.

Herdt, Gilbert. *Same Sex, Different Cultures: Exploring Gay and Lesbian Lives*. Boulder, Colorado: Westview Press/HarperCollins, 1997.

Hoare, Philip. *Oscar Wilde's Last Stand: Decadence, Conspiracy, and the Most Outrageous Trial of the Century*. New York: Arcade, 1997.

Hudson, Rock and Davidson, Sarah. *Rock Hudson: His Story*. New York: William Morrow, 1986.

Ignatieff, Michael. *The Rights Revolution*. Toronto: House of Anansi Press, 2000.

Isherwood, Christopher. *Goodbye to Berlin*. London: Minerva, 1939, 1992.

Jones, Constance, ed. *The Love of Friends: An Anthology of Gay and Lesbian Letters to Friends and Lovers*, research by Val Clark. New York: Simon & Schuster, 1997.

Jones, James H. *Alfred Kinsey: A Public/Private Life*. New York: Norton, 1997.

Jordan, Mark D. *The Invention of Sodomy in Christian Theology*. Chicago: University of Chicago Press, 1997.

Kaiser, Charles. *The Gay Metropolis 1940–1996*. Boston: Houghton-Mifflin, 1997.

Katz, Jonathan Ned. *The Invention of Heterosexuality*. New York: Plume/Penguin, 1996.

Kinsey, Alfred, et al. *Sexual Behaviour in the Human Female*. Philadelphia: W.B. Saunders, 1953.

Kinsey, Alfred, et al. *Sexual Behaviour in the Human Male*. Philadelphia: W.B. Saunders, 1948.

Knight, George Wilson. *The Mutual Flame: On Shakespeare's Sonnets and The Phoenix and the Turtle.* London: Methuen, 1955.

Krafft-Ebing, Richard von. *Psychopathia Sexualis: The Case Histories,* trans. Domino Falls. London: Velvet Publications, 1997.

Lauritsen, John, and David Thorstad. *The Early Homosexual Rights Movement (1864–1935).* New York: Times Change Press, 1974, 1995.

LeVay, Simon. *Queer Science: The Use and Abuse of Research Into Homosexuality.* Cambridge, Massachusetts: The MIT Press, 1996.

Lewis, David Levering. *When Harlem Was in Vogue.* New York: Knopf, 1981.

Loughery, John. *The Other Side of Silence: Men's Lives and Gay Identities – A Twentieth-Century History.* New York: Henry Holt, 1998.

Marcus, Eric. *Making History: The Struggle for Gay and Lesbian Equal Rights, 1945–1990,* An Oral History. New York: HarperCollins, 1992.

Martin, Peter. *Edmond Malone, Shakespearean Scholar.* Cambridge: Cambridge University Press, 1995.

McLeod, Donald W. *Lesbian and Gay Liberation in Canada: A Selected Annotated Chronology, 1964–1975.* Toronto: Homewood Books/ECW, 1996.

Miller, Neil. *Out of the Past: Gay and Lesbian History from 1869 to the Present.* New York: Vintage, 1995.

Monette, Paul. *Becoming a Man: Half a Life Story.* New York: HarperCollins, 1993.

Moore, Thomas. *The Soul of Sex: Cultivating Life as an Act of Love.* New York: HarperCollins, 1998.

Nardi, Peter M. and Beth E. Schneider. *Social Perspectives in Lesbian and Gay Studies: A Reader.* New York: Routledge, 1998.

Norton, Rictor, ed. *My Dear Boy: Gay Love Letters through the Centuries.* San Francisco: Leyland Publications, 1998.

Persky, Stan. *Autobiography of a Tattoo.* Vancouver: New Star, 1997.

Plato. *The Symposium,* trans. Walter Hamilton. Harmondsworth: Penguin, 1951.

Probyn, Elspeth. *Sexing the Self: Gendered Positions in Cultural Studies.*

London: Routledge, 1993.

Pynchon, Thomas. *Gravity's Rainbow*. New York: Viking, 1973.

Queen, Carol, and Lawrence Schimel, eds. *PoMoSexuals: Challenging Assumptions about Gender and Sexuality*. San Francisco: Cleis Press, 1997.

Roscoe, Will, ed. *Radically Gay: Gay Liberation in the Words of Its Founder, Harry Hay*. Boston: Beacon Press, 1996.

Signorile, Michelangelo. *Queer in America: Sex, the Media, and the Closets of Power*. New York: Random House, 1993.

Simpson, Mark, ed. *Anti-Gay*. New York: Freedom Editions/Cassell, 1996.

Spender, Stephen. *The Temple*. London: Faber and Faber, 1988.

Van Gelder, Lindsy, and Pamela Robin Brandt. *The Girls Next Door: Into the Heart of Lesbian America*. New York: Touchstone/Simon & Schuster, 1996.

Vidal, Gore. *Palimpsest: A Memoir*. New York: Random House, 1996.

Ware, Caroline Farrar. *Greenwich Village: 1920–1930 – A Comment on American Civilization in the Post-War Years*. Boston: Houghton Mifflin, 1935.

Watson, Steven. *The Harlem Renaissance: Hub of African-American Culture, 1920–1930*. New York: Pantheon, 1995.

Weeks, Jeffrey, and Kevin Porter, eds. *Between the Acts: Lives of Homosexual Men 1885–1967*. London: Rivers Oram Press, 1991, 1998.

Whisman, Vera. *Queer by Choice: Lesbians, Gay Men, and the Politics of Identity*. New York: Routledge, 1996.

Wilson, John Dover. *An Introduction to the Sonnets of Shakespeare for the Use of Historians and Others*. Cambridge: Cambridge University Press, 1963.

Winny, James. *The Master-Mistress: A Study of Shakespeare's Sonnets*. London: Chatto & Windus, 1968.

Wraight, A. D. *The Story that the Sonnets Tell*. London: Adam Hart, 1994.

## Further Reading

Abramson, Paul R. and Steven D. Pinkerton. *With Pleasure: Thoughts on the Nature of Human Sexuality*. New York: Oxford University Press, 1995.

Amnesty International. *Breaking the Silence: Human Rights Violations Based on Sexual Orientation*. London: Amnesty International, 1997.

Bagemihl, Bruce. *Biological Exuberance: Animal Homosexuality and Natural Diversity*. New York: St. Martin's Press, 1999.

Bakos, Susan Crain. *Kink: The Hidden Sex Lives of Americans*. New York: St. Martin's Press, 1995.

Bawer, Bruce, ed. *Beyond Queer: Challenging Gay Left Orthodoxy*. New York: Free Press, 1996.

Bech, Henning, *When Men Meet: Homosexuality and Modernity*, trans. Teresa Mesquit and Tim Davies. Chicago: University of Chicago Press, 1987, 1997.

Bernstein, Robin and Seth Clark Silberman, eds. *Generation Q: Gays, Lesbians and Bisexuals Born Around 1969's Stonewall Riots Tell Their Stories of Growing Up in the Age of Information*. Los Angeles: Alyson Books, 1996.

Braithwaite, Lawrence Yitzhak. *Ratz Are Nice (PSP)*. Los Angeles: Alyson Books, 2000.

Brodkey, Harold. *This Wild Darkness: The Story of My Death*. New York: Owl/Metropolitan/Henry Holt, 1996.

Bronski, Michael. *The Pleasure Principle: Sex, Backlash, and the Struggle for Gay Freedom*. New York: St. Martin's Press, 1998.

Browning, Frank. *The Culture of Desire: Paradox and Perversity in Gay Lives Today*. New York: Vintage/Random House, 1994.

Burgess, Tony. *Pontypool Changes Everything*. Toronto: ECW, 1998.

Burgess, Tony. *The Hellmouths of Bewdley*. Toronto: ECW, 1997.

Cabaj, Robert P. and David W. Purcell, eds. *On The Road to Same-Sex Marriage: A Support Guide to Psychological, Political, and Legal Issues*. New York: Jossey–Bass/Simon & Schuster, 1997.

Carpenter, C. Tyler and Edward H. Yeatts. *Stars Without Garters: The Memoirs of Two Gay GIs in WWII*. San Francisco: Alamo Square Press, 1996.

Cocteau, Jean. *Le livre blanc*, trans. Margaret Crosland. London: Peter Owen, 1969, 1990.

Collard, Cyril. *Les nuits fauves*. Paris: Éditions J'ai Lu/Flammarion, 1989.

Díaz, Rafael M. *Latino Men and HIV: Culture, Sexuality, and Risk Behaviour*. New York: Routledge, 1997.

Ellis, Bret Easton. *Glamorama*. New York/London: Vintage/Picador, 1999.

Feinberg, Leslie. *Transgender Warriors: Making History from Joan of Arc to RuPaul*. New York: Beacon Press/Farrar, Straus & Giroux, 1996.

Foucault, Michel. *The History of Sexuality: An Introduction*, Volume I, trans. Robert Hurley. New York: Vintage/Random House, 1978, 1990.

Gide, André. *Corydon*. Paris: Folio/Gallimard, 1924, 1993.

Gowdy, Barbara. *Mister Sandman*. New York/London: Harvest/Flamingo, 1996.

Grahn, Judith. *Edward the Dyke and Other Poems*. Oakland, California: The Women's Press Collective, 1971.

Heilbut, Anthony. *Thomas Mann: Eros and Literature*. New York: Knopf, 1996.

Highcrest, Alexandra. *On the Stroll: My Twenty Years as a Prostitute in Canada*. Toronto: Knopf, 1997.

Hillsbery, Kief. *War Boy*. New York: William Morrow/HarperCollins/Perennial, 2000.

Hinsch, Brett. *Passions of the Cut Sleeve: The Male Homosexual Tradition in China*. Berkeley: University of California Press, 1990.

Huizinga, J. *Homo Ludens: A Study of the Play-Element in Culture*. Boston: Beacon Press, 1950.

Hunt, Morton. *Sexual Behaviour in the 1970s*. Chicago: Playboy Press, 1974.

Kahn, Arthur D. *The Many Faces of Gay: Activists Who Are Changing the Nation*. Westport, Connecticut: Praeger, 1997.

LeRoy, J.T. *The Heart Is Deceitful Above All Things*. New York/London: Bloomsbury, 2001.

LeRoy, J.T. *Sarah*. New York/London: Bloomsbury, 2000.

Lopez, Erika. *They Call Me Mad Dog!: A Story for Bitter, Lonely People.* New York: Simon & Schuster, 1998.

Lopez, Erika. *Flaming Iguanas: An Illustrated All-Girl Road Novel Thing.* New York: Scribner, 1997.

Lowenthal, Michael, ed. *Gay Men at the Millennium: Sex, Spirit, Community.* New York: Jeremy P. Tarcher/Putnam, 1997.

Mendelsohn, Daniel. *The Elusive Embrace: Desire and the Riddle of Identity.* New York: Knopf, 1999.

Merla, Patrick, ed. *Boys Like Us: Gay Writers Tell Their Coming Out Stories.* New York: Avon, 1996.

Monette, Paul. *Last Watch of the Night: Essays Too Personal and Otherwise.* New York: Harcourt Brace, 1994.

Mootoo, Shani. *Cereus Blooms at Night: A Novel.* Vancouver: Press Gang, 1996.

Murphy, Timothy F. *Gay Science: The Ethics of Sexual Orientation Research.* New York: Columbia University Press, 1997.

Novick, Sheldon. *Henry James: The Young Master.* New York: Viking, 1996.

Plummer, Ken. *Modern Homosexualities: Fragments of Lesbian and Gay Experience.* London: Routledge, 1992.

Queen, Carol. *Real Live Nude Girl: Chronicles of Sex-Positive Culture.* San Francisco: Cleis Press, 1997.

Roscoe, Patrick. *The Truth About Love.* Toronto, Key Porter Books, 2001.

Roscoe, Patrick. *The Lost Oasis.* Toronto: McClelland & Stewart, 1996.

Rowe, Robert J. *Bert & Lori: The Autobiography of a Cross-Dresser.* New York: Prometheus, 1997.

Sadownick, Douglas. *Sex Between Men.* San Francisco: HarperSanFrancisco, 1996.

Scarce, Michael. *Male on Male Rape: The Hidden Toll of Stigma and Shame.* New York: Insight/Plenum Publishing, 1997.

Sears, James T. *Lonely Hunters: An Oral History of Lesbian and Gay Southern Life, 1948–1968.* Boulder, Colorado: Westview/HarperCollins, 1997.

Sinfield, Alan. *Gay and After.* London: Serpent's Tail, 1998.

Spencer, Colin. *Homosexuality in History*. New York: Harcourt Brace & Company, 1996.

Sprinkle, Annie. *Post-Porn Modernist*. New York: Cleis Press, 1998.

Steele, Valerie. *Fetish: Fashion, Sex & Power*. New York: Oxford University Press, 1996.

Thompson, Mark. *Gay Body: A Journey through Shadow to Self*. New York: St. Martin's Press, 1997.

Turner, Kay, ed. *Between Us: A Legacy of Lesbian Love Letters*. San Francisco: Chronicle, 1996.

deWaal, Frans. *Bonobos: The Forgotten Ape*. Los Angeles: University of California Press, 1997.

Waddell, Tom, and Dick Schaap. *Gay Olympian: The Life and Death of Dr. Tom Waddell*. New York: Knopf, 1996.

Warner, Michael. *The Trouble with Normal. Sex, Politics, and the Ethics of Queer Life*. New York/London: Free Press, 1999/2000.

Warren, Patricia Nell. *Billy's Boy*. Los Angeles: Wildcat Press, 1997.

Weeks, Jeffrey. *Sexuality and its Discontents: Meanings, Myths and Modern Sexualities*. London: Routledge & Kegan Paul, 1985.

Woog, Dan. *Jocks: True Stories of America's Gay Male Athletes*. Los Angeles: Alyson Books, 1998.

## Movies

*Buffy the Vampire Slayer*, dir. Fran Rubel Kugui, written by Joss Whedon, 20th Century Fox, 1992.

*Chasing Amy*, dir. and written by Kevin Smith, Miramax, 1997.

*Cruising*, dir. and written by William Friedkin, United Artists, 1980.

*The Crying Game*, dir. and written by Neil Jordan, Miramax, 1992.

*Partners*, dir. James Burrows, written by Francis Veber, Paramount, 1982.

*Without You I'm Nothing*, dir. John Boskovich, written by Sandra Bernhard and John Boskovich, MCEG Productions, 1990.

## Television

*Absolutely Fabulous*, French & Saunders Productions, BBC, Comedy

Central, 1992–1996, 2001–present.

*All in the Family* (based on the 1966 BBC series *Till Death Do Us Part*, written by Johnny Speight and starring Warren Mitchell), Norman Lear/Tandem Productions, Bud Yorkin Productions, CBS, 1971–1979.

*Bob & Rose*, Red Production Company, 2001.

*Dawson's Creek*, Proctor & Gamble/Columbia Tristar, 1998–present.

*The Drew Carey Show*, Mohawk Productions Inc./Warner Bros. Television, 1995–present.

*Ellen*, Black-Marlens/Touchstone, 1994–1998.

*Friends*, Bright/Kauffmann/Krane Productions/Warner Brothers, 1994–present.

*Queer as Folk*, Showcase, 2001–present.

*Queer as Folk*, Red Production Company, 1999.

*Roseanne*, Carsey-Werner/Viacom, 1988–1997.

*Three's Company*, The NRW Company/D. L. Taffner Syndication Sales, 1977–1984.

*Will & Grace*, Three Sisters/Everything Entertainment/NBC, 1998–present.

# Index

*1999* 286n14
*20/20* 187, 189

abduction, sexual 71
abortion 246n97
*Absolutely Fabulous* 170
*Ace Ventura* 54
Achilles 30, 224
ACT-UP 170
adolescents, sexual practices of
    11, 120–22, 221 ff *see also*
    sexual experimentation;
    situational homosexuality
adoption 23
advertising 32–34, 36, 47, 108,
    135
    male sexuality in 146–47
anti-gay *see* ex-gays
*The Advocate* 24, 58, 92
Affleck, Ben 211
AIDS 1, 169
    and bisexuality 52
    effect on gay 126, 169–70,
        222
    effect on gay community
        145–46, 195
    effect on sex 33, 46, 119,
        147, 162
    and literature 182–83
    and the media 112, 145
    and science 131–34, 136, 143
Alexander the Great 63
Allan, Maud 80 ff
Allen, Woody 222, 235n5
Altman, Dennis 44, 167, 170
Amanda (interviewee) 237n21
*American Gigolo* 147
Anderson, Brett 58
animal sex, and human sexuality
    214 ff, 236n14, 246n101
anti-gay 23, 24, 148 *see also* ex-
    gays
anti-gay movements 77
anti-semitism 31, 64, 140, 145
anti-sexualism 1, 195, 215
'Anything Goes' 86

*Apples and Oranges* 192 ff
appropriation of voice 28
Aquinas, Thomas 67
Araki, Gregg 148
Aristotle 91, 210
'Arms and the Boy' 78
art 28, 48, 83, 86, 198, 212–13,
    239n43
assimilationism 91, 149, 183
attraction *see also* sexual
    attraction
  and fetishism 189, 199 ff
  history of 52
  kinds of 11, 14, 20, 37–38, 54
    ff
  nature of 18, 42–43, 54 ff
Auden, W. H. 46, 81, 83
St. Augustine 66
Austen, Jane 28
*Autobiography of a Tattoo* 11
autobiography, gay 11, 182–83
Avedon, Richard 146

bad sex 18–19, 96, 213, 235n5
Baldwin, James 27–28, 33, 219 ff
Barker, Clive 153 ff
Barkley, Alben 100
Barr, Roseanne *see* Roseanne
bars 10, 50, 59, 91 ff, 207,
    244n84
*Basic Instinct* 70, 184
bathhouses 144
Bayley, John 172
Beatles 2, 48
Beats 88, 93, 144, 198
beauty, and sex 45–47, 52–53,
    78, 97, 146
Bébout, Rick 93, 245n86
*Becoming a Man* 182
being *see* ontology
Benderson, Bruce 86, 215–16
Benetton 34
Bentley, Gladys 86
*Beowulf* 135
Berenger, Tom 95–96
Berlin 75, 81, 97, 213
*Berlin Stories* 82
Bernardo, Paul 70
Bernhard, Sandra 13, 44, 49–51,
    148
Bérubé, Allan 103 ff
bestiality 163, 177, 243n77
billboards 36, 47, 164, 173, 175
Billing, Noel Pemberton 79 ff,
    101, 114
bisexuality
  act vs ontology 189
  and AIDS 52
  celebrity 57–58, 237n20
  definition of 52
  as evolved from gay 191
  Freud and 127
  Marjorie Garber's view of 45,
    51 ff, 213
  as misguided concept 51 ff
  not considering oneself 16, 20
  and polling 138
  as pre-gay phase 12
  theory we all are 44
  as third option 12, 220
Black Panthers 93
Bloomsbury Group 45, 52, 172

blue discharges 110 ff
Blur 57
*Bob & Rose* 139, 170, 175–76
Bobbitt, John Wayne 39
bonobos 214 ff
Boon, L. J. 69
Bornstein, Kate 40 ff, 190
*Borrowed Time: An AIDS Memoir* 182
Boswell, John 63
Bowie, David 44, 58, 147
*Boys Like Her* 190
*A Boy's Own Story* 222
Brand, Adolf 74
Brandt, Pamela Robin 185 ff
Brecht, Bertolt 235n3
British Society for the Study of Sex Psychology 81
*Broadway Brevities* 97
Brooke, Rupert 78, 97
brothels 68, 99
Browning, Frank 55ff, 205–06
Brummel, Beau 45
Bryant, Anita 233
buffet flats 239n29
Bulgars 70
Bülow, Bernhard von, Prince 73
Bunker, Archie 55
Burgess, Guy 70
Burgess, Tony 179
Burroughs, William 93
Burrows, James 29
Burton, William 100
Bynon, Arlene 196 ff
Byrd, James Jr 35
Byron, George Gordon, Lord 212

*Cabaret* 82
cabarets 87, 97, 239n38
Califia, Pat 188–90, 192, 245n92
Cambacérès, Jean Jacques Regis de 238n27
Campbell, Joseph 246n102
Carpenter, Edward 81
Carrington, Dora 45
Carson, Johnny 55
castrati 39
catacombs 189
categorisation
    before sexual identity 26
    and birth of homosexuality 64 ff, 221
    gender as 39 ff
    and Kinsey 120 ff
    and polling 127 ff
    and science 131 ff
    of sexuality 50 ff, 94, 101, 205 ff, 229 ff
Catullus 47, 63
censorship 82, 235n2
*Chances Are* 210–11
Charles, Prince of Wales 74, 107
*Chasing Amy* 211 ff
chat rooms 164–67
Chaucer, Geoffrey 84
Chauncey, George 97
Cheney, Russell 84
children, as sexual beings 85, 94, 164, 193, 222 ff, 232–33
Chomsky, Noam 158
Christian Coalition 196, 228

Christianity 11, 22–23 *see also*
    religion
    and identity 180 ff
    and marriage 163
    and same-sex sex 66 ff, 92,
        194 ff
    and sex 157
Christopher Street 7, 168
Cinderella 227
*City of Night* 222
Clam House 97
Clausen, Jan 192 ff, 232
'Closer' 236n14
the closet 8, 11, 15, 17, 19, 50,
        57, 89–91, 187, 227, 232,
        236n13
Cobain, Kurt 58, 203
Cocteau, Jean 82, 83, 97
Cohn, Roy 117, 144
Cole, Susan G. 186, 188
Coleridge, Samuel Taylor 46
Collis, Rose 99
communism
    born like gay 64
    gone like gay 23
    as half a dichotomy 221
    hated like gay 70, 168
    and identity 182 ff
    and origins of modern
        American gay movements
        112 ff
    as synonym for bad 66
*Consilience* 198
*Controversy* 49
Cornell Selectee Index 106
Cory, Donald Webster (Edward

Sagarin) 144, 241n63
*Corydon* 82, 87
Costner, Kevin 237n17
Cotton Club 87
Craighill, Margaret 98–99, 107
Crisp, Quentin 11
Crittenden Report 242n66
Croce, Arlene 212
Cronenberg, David 55
*The Crucible* 69
*Cruising* 29–30, 70, 95
*The Crying Game* 54–55
Cullen, Countee 45, 86
'The Cult of the Clitoris' 80, 97
*The Culture of Desire* 55

Dalai Lama 177
Damian, Peter 66–67
*Dancer from the Dance* 222
Dante 30
Danziger, Kurt 131, 139
Daughters of Bilitis 144
Davidson, Jaye 54–55
Davies, Ray 53
Davies, Russell T. 139, 175–76
Dawson, Bill 9
*Dawson's Creek* 172–74
*The Dead Poets Society* 197
Dearie, Blossom 13
Defense of Marriage Act 159
Degeneres, Ellen 45, 230
demonstrations, gay 14, 91 ff
Denise (interviewee) 185–86
D'Erasmo, Stacey 2
Descartes, René 85
deviance, sexual 71

*Diagnostic and Statistical Manual of Mental Disorders* 140

dichotomy
  of the closet 89
  gay/straight 201–02, 221
  love/friendship 173 ff
  man/woman 40–41
  nature/nurture 135–37
  of personal responsibility
    179–80
  in polling 130
  sacred/profane 213
  within gay 89–90
Dire Straits 237n15
disco 50, 94, 144, 195–96
Disney 172, 227
Disneyland 148
domestic partnerships 29, 159,
    161, 239n43
'Don't Leave Me This Way' 195
*The Doom Generation* 243n80
Douglas, Alfred, Lord 77
*The Downward Spiral* 236n14
*The Drew Carey Show* 170
Dryden, John 46

*Eclipse* 139
Edward II 26
*Edward II* (film by Derek
    Jarman) 14
*Edward II* (play by Christopher
    Marlowe) 43
effeminacy 67, 70, 73–74, 101,
    104 ff
Effen, Justus van 70
Einstein, Albert 76, 139

Eisenhower, Dwight 114
Eliot, T. S. 28
*Ellen* 17, 44, 167–68, 170
Ellis, Edith Lees (wife of
    Havelock) 172
Ellis, Havelock 126, 172
*The Embroidered Couch* 178–79
'The End of the Homosexual?'
    44
Engels, Friedrich 64
*Entertainment Tonight* 7
Epstein, Brian 2
Equal Rights Amendment
    (ERA) 147
eros 38, 97, 156
etiology, gay 126
Eulenberg, Philip zu 73 ff
ex-gays 127, 193 ff, 207–08, 227
*Execution, Texas: 1987* 246n96
Exodus 196 *see also* ex-gays

family jargon, gay 88–89
Family Research Council 196
Fawcett-Majors, Farrah 45
FBI 114
Featherstone, Grenfel 212
female sexuality, in public
    discourse 122–23
feminielli 54 ff
femininity 29, 55–57, 107–08,
    193
fetishism 189, 199 ff
feudalism, death of 22, 70–71
Ficino, Marsilio 91
fiction 218, 220, 240n53
Fielding, Henry 28

film *see also* pornography
  dissolution of sexual identity
    in 148, 211–12, 236n9,
    243n80
  female sexuality in 49–50,
    239n38
  gay 14, 26, 235n3, 245n88
  male sexuality in 29 ff, 42,
    147, 237n17
  reflux sexuality in 197
  sex in 36
  sexual identity in 49–50, 54,
    82, 95, 139, 184, 236n9,
    245n88
  transvestism in 54, 59
Fitzgerald, F. Scott 82
Ford, Harrison 237n17
Forster, E. M. 29, 81
Foucault, Michel 63, 67, 71, 179
free love 95, 188
Freud, Sigmund 81, 83, 180
  and identity 180
  on sexuality 38, 51, 57, 85,
    126, 199–200, 245n86
  vs Kinsey 126
Freudianism, death of 23
Friedkin, William 29
*Friends* 170–72, 174, 245n87
friendship
  childhood 202, 232
  as a goal 2
  historically variable notions of
    71–75, 238n25
  and love 170 ff, 245n87
  and sexual attraction 170 ff
friendships, sexual 16, 212–13,
  217, 230
*The Front Runner* 105, 222
Frye, Northrop 36
Fussell, Paul 78

Gabe, Ron 91
Gallant, Mavis 212
Garber, Marjorie 45, 51–53, 204,
  209, 213
Gardiner, Mr. (biology teacher)
  135
Gaveston, Piers 26
gay *see also* homosexual
  appropriation of historical
    figures as 26, 45, 51–52,
    63, 71 ff, 238n25 & 26
  beginning of 63 ff, 232
  nature of 134 ff
Gay and Lesbian Alliance
  Against Defamation
  (GLAAD) 184–85
gay brain 133–34
gay community
  activism in 73, 75, 93, 112,
    133, 145, 147–48, 160,
    184–85, 187, 192, 195–96,
    208, 235n4
  crystallised by AIDS 145–46
gay culture, fall of 148
gay gene 126 ff
gay identity
  formation of 33, 68 ff, 112,
    145
  as marketing tool 146 ff
'gay is good' 17, 34, 92
gay liberation 93–94, 110

Gay Liberation Front 93, 94
gay movement
  as bifurcated 147–48
  birth of 75 ff, 115 ff
  in Germany 64 ff, 80 ff, 106
  as a phase 24
  in Prussia 75
*Gay New York* 97–98
gay people
  attracted to straightness 14–15
  as consumer market 146–49,
    168
  as cultural minority 112
  and opposite-sex sex 18–19,
    198–206
gay purges
  in Germany 101
  in Holland 68 ff
  in United States 113 ff, 209 ff
gay science *see* science
gay separatism 94–95
gay studies 26, 63, 72, 223
*Gay Times* 49
Geer, Will 241n64
gender
  as continuum 38 ff
  dichotomous notions of
    40–41
  playing with 38 ff
  and sexuality 104 ff
  stereotypes of 104 ff
gender difference 190
gender dysphoria 39, 104, 230
gender identity
  and gayness 104 ff
  and same-sex sex 98

*Gender Outlaw* 42
General Idea 91
Genesis, Book of 65–68
Gere, Richard 147
G. I. Bill 107, 111
Gide, André 82, 97
Gilbert, Sky 31 ff
Ginsberg, Allen 93
'Girls and Boys' 57
*The Girls Next Door* 185 ff
Glaze, Lee 92
*Globe and Mail* 207
Goethe, Johann Wolfgang von
    26, 71 ff
Grable, Betty 45
*The Graduate* 42, 147
Graham, Stephen 88
Grant, Hugh 20
*Gravity's Rainbow* 96–97
Greenwich Village 85 ff, 243n76
Gregory the Great 66
Grein, Jack 80
Greyson, John 235n3
Griffin, John 9
Grimm brothers 227
Guns 'N' Roses 48

Hall, Radclyffe 82
Hamburg 81
Hamer, Dean 133, 134–38
  on social constructionism
    136–37
Hamilton, Gilbert 236n12
Hamlet 224
happiness
  and pleasure 77

Aristotle's theory of 210
as purpose of life 2, 77, 176, 231
and sex 25, 38, 176
as social goal 141
as societal goal 197
Harden, Maximillian 73 ff
Harlem 45, 85 ff, 94
Harlem Renaissance 45, 86 ff, 94
Harwood, Gean 241n63
Hawking, Stephen 39, 140
Hay, Harry 112, 115, 144, 230
Hedegard, C. D. 70
Heisenberg Identity Principle 181
Heisenberg Uncertainty Principle 137
Hemingway, Ernest 82
*Henry James: Young Master* 238n26
*Hero of a Thousand Faces* 246n102
Hershey, Lewis B. 103
Hesse, Hermann 76
heterosexuality
    definition of 24, 51, 137, 246n98, 247n104
    historical development of 33, 221, 231
    as nonexistent 47, 118 ff, 136–37, 206
    presumption of 72, 138–39, 204, 210–11, 243n75
Hill, Lister 113
Hinthaus, Tony 147
Hirschfeld, Magnus

burnt in effigy 87
    and gay movement 67, 73, 75–78, 81, 87, 90, 101, 116, 126, 230
*History of Sexuality* 63
Hite, Shere 126
*Hite Report* 242n73
Hitler, Adolf 101, 114
Hoare, Philip 80
Hoey, Clyde 113
Hoey Committee 113–14
Hoffman, Abbie 93
Holland, Vyvyan 81
*De Hollandsche Spectator* 70
Holmes, Oliver Wendell 238n26
Holocaust 145
Homer 219
*Homework* 243n79
homoeroticism 78–79 *see also* poetry
homophiles 17, 91–92, 115, 235n4
homophobia
    created by US military 99 ff
    in film 29–30
    and identity 31
    as a lament 96–97
    mainstream 20
    as overcompensation 50, 236n13
    related to homosexism 175–76
    at St. Michael's College 8, 9
*The Homosexual in America: A Subjective Approach* 241n63
homosexuality *see also* gay

people
as biological 75 ff, 101–02,
    125 ff, 215
and communism 64, 66, 70,
    112–15, 168, 182–83
historical development of 33
    ff, 63 ff, 97 ff
and *The Kinsey Report* 118 ff
media image of 127–28
as a moral issue 129–30,
    193–94, 196
as nonexistent 206
perceived need for non-sexual
    defences of 77
public discussion of 30–36
as scary 43, 236n12
situational *see* situational
    homosexuality
as unchangeable 135 ff
visibility of 99, 112
'Homosexuality in a Woman' 57
homosexuals *see also* gay;
    lesbians
defined by US military 98 ff
as effeminate men 70, 73–74,
    101, 104 ff
oppression of, as a group 25,
    90, 110, 222, 240n48
as perverts 70, 74, 101 ff,
    110–14, 120, 226
popular idea of 33, 109 ff
as psychopaths 100 ff
as security risk 70, 113
self-identified 111, 117, 138
settled 11, 88
as third sex 75, 238n28

as a type 64–65, 103, 105–06,
    139, 174, 204, 218 ff,
    240n55
'The Homosexuals' (by Mike
    Wallace) 95
Hooker, Evelyn 126
Hoover, J. Edgar 114
Housman, A. E. 78
*The Howard Stern Show* 7, 235n2
Hudson, Rock 125
Hughes, Langston 45, 86
Hughes, Robert 32
Human Genome Project 136,
    143
Humphries, Wilberforce
    Clayborne 167
Hurley, Elizabeth 20
Hurston, Zora Neale 45
Hurt, John 29

'i love u in me' 49, 237n16
identity *see also* gay identity;
    sexual identity
before sexual identity 26, 73,
    97
construction of 14 ff, 26, 41,
    83 ff
getting in the way 200–05
historical development of 1,
    26, 43, 60, 64 ff, 180 ff
and the Internet 164–67
reason for its importance 126
identity politics 27 ff, 58
identity reconstruction 20, 50,
    188 ff
'Identity Sedition and

Pornography' 189
'if i was your girlfriend' 49
Ignatieff, Michael 31, 188
*The Iliad* 135
imagination 28–29, 166
*The Imperialist* 79
*International Journal of Opinion and Attitude Research* 118
'International Lover' 48
Internet
    pornography 163–64, 237n21, 244n84
    sexual role-playing on 164–67
introspection 2, 108, 127, 162, 180–81, 202, 204, 224–25
*The Invention of Sodomy in Christian Theology* 66
Isabella, Queen 26
Isherwood, Christopher 81–82, 83

Jacobi, Friedrich Heinrich 71–72
Jagger, Mick 58, 147
Jarman, Derek 14
St Jerome 66
Jesus 224
*Jocks* 223
John, Elton 44, 147
Jones, Bill T. 212
Jones, James 124
Joplin, Janis 147
Jordan, Mark 66
Jordan, Neil 54
Jorgensen, George/Christine 39
Jorie (interviewee) 191–92, 205

Josh (as we'll call him) 15 ff
Joyce, James 82
Jung, Carl 246n102
Jungian psychology 156
'Justify My Love' 7

Kaiser, Charles 99
Kano, Takayoshi 214
Katz, Jonathan 167, 170
Keaton, Diane 95
Kenner, Hugh 56
Kertbeny, Karl Maria 63 ff, 115, 230, 231, 242n74
Kettle, Michael 238n32
Keynes, John Maynard 45
King, Martin Luther Jr 35
Kingsolver, Barbara 246n99
Kinks, The 53 ff
Kinsey, Alfred 116–17, 124
    sexuality of 116–17, 242n68
Kinsey, Clara 117, 124
*The Kinsey Report* 112, 116 ff, 134, 143–44, 235n1 *see also Sexual Behaviour in the Human Female*
    bestiality in 243n77
    on categorisation 118 ff
    effects of 118–20, 122–26, 143–44
    on homosexual experience (the 10 percent) 120–25, 128, 133
    misuse of 123, 134, 144
    as scientific study 116 ff, 134
Kinsey scale 51, 138
*Kiss of the Spider Woman* 30

Klein, Calvin 34, 36, 47, 146–47
Klinck, Todd 51, 187, 192,
     204–05
Krafft-Ebing, Richard von 71,
     85, 115
Kramer, Larry 35, 115, 230
Kristol, William 246n97
Krupp, Alfred 73, 75, 77

*La cage aux folles* 236n8
labelling, sexual
     as accusatory 101, 111
     bisexuality not one 52
     as bulwark 35
     and ex-gays 196
     as obstacle to comprehension
          46–47, 219 ff, 231, 238n23,
          246n98
     as practical 70
     problems with posthumous
          133
     rejecting 207
     related to ontology 63 ff, 175
     related to self-perception 112,
          220–21
     scientific 133, 138
LaBruce, Bruce 148
Lancelot (character) 219, 221
language, and sentiment 72 ff
*Last Watch of the Night* 182
Lauren, Ralph 146
Lawrence, D. H. 37, 82, 219
Lennon, John 2
lesbians *see also* Sapphism
     in conflict with sexual
          identity 18, 185 ff 211–12

definition of 188 ff
divorce 158–59
and ex-gays 196
in film 49 ff, 211–12
gay male denigration of 89
role in early gay movement
     94
as scandalous 79–81
as stereotype 43
on TV 44 ff, 170, 174
in U.S. military 99
LeVay, Simon 132–34
Lewis, C. S. 89–91
Lewis, David Levering 87
Liberace 44
literature 28, 72–73, 78–81,
     89–91, 166, 197–98,
     212–13, 221 ff, 246n102
     *see also* fiction; poetry
     of same-sex sexuality 45–47,
          98, 204
     sex in 84, 89, 144, 179
Little Richard 44
*Le livre blanc* 82, 94
'Lola' 53 ff
London 11, 46, 68, 70, 80, 81,
     83, 86, 93, 175
Lone, John 55
Lonergan, Wayne 100 ff, 110
     wife of 100
*Looking for Mr Goodbar* 95–96
Loughery, John 236n12
Loulan, JoAnn 187 ff, 192, 232
love
     and Ecstasy 57
     and friendship 30, 71 ff, 84,

98, 171 ff, 245n87
as a goal 2
and the Internet 164, 167
male expression of, for other
    men 45–47, 78
and marriage 160
and science 143
and sex 25, 96–97
and sexual boundaries
    175–76, 187–92, 211–12
Lowenthal, Mark 245n92
Lyons, Phyllis 144

*M. Butterfly* 55
*M v. H* 158–59
Madonna 7–8, 13, 45, 49, 50, 55,
    57, 148
*The Making of Monsters* 235n3
male sexuality
    in advertising 47, 146 ff
    in films 29 ff, 54–55, 58,
        211–12, 237n17, 243n80,
        245n88
    and *The Kinsey Report* 124 ff
Malory, Thomas 219
Mann, Thomas 76, 83
Mark 8–10, 13, 14, 20
Marlowe, Christopher 45
marriage
    alternatives to 160–62
    fundamentality of 25, 65, 160
    as no longer necessary
        160–62
    same-sex 23, 63, 158–62
    and same-sex legislation
        158–59

Martin, Clyde 117
Martin, Del 144, 230
Marx, Karl 64
marxism 93, 115, 241n64
masculinity, in women 105, 107
masturbation 36, 172, 194,
    243n74
Mattachine Society 17, 110 ff,
    235n4, 241n64
Matthiessen, F. O. 84
McCarthy, Joseph 70, 101, 144
McKellan, Ian 44
'Me and Mrs. Jones' 49
media
    and AIDS, effect on gay 145
        ff
    discussion of sex in mass
        36–38
    and ex-gays 193–94
    gay 240n45
    and gay science 133–34, 136
    and GLAAD 184–85
    image of homosexuality in
        38, 70, 74, 76–77, 83,
        106–07, 112, 138, 168, 204
    sexuality in 3, 83, 119,
        127–30, 145, 201
Medical Circular Number One
    102
Mepsche, Rudolph De 69–70
Mero, Bruhs 241n63
Metropolitan Community
    Church 240n44
Michelangelo 26, 63
Miller, Arthur 69
Miller, Henry 144

ministries, ex-gay 193–94
misogyny 8, 31, 43, 220
Mitchell, Broadus 87–88
molly houses 68, 106
Moloko, Brian 237n20
Moltke, Kuno von, Count 73 ff, 79
  wife of 74
Monette, Paul 182–83, 185
'Money for Nothing' 237n15
monogamy 161, 190, 216–17
Monroe, Marilyn 45
Moore, Thomas 51, 155-58
moral purity, oaths of 114
Morrissey 13
Moss, Kate 47
*Mother Jones* magazine 155
movies *see* film
MTV 7
Murdoch, Iris 172
*My Gender Workbook* 40 ff
*My Tutor* 243n79

*Naked Gun 33 ¹/₃* 54
Napoleonic Code 75
Narnia 89–91
narrative 217 ff
National Institutes of Health 136
nature/nurture 128, 135–36
Nederlandsch Wetenschappelijk Humanitair Komitee 81
neoplatonism 63, 91
nerve.com 214
*The New Republic* 7
*New York Blade* 167

New York City 7, 29, 83, 85, 87 ff, 100, 111, 112, 132, 168, 192, 231 *see also* Greenwich Village; Harlem
*New York Journal-American* 101
*New York Nights* 88
*New York Times* 127–28, 130, 193–94
*New York Times Book Review* 118
*New York Times Magazine* 2, 145, 194–95
*The New Yorker* 212
Newton, Isaac 140
*Nicomachean Ethics* 210
Nietzsche, Friedrich 87, 126, 180
*Nightline* 7, 235n2
'Nikki' 236n14
Nine Inch Nails 236n14
Nolen, Stephanie 207
North American Conference of Homophile Associations 92
Novick, Sheldon 238n26
*NOW* magazine 188
*Nowhere* 243n80
Nugent, Bruce 89, 239n36

Odysseus 30, 219
Oedipus 224
Olsdal, Stefan 237n20
*On a Clear Day* 171
O'Neal, Ryan 29, 211
*Oprah* 130, 133–34
*Oscar Wilde's Last Stand* 80
*The Other Side of Silence* 236n12
*OUT/LOOK* 192

*An Outline of Psycho-Analysis* 51
OutRage! 17, 170
Overholser, Winfred 101–02, 107
Owen, Wilfred 78, 79, 83, 97

Pacino, Al 29
paedophilia 71
*Palimpsest* 236n6
pansexuality 92
pansy craze 97, 100
Paragraph 175 75–76, 81
*Partners* 29–30, 236n8
Patch, The 91
Paulk, Anne 193–94
Peck, Dale 179
Pepperdine University 146
Perry, Troy 92, 240n44
Persky, Stan 11–12
Peter (the Apostle) 224
Peterkin, Allan 197
Peurifoy, John 113
*Phaedrus* 47
*Philadelphia* 30
Phillippe, Ryan 20
the pill 11, 95, 166
Pip (character) 224
Pitt, Brad 44, 237n17
*Pittsburgh Courier* 111
Placebo 237n20
Plato 47, 91
pleasure
    adolescent discovery of 224
    in animals 215
    anti-social nature of 157
    and happiness 77, 175

homosocial 171
    as learned 154, 209–10
    pursuit of 77, 154, 171, 198, 232
    sex education and 163
    and sexuality 38, 53, 60, 64, 176, 177, 207, 209, 230, 233, 245n86
Podeswa, Jeremy 139
Poe, Edgar Allen 52, 73
poetry
    homoerotic 47, 176
    and male appreciation of male beauty 46
    of World War I 78–79, 82, 97
    of World War II 78
*The Poisonwood Bible* 246n99
polling
    problems with 1–2, 84, 127 ff, 143, 202
    and sex 76, 126, 127 ff, 138
Pomeroy, Wardell 117
*PoMoSexuals* 42, 190
pornography 162–64
    vs actual sex 244n82
    gay male, made by lesbians (and vice versa) 190
    and the Internet 166, 244n84
    Ming dynasty 178–79
    vs science 118, 145
    trials as 69
Porter, Cole 86, 119
*Post-Porn Modernist* 244n83
Pound, Ezra 28
Presley, Elvis 48
pride marches 14, 223

Prince 13, 47, 48–49, 237n17
*The Prince* 34
*The Prisoner* 154
*Private Lessons* 147
Probyn, Elspeth 49–50
Prohibition 82, 87
prostitutes
    boy 68, 70
    transsexual/she-male 59–60,
        237n21
    transvestite/feminielli 55–56
Proust, Marcel 83
Pruys, Karl Hugo 71–72
*Psychopathic Sexualis* 85
Pu Yi (the last emperor of
    China) 182–83, 185
*Publishers Weekly* 21
Puig, Manuel 30
*The Purloined Letter* 52, 73
Pynchon, Thomas 96–97

Queensberry, John Douglas,
    Marquess of 80
queer 208 ff
    and 'Lola' 53
    sensibility 205, 208 ff
    theory 23, 25, 31, 63
    TV 45, 170
*Queer as Folk* 17, 174–75
*Queer by Choice* 208–09
*A Queer Geography* 55 ff, 205–06
*Queer in America* 14, 90
Queer Nation 17, 209

racism 8, 31 ff, 220
Rafe/Renée (interviewee) 59 ff

Rainey, Ma 45, 86
Ratzinger, Cardinal 194
Rea, Stephen 54
Red Hot Chili Peppers 48
Redford, Robert 237n17
*Reel Time* 139
religion *see also* Christianity
    control of sexuality 2, 25,
        53, 126, 144, 158, 160,
        176–77, 215
    crumbling 179, 231
    and marriage 160
religious right, American 21, 77
*Remembrance of Things Past* 34
*A Research in Marriage* 236n12
Reznor, Trent 236n14
Rilke, Rainer Maria 76
*Risky Business* 53
Rodd, Rennell 78–79
Rodriguez, Alexa (interviewee)
    187
role-playing, sexual 164
Roman Catholic Church, and
    identity 66 ff, 180
Romantics 198
Roosevelt, Eleanor 139
Roosevelt, Franklin Delano 99 ff
Roscoe, Will 112, 235n4
Rose, Axl 49
Roseanne 45, 245n87
*Roseanne* 44, 170
Ross, Robbie 80
Royal Canadian Mounted Police
    101
*Rubyfruit Jungle* 222
Rule, Jane 179

Rusk, Howard 118–19

S/M (sado-masochism) 116, 189, 190, 203
Sackville-West, Vita 45
Sagarin, Edward 144, 241n63
Saia, Jorge 91
St. Michael's College 7 ff
*Salome* 80
*Salome's Last Veil* 238n32
same-sex sex *see also* situational homosexuality; sodomites; sodomy
and AIDS 146
before homosexuality 74, 83
distaste for among other activist groups 93
early experiences of 202, 223
and effeminacy 96
and ex-gays 194
and gender identity 98, 105, 230
lack of effect on society 231
laws against 75, 91, 111, 113, 114, 241n62, 242n74
and non-gay-identified people 8, 45, 52, 98, 202
*Same-Sex Unions in Premodern Europe* 63
San Francisco 85, 92, 112, 240n54
*Sandra Bernhard – Confessions of a Pretty Lady* 50
Santé, Luc 7
Sapphism 98
Sassoon, Sigfried 78, 83, 97

*Saturday Night Live* 7, 235n2
Savoy 87
Schorer, Jacob 81
science 60, 67, 103, 119, 125, 126 ff *see also* gay science
*Science* 132, 133, 134, 135
*The Science of Desire* 134–38
Scientific Humanitarian Committee 75
scientism 137
Scott, D. Travers 179, 192, 245n92
screening, military 99, 102–04, 106–09, 112–13, 117
sentiment, and language 72–74
serial killing 70
sex
as activity 189, 192
and AIDS 52, 112, 119, 146, 147, 162, 169
as amoral 144
anal 104, 146, 177, 178, 237n21
as appetite 153–54
and death 35, 145, 162, 169
diversity of 38
and everyday life 2, 51–52, 81, 154–55, 156, 212
experimentation with 11, 22
as fun 14, 15–16, 26
and identity 2, 11, 22, 24, 26
and love *see* love, and sex
oral 10, 54, 55, 144, 162, 177
and pain 154, 196
and pleasure *see* pleasure, and sexuality

for practical purposes 212, 213, 228
and reproduction 25
as sacred/profane 213
seeing, effect of 163, 186
as taboo 153–54, 246n103
talk about 1, 25, 36 ff
sex education 163–64
sex radicals 25, 35, 44, 93–94, 239n43
sex shows, live 239n39
*Sexing the Self* 49
sexologists 73, 75, 83, 104–05, 106
motivations of 76, 115–16
sexual attraction *see also* attraction
as basis of all relationships 37–38, 154–55
as changeable 54, 59, 164, 166, 174, 187, 191, 197–99, 202–03, 204, 207–08, 227–29, 233
as contextual 11, 56, 59–60, 226
depiction of 204
as fetishistic 199 ff
and identity 55, 200–01, 206
learning from animals 215
non-exclusive 18
as overdetermined 57, 201–03
sexual behaviour
complexity of 51, 135, 139, 142, 213, 215, 221, 226, 228
evolution of 24, 119, 143, 158, 208, 216–17

regimented 143
*Sexual Behaviour in the Human Female* 122–23
*Sexual Behaviour in the Human Male see The Kinsey Report*
*The Sexual Brain* 132
sexual compatibility 204–05
sexual difference 19, 101, 113, 190, 220, 226–27, 232
sexual experimentation 23–24
sexual friendship 75, 172–73, 212, 230, 245n87
sexual identity *see* gay identity; identity
sexual liberation 48, 93, 246n97
Sexual Offences Bill 240n47
sexual role-playing 7, 164
sexuality *see* female sexuality; male sexuality
Shakespeare, William 45 ff, 52, 71, 72
the sonnets 45–47, 212
Shaw, George Bernard 81
'She walks in beauty, like the night' 212
Shepard, Matthew 35, 184–85, 194
Shepherd, Cybill 211
Sherr, Lynn 187
Shields, Brooke 146, 243n78
*Showbiz Today* 7, 235n2
sickle-cell anaemia 140
Signorile, Michelangelo 14, 20, 24, 184, 195
*Silence of the Lambs* 70
Simmons, Gene 49

Simpson, Mark 245n92
'Sissy Man Blues' 86
situational homosexuality
   in adolescence 11, 16
   and 'elsewhere' 56
   in the military 11, 16, 207
   in prison 16, 56, 207
   in residential schools 16, 207
slavery 28, 53, 145, 220
Small, Meredith 214 ff
Smalls' Paradise 87
Smith, Bessie 45, 86, 239n39
Smith, Kevin 211
Smith, Ruby 239n39
social constructionism 21,
   136–37
Socrates 52, 63
sodomites 65 ff, 81
sodomy
   and identity 33
   invention of 66 ff
   scapegoating of 68
Solomon, King 142
Somerville, Jimmy 195
*The Soul of Sex* 51–52, 155–58
Spender, Stephen 81–83
sports, and gay identity 201, 223
spousal benefits 14, 23, 161
spouse, definition of 23, 159
Sprinkle, Annie 163
spying 70
Stalin, Joseph 112
stalking 142–43
*Star Trek* 173
*Star Wars* 246n102
*States of Desire: Travels in Gay*

*America* 185, 186
Steinem, Gloria 35
'Still/Here' 212
Stipe, Michael 13, 148
Stone, Sharon 58
Stonewall 7, 91, 147, 192
   twenty-fifth anniversary of
   168
Strachey, Lytton 45
Studio 54 82, 147
Suede 58
suicide, teen 76–77, 197
Sullivan, Andrew 145, 194–95
Sullivan, Harry Stack 101–03,
   107, 241n56
survival couples 145
*Switch Hitters* 190
*The Symposium* 16, 47

taboo, sexual 53, 153, 154,
   236n12, 246n103
*Tacones* 246n95
*Tales of the City* 222
Tatchell, Peter 36
Taylor, Elizabeth 50, 160
television
   depiction/discussion of
      sex/sexuality on 36, 95,
      107, 130, 167
   gay *vs* queer 45, 168 ff
*The Temple* 82
Terence 27–28
Thatcher, Margaret 39
*Thelma & Louise* 237n17
*This* magazine 31 ff
*Three Essays on the Theory of*

*Sexuality* 199
Thurman, Wallace 45, 86, 239n36
*Time* magazine 7, 118
Tims, Michael 91
'To Eros' 79, 98
Tönnig, Ferdinand 179
*Toward the New Degeneracy*
    215–16
transgendered 51, 189
transsexuals 25, 43, 59–60, 171,
    245n92
transvestites 54–55, 58 ff
'Trials of a Gay-seeming Straight
    Male' 246n98
Trilling, Lionel 125–26
Tripper, Jack 167
Trudeau, Pierre 92

Ueland, Lief 246n98
Ulrichs, Karl Heinrich 75, 77, 90
*Ulysses* 82, 118
University of Montreal, massacre
    35
University of Toronto 8
US government *see also* G. I. Bill
    hiring practices of 113
US military *see also* screening,
    military
    blue discharges 110 ff
    defines homosexuals 106 ff
    develops homophobia 99, 109
*USA Today* 218

Van Gelder, Lindsy 185 ff, 205
*Vanity Fair* 88
*Variety* 88, 239n39 & 40

Veber, Francis 236n8
Versace, Gianni 146
Veterans Benevolent Association
    110–12
*le vice allemand* 74–75
*Vice Versa: Bisexuality and the
    Eroticism of Everyday Life* 45,
    51 ff, 204
Victoria, Queen 64–65, 98
Vidal, Gore 23, 92, 179, 236n6,
    246n103
*The Vigilante* 80
Vince Incident, the 7–8, 10–13,
    18, 60
Virgil 47
Vulpius, Christiane 71

Wagner, Richard 82
Wahlberg, Mark 47
Wainwright, Rufus 13, 237n20
Walcott, Rinaldo 31 ff
Walker, Gerald 30
Wallace, Mike 95
Walsh, David I. 99–100
Walters, Barbara 187
Ware, Caroline 243n76
Warren, Patricia Nell 105
webcams 166, 187, 244n84
Weber, Bruce 146–47
*Webster's Dictionary* 247n104
*The Weekly Standard* 246n97
Weill, Kurt 235n3
Weimar Republic 75, 82, 85,
    87, 100
*The Well of Loneliness* 82, 222
*When Harlem Was in Vogue* 87

'When Plagues End: Notes on
the Twilight of an
Epidemic' 145
Wherry, Kenneth 113
Whisman, Vera 209–10
White, Edmund 185, 186, 204,
206
White, Reggie 193
Whitman, Walt 78, 197
Wilde Affair 79 ff, 101, 106
Wilde, Oscar 26, 45, 75, 138–39,
208
Wilhelm II, Kaiser 73
*Will & Grace* 44, 168, 236n8
Willis, Julia 139, 243n76
Wilsma, Zacharias 68 ff
Wilson, Edward O. 198
witches 65, 69
*Without You I'm Nothing* 49–50
Women's Army Corps 99
women's liberation 36, 93,
246n97
Woog, Dan 223

Woolf, Leonard 172
Woolf, Virginia 45, 52, 172
Wordsworth, William 46, 198
World War I
in history of homosexuality 1,
75, 78 ff, 96
poetry of 78–79
sexuality in 78 ff, 82, 96–97
World War II *see also* screening,
military; US military
conscientious objectors
241n60
gay activists like veterans of
232
in history of homosexuality 1,
11, 96 ff
identity construction like
housing after 222
poetry of 78
same-sex sex in 11, 98 ff
women in 98–99, 107–08

*Die Zukunft* 73